Problems of Rationality

Other volumes of collected essays by Donald Davidson

Essays on Actions and Events
Inquiries into Truth and Interpretation
Subjective, Intersubjective, Objective
Truth, Language, and History (forthcoming)

Problems of Rationality

DONALD DAVIDSON

CLARENDON PRESS · OXFORD

OXFORD
UNIVERSITY PRESS

Great Clarendon Street, Oxford OX2 6DP

Oxford University Press is a department of the University of Oxford.
It furthers the University's objective of excellence in research, scholarship,
and education by publishing worldwide in

Oxford New York

Auckland Bangkok Buenos Aires Cape Town Chennai
Dar es Salaam Delhi Hong Kong Istanbul Karachi Kolkata
Kuala Lumpur Madrid Melbourne Mexico City Mumbai Nairobi
São Paulo Shanghai Taipei Tokyo Toronto

Oxford is a registered trade mark of Oxford University Press
in the UK and in certain other countries

Published in the United States
by Oxford University Press Inc., New York

© in this volume Marcia Cavell 2004
Interview with Donald Davidson © Ernie LePore 2004

British Library Cataloguing in Publication Data
Data available

Library of Congress Cataloging in Publication Data
Data available
ISBN 0–19–823754–5
ISBN 0–19–823755–3 (pbk.)

1 3 5 7 9 10 8 6 4 2

Typeset by Newgen Imaging Systems (P) Ltd., Chennai, India
Printed in Great Britain
on acid-free paper by
Biddles Ltd., King's Lynn, Norfolk

To my Daughter, Elizabeth Davidson

Contents

Provenance of the Essays and Acknowledgments

Essay 1, 'The Problem of Objectivity', was published in *Tijdschrift voor Filosofie* (Leuven, June 1995), 203–20.

Essay 2, 'Expressing Evaluations', was delivered as the Lindley Lecture and published as a Lindley Lecture monograph at the University of Kansas, 1984.

Essay 3, 'The Objectivity of Values', was first published in *El Trabajo Filosófico de Hoy en el Continente*, edited by Carlos Gutiérrez (Bogatá, Editorial ABC, 1995), 59–69. Translated into Serbo-Croatian by D. ö. Mileusnić, it was later published in *Belgrade Circle*, 1–2 (1995), 177–88, both in English and Serbo-Croatian.

Essay 4, 'The Interpersonal Comparison of Values', is a slightly altered version of 'Judging Interpersonal Interests', published in *Foundations of Social Choice Theory*, edited by J. Elster and A. Hylland (Cambridge University Press, 1986), 195–211.

Essay 5, 'Turing's Test', was published in *Modelling the Mind*, edited by W. H. Newton-Smith and K. V. Wilkes (Oxford University Press, 1990), 1–11.

Essay 6, 'Representation and Interpretation', was published in *Modelling the Mind*, edited by W. H. Newton-Smith and K. V. Wilkes (Oxford University Press, 1990), 13–26.

Essay 7, 'Problems in the Explanation of Action', was published in *Metaphysics and Morality: Essays in Honour of J. J. C. Smart*, edited by P. Pettit, R. Sylvan, and J. Norman (Oxford: Blackwell, 1987), 35–49.

Essay 8, 'Could There Be a Science of Rationality?', was first published in *International Journal of Philosophical Studies*, 3 (1995), 1–16. Translated into Spanish by A. Nudler and S. Romaniuk, it was published in *La Rationalidad: Su Poder y sus Límites*, edited by O. Nudler (Buenos Aires: Paidós, 1996), 273–93.

Essay 9, 'What Thought Requires', was first published in *The Foundations of Cognitive Science*, edited by J. Branquinho (Oxford University Press, 2001), 121–32. Translated into Chinese by Whi-Chuan Fang, it was reprinted in *Con-Temporary*, 1 1 (2003).

Essay 10, 'A Unified Theory of Thought, Meaning, and Action', was first published as 'Toward a Unified Theory of Meaning and Action' in *Grazer Philosophische Studien*, 11 (1980), 1–12. It was subsequently published in *Essays on Truth, Language and Mind*, edited and translated into Polish by B. Stanosz (Warsaw: Wydawnictwo Naukowe, 1992).

Essay 11, 'Paradoxes of Irrationality', was first published in *Philosophical Essays on Freud*, edited by R. Wollheim and J. Hopkins (Cambridge University Press, 1982), 289–305. It was published in Serbo-Croatian in *Filozofskočitanje Frojda*, edited by O. Savić, who also translated the essay (Belgrade: IIC SSO Srbije, 1988). Translated into French by Pascal Engel, it was published in *Paradoxes de L'Irrationalité* (Combas: Éditions de L'Éclat, 1991). Translated into German by G. Grünkorn, it was published in *Motive, Gründe, Zwecke: Theorien praktischer Rationalität*, edited by S. Gosepath (Frankfurt am Main: Fischer Taschenbuch Verlag, 1999), 209–31. A precursor of this paper was delivered as the Ernest Jones Lecture before the British Psyohoanalytic Association on April 26, 1978.

Essay 12, 'Incoherence and Irrationality', was presented at the Entretiens between Oxford and the Institut International de Philosophie, 3–9 September 1984. It was published in *Dialectica*, 39 (1985), 345–54.

Essay 13, 'Deception and Division', was first published in *The Multiple Self*, edited by J. Elster (Cambridge University Press, 1986), 79–92. It was reprinted in *Actions and Events: Perspectives on the Philosophy of Donald Davidson*, edited by E. LePore and B. McLaughlin (Oxford: Blackwell, 1985), 138–48. Translated into French by P. Engel, it was published in *Paradoxes de L'Irrationalité* (Combas: Éditions de L'Éclat, 1991). It was published in Spanish in *Mente, Mundo y Acción* (Barcelona: Ediciones Paidós, 1992). Translated into Serbo-Croatian by Z. Lazović, it was published in *Metafizićki Ogledi* (Belgrade: Radionica Sic, Edicija Teorija, 1995).

Essay 14, 'Who is Fooled?', was published in *Self-Deception and Paradoxes of Rationality*, edited by J.-P. Dupuy (Stanford, Calif.: CSLI, 1997), 15–27.

Introduction

This volume of essays has been virtually ready for publication for three years. In the summer of 2000, Ernie LePore came to Berkeley to stay with us for a week. Except for walks in the hills, meals, an excursion or two, Ernie LePore and my husband spent the entire time going through his unpublished essays, deciding which ones to keep, and how to place and order them in the forthcoming volumes of collected essays. They put together Volumes 3, 4, and 5 at that time. Ernie and I thought the volumes were ready to go. But Donald never let things out of his hand for publication until he had taken them as far as he thought he could. He was clearly not ready to let the last two volumes of collected essays escape just yet. He died unexpectedly before he had made the final changes and written an Introduction.

At my request, immediately after Donald died Ernie came to Berkeley for three days. He helped me locate the essays and the volumes and make a number of preliminary arrangements. But there was a bit left to be done. When Ernie left, Arpy Khatchirian, who has been of enormous help to me, and I were not in every case sure which of several versions of an essay was the 'final' one. Then what little idea I had of the changes Donald might have made came from sets of comments Arpy and I had independently given him and that Donald had kept among the papers but had not incorporated into the text. All the changes we suggested were minor. Some he clearly would have accepted; with a few others I had to make a judgment call. And of course there may have been many changes he would have made had he been given the time. There is some overlap in the essays, but except for exact duplications (noted at the end of Essay 3), Donald might well have wanted the overlap to remain.

Donald's Introduction to Volume 3, *Subjective, Intersubjective, Objective*, begins with a paragraph stating the themes that connect

the essays. He follows this with a brief paragraph on each of them
individually. I have taken this as my model here. Many of these essays
I knew well, and Donald and I had discussed them; all, I had at
least heard him give. The Introduction is of course in my words. (In
two cases Donald preceded the essay with a summary, as required
by the publication in which the essay appeared. I have incorporated
these summaries into my introductions.) I may have made errors of
emphasis, even of content.

I am grateful beyond words to Ernie LePore. My thanks also to
Branden Fitelson, who read those of Donald's essays that draw on
decision theory (essays 2, 8, and 10), suggesting a few changes in
my own paragraphs in the Introduction; and, once again, to Arpy
Khatchirian.

The essays in this volume take up some of the implications of the
theory of meaning that Davidson laid out in the first three volumes
of his collected essays. All the implications concern various aspects
of rationality, some degree of which Davidson's theory of *radical
interpretation* attributes to any creature that can be said to have
a mind.

The first group of essays, *Rationality and Value*, carries Davidson's thesis about the sense in which our interpretations of another
person's mental states and actions can bring objectivity into the realm
of values: value judgments, and our understanding of them, he argues,
are as objective as any judgments about the mind can be. (Davidson's
title for this section was simply *Rationality*. My proposal to change
it to *Rationality and Value* was among the notes I found with his
manuscript.)

Problems and Proposals, the second part, is primarily concerned
with what the minimal conditions are for attributing mental states
to an object (say a computer) or creature. Several of these essays
develop Davidson's Unified Theory for interpreting thought, meaning, and action, a theory that draws on certain forms of decision
theory.

The third part, *Irrationality*, grapples with the problems raised by
those thoughts and actions that seem in a fundamental way to violate
the constraints of rationality. Since these constraints are, according to Davidson, among the necessary conditions both for mind and
interpretation, irrationality poses a peculiar puzzle.

Essay 1, 'The Problem of Objectivity', points out that the traditional (Cartesian) idea that all knowledge is based on data given to the individual mind runs together two problems. One asks how we can justify belief in a world independent of our minds. The other, which lies behind this epistemological problem, asks how we come to have an idea of an objective reality in the first place. This is an interesting, neglected, and difficult question; shedding light on it has long been, and in this volume continues to be, one of Davidson's chief projects. In this essay he is at pains to distinguish the many abilities that we and other creatures have to move around in the world successfully and to make discriminations essential to our lives from those more specific activities that require thought. Thought requires, Davidson argues, that the creature have the concept of error, of making a mistake *by the creature's own lights*. Only if it has the concept of error can it be said to have any other concepts. The concepts of objective reality and truth are presumptions of thought itself, so of the ability to raise Cartesian doubts. If this is right, *general* skeptical claims are simply unintelligible.

Though he begins, like Descartes, with the fact of thought, Davidson argues for a total revision of the Cartesian picture. All propositional thought, positive or skeptical, of the inner or of the outer, requires possession of the concept of objective truth, and this concept is accessible only to those creatures that are in communication with others. Knowledge of other minds is thus basic to all thought. But such knowledge requires and assumes knowledge of a shared world of objects in a common time and space. Thus the acquisition of knowledge is not based on a progression from the subjective to the objective; it emerges holistically, and is interpersonal from the start.

Essay 2, 'Expressing Evaluations', brings the attitude of the interpreter—Davidson's strategy for a theory of meaning in general—to the issue of evaluative judgments. Just as the questions of belief and meaning are entwined, so are belief, meaning, and valuing, where valuing includes attitudes like desire. Though interpretation is always a holistic act in which the interpreter weighs a speaker's attitudes against each other so as to render them largely intelligible, or rational, by the interpreter's lights, Davidson argues that desire is the most basic attitude in this interpretive process. The thrust of the essay is that understanding another presumes a shared body of evaluations as well as beliefs.

Essay 3 draws out one of the implications of Essay 2: values are as objective as beliefs, since interpreting another requires a common framework of belief, desire, and valuation, within which, and only within which, disagreement about values becomes possible. The denial that values are objective should not be confused with relativism: of course what is valuable or right is relative to time, place, local custom, and so on. This is not in itself a denial of the objectivity of values; rather, it spells out what the interpreter must come to understand about the other in order to know whether they disagree or not. Nor should objectivism about values be confused with realism, the ontological position that one or another sort of object—in this case, values—exists.

The appendix to this chapter consists of the opening pages of another essay entitled 'Objectivity and Practical Reason', omitting the later pages, which duplicate verbatim material in Essays 2 and 3.

Essay 4, 'The Interpersonal Comparison of Values', asks whether it is possible to find a basis on which to make objective judgments comparing the interests of two or more people. Such a basis would not decide the difficult cases; it would rather give content to the idea of objectivity in relation to this question. The argument, which again takes the nature of interpretation as the point of departure, makes the following claims: (1) beliefs and desires are inextricable from evaluations; (2) in making the propositional attitudes of another intelligible, the interpreter has no choice but to fit them to some degree to his own scheme, including his own evaluations. Thus the basis for interpersonal comparisons is inherent in the very activity of interpretation.

This may seem to imply that interpersonal comparisons of value are subjective, since the interpreter cannot help using his own evaluations in the interpretive process; but this inference would be justified only if we had some other concept of what beliefs and desires are 'really' like. Since we do not, the best interpretation an interpreter can devise is as objective as possible.

Essay 5, 'Turing's Test', takes another direction from the traditional one toward the question, What is thought? One way to inquire into its nature is to assume that the contents of the mind are fully determined at any moment by what is inside the skull; this is where most Western philosophy, starting from Descartes, has begun. But if the assumption is right, knowledge of anything outside the skull is based on inference, and so open to doubt. Indeed, if we start with the mind, even the knowledge that one has of a skull is threatened. For this reason it is interesting to approach the question of the nature of thought from another direction.

'Turing's Test' examines Turing's answer to the question, 'Can a computer think?' Turing answered: Yes, if an interpreter is unable to discriminate a computer from a person by the answers each gives to the interpreter's questions. Against Turing, Davidson argues that while the Test gives evidence that the object has the syntax of the language in which it is responding right, the Test tells us nothing about whether the object has a semantics. Without knowing this, we have no reason for believing that the computer *means* anything by what it says, i.e. that it is thinking. *Understanding* the semantics of an object or creature requires that the interpreter be able to observe what in the world that is shared by interpreter and interpretant causes the latter's responses; *having* a semantics (on the part of interpreter or interpretant) requires a history of engagement with others and with objects in the world. Turing's test for thinking is inadequate not because it restricts the evidence to what can be observed about the computer from outside (the objection against behaviorism), but 'because it does not allow enough of what is outside to be observed'. This answer to Turing opens the way for Davidson's own view into the nature of thought, set forth in essays in Volume 3 of the collected papers, *Subjective, Intersubjective, Objective*, and developed further in the essays in this volume.

Essay 6, 'Representation and Interpretation', extends the implications of Essay 5 into the claim that the concepts used to explain actions of thinking creatures are irreducibly causal, while a science like physics seeks explanations and laws in which causal concepts (like 'soluble', but also 'believes') no longer figure. Further, the explanatory causal vocabulary that we call upon to interpret the semantics of a thinking object or creature is normative, relying on the interpreter's own norms of rationality in ways that explanations in a thoroughly physicalist language do not. Knowledge of the (syntactical) program of a computer resembles knowledge of the neurophysiology of an organism, in that neither, by itself, warrants our attributing to the object or creature a holistic, normative, or largely rational, network of concepts, acquired through its (or his) interactions with the surrounding world. Without that warrant, 'we can say that information, even ends, or strategies, can be represented in the system, but the system can't be *interpreted* as having the information, ends or strategies'.

The difference Davidson sees between mind and body, it must be emphasized, is not an ontological difference between types of entities, but a difference between schemes of classificatory concepts.

Essay 7, 'Problems in the Explanation of Action', tries to answer several objections that have been made to Davidson's causal theory of action. The claim that if one person kills another by shooting him, the shooting and the killing are one and the same event is defended. Hume's contention that a desire or pro-attitude is always involved in the causality and explanation of an action is upheld. It is argued that though reason explanations of actions cannot be backed by strict laws, this does not imply that reasons (beliefs and desires) are causally ineffectual.

Essay 8, 'Could There Be a Science of Rationality?', proposes in answer the 'Unified Theory' of speech and action which draws on formal decision theories for explaining intentional action laid out by Frank Ramsey and Richard Jeffrey. Davidson's theory differs from theirs in including a theory of meaning. He then considers the criticisms leveled by Fodor and Chomsky against the Unified Theory and the method for interpreting it empirically that Davidson has elsewhere called *radical interpretation*.

Essays 9 and 10, 'What Thought Requires' and 'A Unified Theory of Thought, Meaning, and Action', expand on the relations between thought and language and the world, on the one hand, and the sort of structure that thought and language require, on the other, in order to judge the criteria for thinking. Essay 10, in particular, spells out more precisely the Unified Theory of thought and action proposed in Essay 8.

Essays 11–14 take up a problem that has emerged from the rest of the essays. It has been argued that large-scale rationality on the part of the interpretant is an essential background of his interpretability, and therefore, in light of Davidson's argument both in the earlier essays in this volume and elsewhere (*Inquiries into Truth and Interpretation*), of his having a mind. Rationality comes with the propositional attitudes, since any one attitude means what it does, makes sense, only given its place in a network of other propositional attitudes, and only as they can more or less be mapped onto the interpreter's own norms of rationality.

Yet in the form of *akrasia* or weakness of the will and self-deception, cases of irrationality, *as judged by the interpretant's own standards*, do exist. How can we explain them without falling into inconsistency ourselves, as we would, for example, in attributing to an agent both a belief and a disbelief in the same proposition?

Davidson is careful to locate just what the cases of irrationality are that threaten paradox. Simple wishful thinking, for example, is not such a case, since one may genuinely come to believe what it is one wants to believe. It is synchronous belief and disbelief that is problematic. To avoid paradox we must 'distinguish firmly between accepting a contradictory proposition and accepting separately each of two contradictory propositions' which are held apart. This distinction implies the scheme that Davidson proposes.

First, we must allow for a hybrid form of explanation of mental phenomena, one that is causal but not rationalizing in the sense of giving a reason for holding a belief to be true. While mental events typically function both as reason and as cause in relation to the other mental events or actions they explain, they need not do so in every case. In the 'normal' case there is a large-scale consistency among the holistic mental structures; and one's attitudes are formed in the light of what one judges is, overall, the most reasonable thing to believe or to do. Further, in the 'normal' case, a belief–desire structure, say, acts both as cause and reason in relation to an intention or action of the agent. But in the puzzle cases cause and reason come apart, and the overall judgment—'This is the best thing to do, all things considered'—is somehow put out of bounds of the reasoning process.

Second, we must conceive the mind as containing a number of semi-independent structures of interlocking beliefs, desires, emotions, memories, and so on. (*Essay 11*, 'Paradoxes of Irrationality', suggests that Freud's explanation of irrationality can be understood along these lines.)

Essay 14, 'Who is Fooled?', discusses scenes from Joyce's *Portrait of the Artist as a Young Man* and Flaubert's *Madame Bovary* to show how self-deception of the puzzling sort can emerge from fantasizing and the imagination, mental activities that do not in themselves generate self-deception, since one can fantasize that something is the case while knowing full well it is not. But in the following scenario from *Madame Bovary* we begin to approach the divided mind: Emma's longing for another reality than her own generates vivid imaginings of what she hopes for; she more and more acts as if this were the case; gradually she begins to believe that what she imagines is real; but since it is the actual world, which she detests, that motivates the whole fantastic construction, 'we must suppose—and this is how

Flaubert describes it—that the two worlds, real and imagined, somehow occupy the same mind. Through the enormous energy of desire and weakness of the will, the conflicting parts of the two worlds are kept from confronting, and so destroying, one another until the end.'

Emma was self-deceived. Flaubert, in conceiving her, presumably was not. Yet he famously identified with her. In the process of deceiving oneself no clear line can be drawn, Davidson suggests, between imaginative activities that are not yet self-deceptive and those that are.

MARCIA CAVELL
Berkeley, October 1, 2003

RATIONALITY AND VALUE

1 *The Problem of Objectivity*

Starting with Descartes, most philosophers have assumed that all knowledge is based on data immediately given to the individual mind. For Descartes, the starting point was clear beliefs he found it impossible to question; for the British empiricists it was non-propositional presentations such as percepts, impressions, sense-data, sensations, the uninterpreted given of experience. What empiricists share with Descartes is the conviction, or assumption, that only what is in, or immediately before, the mind is known directly and without inference. Whatever other knowledge we pretend to have must be based on what is certain and immediate, the subjective and personal.

Despite the simplicity and intuitive appeal of this idea, it runs together two problems. One problem, the one that has dominated the history of philosophy since Descartes, is the problem of knowledge; it asks: how can we justify our belief in a world independent of our minds, a world containing other people with thoughts of their own, and endless things besides? The other problem, concealed behind the epistemological problem, and conceptually prior to it, is: how did we come by the concept of an objective reality in the first place? It is one thing to ask how we can tell if our beliefs are true; it is another to ask what makes belief, whether true or false, possible. This question concerns not just belief, but everything we call thought. It concerns our doubts and our hopes, our intentions and our reasonings about how to act. For all thought, whether in the form of beliefs or intentions, desires, fears or expectations, has propositional content, the kind of content that is paradigmatically expressed by sentences. Propositions are characterized by their truth conditions; we cannot have a thought without understanding that its propositional content may be true or

This was the first of ten Francqui Chair Lectures given at the Institute for Philosophy, the Catholic University of Leuven, October–December 1994.

false. (Our beliefs may be true or false; what we intend may or may not come about; the state of affairs we desire, hope for, or expect, may or may not be realized.) It is a deep question what makes it possible for us to form such judgments. How have we come to be able to appreciate the fact that our beliefs may be false, that there is a basic difference between what we believe and what is the case? This is the topic of my lectures: What explains our grasp of the concept of objective truth? It may be that the epistemological question will be solved if we can answer the apparently simpler question how thought is possible. If we can understand what makes error possible, we may then see how, given the existence of thought, it must be the case that many of our beliefs are true and justified, and so constitute knowledge.

Suppose you were designing a robot for survival, a machine threatened by weather, by a hostile terrain, by competitors and enemies, and dependent on its own resources to collect the energy needed to continue. You would give it many of our attributes: an ability to move about, to manipulate objects, to take advantage of many energy sources. You would give it sensing devices, defensive strategies, the capacity to learn, and therefore the ability to make numerous distinctions between the stimuli recorded by its sensing devices.

None of this, however, amounts to thought. What is missing? Our mechanical toy could, of course, make mistakes—but these would be mistakes only from *our* point of view (since we designed it with a purpose—our purpose). But nothing I have described would justify our attributing to the robot the concept of error or mistake, and lacking such a concept, it could not have the idea of the difference between how something seems and how it is, the concept of truth or objectivity.

It is not my purpose to speculate on whether or why thought has survival value; my point is only to emphasize how much of our competence in dealing with the world does not require thinking, and how difficult it therefore is to account for it. Not account for its *existence*, which is odd enough, but for its *nature*. To account for its nature calls for a description, perhaps what used to be called an analysis of the concept.

It is easy to state a necessary condition: thought would not be possible for a creature that did not have a grasp of the concept of objective truth, an awareness, no matter how inarticulately held, of the fact that what is thought may be true or false. But a grasp of the concept of truth is also sufficient for thought. Of course: but to see this is hardly progress, for it is no easier to say what it is to have the concept of truth than to say what is required for thought: these are just two ways of pointing to the problem of objectivity.

Here I must pause to emphasize again the distinction between the traditional problematic, on the one hand, which seeks to justify our belief in what lies beyond the scope of what is, as one says, immediately given in experience, and the problem of objectivity, on the other, which asks how belief is possible in the first place.

Ironically perhaps, my starting point is the same as Descartes': what I know for certain is that thought exists, and I then ask what follows. Here, however, the similarity with Descartes ends. For I see no point in pretending to doubt most of what I think I know; if I could carry out the pretense I would have to deprive the remaining beliefs of so much of their substance that I would not know how to answer the question, or, for that matter, to entertain it. I should begin, then, as I think we clearly must, *in medias res*, assuming that we have a roughly correct view of our surroundings and of the existence of other people with minds of their own. I do not question that we are, often enough, justified in these beliefs: we *know* there are mountains and seas, fish and serpents, stars and universities. Of course we are apt to be wrong about many things; but the possibility of error depends on a generous supply of truths: indeed, the more numerous our errors, the more we must have right in order to give substance to our mistakes. In thus accepting the deliverances of science and common sense, I do not, however, suppose it is obvious what puts us in a position to entertain or accept such deliverances.

This attitude and method have sometimes been called *naturalism* because naturalism starts by accepting common sense (or science) and then goes on to ask for a description of the nature and origins of such knowledge. A successful outcome of the attempt to give such a description will, I think, show why certain common forms of skepticism (that is, general skepticism of the senses—skepticism about other minds and an external world) are unintelligible. If this is right, there is no point in trying to give a constructive *answer* to such skeptics; all we can hope to do for the skeptic is to show him why his doubts are empty, that he does not understand his own doubts. In saying this I am altering, or at least changing the emphasis of, what I have said elsewhere. I have in the past claimed to have a *refutation* of skepticism. Richard Rorty has scolded me for saying this; he thinks that if I were right in so describing my position, I would be aligning myself with all the other philosophers who have tried to give a constructive answer to Descartes or Hume. Rorty says that, properly interpreted, my message to the skeptic is to 'tell him to get lost', thus aligning myself with the later Wittgenstein or the early Heidegger. I am now inclined to go along with Rorty. If one can show, as I think is possible, that in order to have a thought, even a doubt, one must already know that there are other minds and an environment we share with them, then this amounts to saying that it is impossible seriously to doubt these things—we cannot give a coherent content to such doubts. It is better to describe such a view as dismissing rather than answering the skeptic.

Nevertheless, dismissing the skeptic is not a simple matter. An argument is needed to see what is wrong with skepticism, and this requires a correct understanding of the essential nature of the concepts of judgment and of truth. Beginning, as I have, by assuming that most of our world picture is true, in itself begs no question against skepticism. This is because, as Russell pointed out, we may find that if what we believe is true, then it must be false. Science, he said, shows us that what we think to be our knowledge of the world depends on the mediation of the senses, and this in turn shows that our claim to knowledge is groundless because there can be no valid inductive argument from the known to the unknown. So it seems that skepticism follows from the assumption that science is true. I do not accept a vital step in Russell's argument, so I do not accept his conclusion, but the fact that one can argue in this way is enough to show that the naturalistic approach does not beg the question against the skeptic.

Like Descartes, then, I start with the fact that we cannot doubt the existence of thought, and ask what follows. We cannot doubt the existence of thought because even a doubt is a thought, and it is impossible to have a doubt without knowing that it is a doubt. A great deal follows from the fact that thought exists.

We should be astonished that there is such a thing as thought. By thought I mean not only affirmation and denial, but doubt, intention, belief, desire, or the idle contemplation of possibilities. What defines thought as I use the word is propositional content, and what defines propositional content is the possibility of truth or falsity: a propositional content has truth conditions, even if it is neither true nor false.

There are at least two reasons why we should be astonished at the existence of judgment. The first is that it is unclear why it exists at all; the second is that it is hard to understand what even makes it possible. On the first point I have little to say, since the answer to the question why judgment exists would have to tell us why evolution has produced creatures that can entertain propositions, and this is a matter for the speculation or discovery of scientists. The cause for wonder is (as Kant said) that it seems that we could operate in the world at least as efficiently as we do without the use of propositional attitudes. The ability to discriminate, to act differentially in the face of clues to the presence of food, danger, or safety, is present in all animals, and does not require reason. Nor does the learning, even of complex routines, require reason, for it is possible to learn *how* to act without learning *that* anything is the case. A creature as capable as we are of unrehearsed, adaptive behavior could be programmed by nature to evade its enemies and preserve its health and comfort without what we call thought.

I am not concerned with the scientific explanation of the existence of thought; my interest is in what makes it possible. Let me state the problem a little more carefully. A thought is defined, at least in part, by the fact that it has a content that can be true or false. The most basic form of thought is belief. But one cannot have a belief without understanding that beliefs may be false—their truth is not in general guaranteed by anything in us. Someone who believes there is a dragon in the closet opens the door and sees there is no dragon. He is *surprised*; this is not what he expected. Awareness of the possibility of surprise, the entertainment of expectations—these are essential concomitants of belief.

To recognize the chance that we may be wrong is to recognize that beliefs can be tested—belief is personal, and in this sense subjective; truth is objective. The problem is to account for our having the concept of objectivity—of a truth that is independent of our will and our attitudes. Where can we have acquired such a concept? We cannot occupy a position outside our own minds; there is no vantage point from which to compare our beliefs with what we take our beliefs to be about. Surprise—the frustration of expectation—cannot explain our having the concept of objective truth, because we cannot be surprised, or have an expectation, unless we already command the concept. To be surprised is to recognize the distinction between what we thought and what is the case. To have an expectation is to admit that it may be faulted.

Here is another way—a familiar way—to view the problem. We would never know anything about the world around us if it were not for the stimulation of our sensory organs. (There may be exceptions, but they are not important here.) Why should, or how can, such stimulations generate thoughts of anything beyond? And if beliefs of something beyond were prompted, what conceivable test could there be that such beliefs were true, since the test could only involve more sensory stimulations? (It is as if all we know of the outside world is brought to us by messengers. If we doubt the veracity of what they tell us, how can it help to ask further messengers? If the first messengers are untrustworthy, why should the later ones be any more truthful?) The idea that since we do not will the stimulations of our sensory organs we must suppose they have an external cause is no help, for at what distance must the posited cause lie? Why not at the surface of the skin, or even in the brain? Without an answer to this question, there is no answer to the question what our beliefs are about; and without an answer to this question, it makes no sense to talk of belief—or thought in general.

There are many people, including philosophers, psychologists, and particularly those who admire the amazing cleverness of speechless animals, who identify the ability to discriminate items having a certain property with having a concept—with having the concept of being such an item. But I shall not use the word 'concept' in this way. My reason for resisting this usage is that if we were to accept it we would be committed to holding that the simplest animals have concepts: even an earthworm, which has so little brain that, if cut in two, each part behaves as the undivided whole did, would have the concepts of dry and moist, of the edible and inedible. Indeed, we should have to credit tomato plants or sunflowers with the concepts of day and night.

I should therefore like to reserve the word 'concept' for cases where it makes clear sense to speak of a mistake, a mistake not only as seen from an intelligent observer's point of view, but as seen from the creature's point of view. If an earthworm eats poison, it has not in this sense made a mistake—it has not mistaken one thing for another: it has simply done what it was programmed to do. It did not mistakenly classify the poison as edible: the poison simply provided the stimulus that caused it to eat. Even a creature capable of learning to avoid certain foods cannot, for that reason alone, be said to have the concepts of edibility and inedibility. A creature could construct a 'map' of its world without having the idea that it was a *map* of anything—that it was a map—and so might be wrong.

To apply a concept is to make a judgment, to classify or characterize an object or event or situation in a certain way, and this requires application of the concept of *truth*, since it is always possible to classify or characterize something wrongly. To have a concept, in the sense I am giving this word, is, then, to be able to entertain propositional contents: a creature has a concept only if it is able to employ that concept in the context of a judgment. It may seem that one could have the concept of, say, a tree, without being able to think that, or wonder whether, something is a tree, or desire that there be a tree. Such conceptualization would, however, amount to no more than being able to discriminate trees—to act in some specific way in the presence of trees—and this, as I said, is not what I would call having a concept. To revert to an earlier point: given the theory of evolution, it is not difficult to imagine a primitive explanation of the faculty of discrimination: a humming bird, for example, survives because it is programmed to feed on flowers in the red and infrared range of colors, and these are the flowers that contain the foods that tend to sustain a humming bird. It is not easy to say what must be added to the power of discrimination to turn it into command of a concept.

These mental attributes are, then, equivalent: to have a concept, to entertain propositions, to be able to form judgments, to have command of the concept of truth. If a creature has one of these attributes, it has them all. To accept this thesis is to take the first step toward recognizing the holism—that is, the essential interdependence—of various aspects of the mental.

Let me dwell briefly on the centrality of the concept of truth. It is not possible to grasp or entertain a proposition without knowing what it would be for it to be true; without this knowledge there would be no answer to the question what proposition was being grasped or entertained. I do not mean that all propositions necessarily *have* a truth value. If I say, "This man is tall", and I indicate no man, then the proposition I express is neither true nor false (according at least to some theories). Nevertheless, what I have said is intelligible, because I know, and you know, under what conditions my utterance would be true or false. To know what it would be for a proposition to be true (or false), it is not necessary to be able to *tell* when it is true or false (much less to *know* whether it is true or false). If the world will come to an instantaneous and unforeseen end, no one will or could know that it came to an end at that instant. This does not prevent our understanding the proposition that the world will come to an end at that instant.

In order to understand a proposition, one must know what its truth conditions are, but one may or may not be concerned with the question whether it is true. I understand what would have to be the case for it to have rained in Perth, Australia, on May 1st, 1912, but I do not care whether or not it did rain there on that date. I neither believe nor disbelieve that it rained in Perth on May 1st, 1912; I don't even wonder about it. The *attitude* I have towards a proposition—of belief, doubt, wonder, hope, or fear—determines how, if at all, I regard its truth. But if I have *any* attitude towards it, even one of total indifference, I must know its truth conditions. Indeed, there is a clear sense in which I know the truth conditions of every proposition I am capable of expressing or considering.

To know the truth conditions of a proposition, one must have the concept of truth. There is no more central concept than that of truth, since having any concept requires that we know what it would be for that concept to apply to something—to apply truly, of course. The same holds for the concept of truth itself. To have the concept of truth is to have the concept of objectivity, the notion of a proposition being true or false independent of one's beliefs or interests. In particular, then, someone who has a belief, who holds some proposition to be true or false, knows that that belief may be true or false. In order to be right or wrong, one must know that it is possible to be right or wrong.

Entertaining any proposition, whatever one's attitude toward the proposition may be, entails believing many other propositions. If you wonder whether you are seeing a black snake, you must have an idea of what a snake is. You must believe things such as: a snake is an animal, it has no feet, it moves with sinuous movement, it is smaller than a mountain. If it is a black snake, then it is a snake and it is black. If it is black, it is not green. Since you wonder what you are seeing, you must know what seeing is: that it requires the use of the eyes, that you can see something without touching it, and so on. I do not wish to give the impression that there is a fixed list of things you must believe in order to wonder whether you are seeing a black snake. The *size* of the list is very large, if not infinite, but membership in the list is indefinite. What is clear is that without many of the sort of beliefs

I have mentioned, you cannot entertain the proposition that you are seeing a black snake; you cannot believe or disbelieve that proposition, wish it were false, ask whether it is true, or demand that someone make it false.

These remarks about holism give little idea of the scope and importance of the subject. Since the truth of holism has recently been conspicuously questioned by Jerrold Fodor and Ernest Lepore,[1] I should say something more at this point about holism, its varieties, and the reasons for embracing it.

One might first consider dividing holisms into those that concern thought and those that concern language. But it is, of course, a form of holism to hold that there is no point in making such a distinction; and this is my position. I have given an account of my reasons for this view elsewhere, but for now it may suffice to point out that the cognitive distinctions we are capable of expressing in language must be distinctions we are capable of making in thought. If one thought logically entails another, or provides a degree of rational support for it, the same logical and confirming relations hold between the sentences that express these thoughts. If a thought is true or false (or neither), then so is the corresponding sentence. These obvious facts are enough to make it highly plausible that whatever holistic constraints hold for thought hold also for language, and vice versa. There remains the consideration that some thoughts may be beyond our verbal powers to express, or perhaps beyond the power of *any* language to express, but it is unlikely that, even if this were the case, it would affect the application of holistic concepts without regard to the distinction between thought and language. I shall assume that this is the case: I intend what I say about holism to hold indifferently for thought and language.

One holistic thesis is that the identity of a given thought depends in part on its relations to other thoughts. The simplest question we can raise about holism, therefore, is whether a creature could entertain a single thought, since if a creature could entertain a single thought, it would be plausible to hold that even given more than a single thought, each thought might be essentially independent of other thoughts: there might be no constraints on the *combinations* of thoughts that were possible. In this case, the relations among thoughts might be irrelevant to the content of the thought.

---

[1] Jerrold Fodor and Ernest Lepore, *Holism: A Shopper's Guide*, Blackwell, 1992.

What would it be like to have a single thought, a belief, say, that the sun is now shining here? Clearly a creature might act as if it believed the sun were shining: it might inhabit sunny places and eschew the shade, reduce its clothing, put things to dry in the sunlight, even put on its sunglasses. But it would be easy to design a machine to which we would not attribute even a single thought, but which would 'act' in this way. Most of us are not seriously inclined to say that the thermostat or the thermometer *thinks* its environment is at a certain temperature, or that the dislodged stone believes the center of gravity of the earth is in the direction in which it is traveling. Before we say a creature believes the sun is now shining, we should ask for evidence that the creature *understands* what it is for the sun to be shining. There could be such evidence (whether or not we as observers have it) only if the creature is able to demonstrate that it can believe falsely that the sun is shining. This it might do by showing an independent understanding of the concept of the sun and of the concept expressed by the word 'now', of the concept of shining, and of course of how these concepts may be deployed in propositional combination. But it is clearly impossible for a creature to have such understanding without having many beliefs besides the belief that the sun is shining. I do not think anything less should be taken to show that a creature has a thought.

It may be suggested that a creature might have a thought, and yet there be nothing in its behavior, actual or potential, that would distinguish it from a creature without thought that was simply programmed to react in a way appropriate to that thought. But this suggestion begs the question by assuming that having a thought does not require even the possibility of demonstrating a grasp of the content of the thought.

We must conclude, I think, that it is not possible for a creature to have a single, isolated, thought.

How many thoughts are necessary if a creature is to have any? There can be no strict or clean answer; there is a continuum of cases, and little point in deciding just where thought begins. There are certain conditions of thought that must be satisfied if there is to be thought, and some of these can be satisfied in the absence of fully developed thought. There also are many degrees of conceptual sophistication a creature can have, depending on the size and character of its repertory of concepts. To have a repertory of concepts, however, demands the capacity to employ concepts in the formation of thoughts and judgments, and this requires a mental vocabulary corresponding to such devices as predication, quantification, the formation of descriptions, the assembly of complex predications, mastery of the concept of equality, and much more. In any case, once such devices come into play, it makes little sense to speak of counting thoughts, because of the essential creativity of thought, which parallels that of language. Thought is creative because of our ability to combine a limited repertoire of concepts in a potentially infinite number of ways. To take the simplest example: if we can frame one judgment, say the judgment that this water is potable, and we have the concept of negation, we already have (rather trivially) an infinity of possible judgments: this water is not potable, it is not the case that this water is not potable, etc. Other connectives, like conjunction and alternation, add to the infinities; the possibility of predicating redness or solidity to any of an endless number of items swells the list, and so on. We must also suppose that developed thought includes the analogue of the device of quantification in logic, the command of the ideas of some and all. Without these ideas there is no ground, as Quine maintained, and Tarski proved, for imputing an ontology to a creature.

We would not recognize as capable of thought a mind that did not conceive of a supply of familiar objects and properties. Just which objects and properties is not fixed, though no doubt there are some we could not do without. In any case, all this merely hints at the variety and richness that the existence of a single thought entails.

I come now to some further aspects of holism: intra-attitudinal and inter-attitudinal. The first concerns the relations among the various beliefs, within the category of belief, or the relations among desires, within the category of desire. The second concerns the relations between one category of thought or judgment and another: for example, the relations between beliefs and desires, or between both of these and intentions. By an attitude I mean a way of taking or entertaining a propositional content. Examples are holding the proposition to be true (belief), wanting it to be true (desire, and its many varieties), hoping or fearing that it is true. Further examples are demanding that a proposition be made true, intending to make it true, saying something that expresses the proposition. Consider first the intra-attitudinal aspects of holism. By intra-attitudinal holism I mean not only the necessity of a multitude of thoughts within an attitude. We have already seen that there must be a multitude of thoughts belonging to any one attitude. What I now have in mind is the ways in which these thoughts must be related to each other, the sort of structure we can expect to find that constitutes the architecture of belief or the architecture of intention or of any other attitude.

Such interdependence is already supported by the arguments for a multitude of thoughts. Thus if to believe one is seeing a snake requires that one have many beliefs about the nature of snakes, then it follows that if enough of those further beliefs were to change, so would the belief that one is seeing a snake. It does not follow, of course, that if a single belief changes, all others must change. Some partisans of holism, for example Kuhn and Feyerabend, may have made such a claim, but I think that more often it has been the readers of Quine and other holists who have read this consequence wrongly into the holist doctrine. Quine did, of course, emphasize holism in "Two Dogmas of Empiricism" and in many later writings. But he never asserted that a change in one belief (or in the meaning of a single sentence) entailed a change in all the rest. His express views in fact directly refuted such an implication, for he emphasized that if the totality of one's beliefs implied a consequence which experience then forced one to abandon, one could make changes in one's total theory in many different ways, all of which would normally leave much of the original structure intact. In other words, a change in one place would necessitate other changes (this is obvious, since beliefs recognized as directly tied by logic to the altered belief would change), but in general these changes would be far from universal. The prudent theorist, Quine maintained, would strive to conserve as much of the old as he could when adjusting his views to new evidence. Here is an analogy: any *one* change in the tension on one part of a spider's web will change the position of many parts of the web (all, in fact, except the anchor points). But given one change, many possible adjustments in the tension elsewhere would preserve the position of most parts. Or consider adjustments in the center of gravity of an airplane. If some person changes his seat in an airplane, the relation of every object in the plane and every part of the plane to the center of gravity changes. But a single compensatory move will restore the center of gravity, and hence the relations of all objects to that center.

Holism should not, then, be thought to entail that *everything* we believe and intend and desire is in constant flux with the input of new information, or the impact of reflection. Much does, of course, change from moment to moment, even as we shift our gaze, or lose concentration, or recognize unexpected connections. But as we know, serious changes in our world outlook, ambitions, and taste are for the most part glacially slow. A change in many everyday beliefs, though it may call for much change, may have very little influence on what matters to us most. The importance of holism rests only in small part on its dynamic flow. Its real importance rests on the fact that the content of any given attitude depends on its place in the whole network. I have been talking as if there were a hypostatizable content to individual thoughts or utterances. This is a mistake: the process of *specifying the content* of a thought or utterance does not require that we suppose there is a definite, or indeed any, object before the mind of the thinker or speaker. When we say two people have the same thought, we mean their states of mind are similar enough to enable each to interpret the other; up to a point, at least, they are able to understand each other. For two people to think alike does not require that there be *things*—actual entities—which are or could be identical. The bugbear of anti-holists is the worry that if we are holists we can no longer compare what is in one mind with what is in another. If comparison necessarily rests on relevant similarity rather than identity, however, the worry evaporates. It's the difference between putting the emphasis on *identity* of thoughts and putting the emphasis on acceptable *interpretation*.

The principle behind intra-attitudinal holism is simply this: one of the ways the states of mind we call propositional attitudes are identified and individuated is by their relations to other such states of mind. When these relations are limited to obvious logical relations, few would disagree. The point becomes important when, with Quine, we give up the analytic–synthetic distinction, for then we have no way of distinguishing between the relations that define the state of mind (or the meaning of an utterance) and those that are "merely" contingent, and so do not touch content. But it is well to remember that giving up the idea of a firm line between the analytic and the synthetic does not mean giving up the idea of a continuum in which some connections among thoughts are far more important to characterizing a state of mind than are others. Thus my belief that it is raining today probably contributes essentially nothing to the content of my other beliefs about rain except those that are logically related, while my belief that rain is caused by the condensation of drops in water-saturated air contributes a great deal.

It follows from what I have said that many of our beliefs must be true. The reason, put briefly if misleadingly, is that a belief owes its character in part to its relations to other, true, beliefs. Suppose most of my beliefs about what I call snakes were false; then my belief that I am seeing what I call a "snake" would not be correctly described as being about a snake. Thus my belief, if it is to be about a snake, whether it is a true belief or a false one, depends on a background of true beliefs, true beliefs about the nature of snakes, of animals, of physical objects of the world. But though many beliefs must therefore be true, most beliefs can be false. This last remark is dangerously ambiguous. It means: with respect to most of our beliefs, any particular one may be false. It does not mean: with respect to the totality of our beliefs, most may be false, for the possibility of a false belief depends on an environment of truths. But this point needs more showing.

Inter-attitudinal holism is equally important, and completes the story of the holism of the mental. The various attitudes require one another. All the attitudes, desire, hope, intention, despair, expectation, depend on belief to give their contents substance. Most of our desires, for example, depend on our beliefs. We would not want to make money unless we believed it would put us in a position to obtain things we need or value; we would not want to go to the opera unless we thought we would enjoy it (or that someone else wants us to be there, etc.). We would never act on a moral principle except that we believe some action is sustained by it. The plainest practical reasoning requires the collusion of values and cognitive judgments. ("Sharp knives are better than dull knives; this is a sharp knife and that is a dull knife; so this knife is better than that knife.") Since intentions and actions follow from, and require, practical reasoning, no matter how implicit, intentions and intentional planning and their execution are also caught up in the web of evaluative attitudes and practical knowledge.

The list goes on. Many of the attitudes, like being pleased, proud, or angry that something has happened, depend on the true belief that it has occurred. We cannot be worried lest something will befall us unless we think it may, or hopeful that we will win a prize unless we know, or at least believe, we may.

It is less obvious that belief could not exist without the conative attitudes, but there is a clear sense in which it emerges from the study of decision theory that subjective probabilities, that is, beliefs, are ultimately distilled out of preference or choice, though this is not to say, with Hume, that belief "is, and ought only to be the slave of desire". Finally, I want to argue that belief and desire, and all the other propositional attitudes, depend on language. This connection has, in fact, often been taken for granted by philosophers, including in particular the American pragmatists: Mead, Dewey, James, Peirce, Wilfred Sellars, are all to be found saying, in effect, "Thought of any complexity clearly requires language." A. J. Ayer also held this view. I shall not take it for granted, however, but shall present what I think is a powerful argument.

My strategy, as I remarked at first, is in an important respect Cartesian. I have begun with the fact that I think, and I have asked what follows from that fact. Among the things that follow, I have suggested, are the existence of a multitude of beliefs, many of which must be true, and command of the concept of objective truth, the idea that beliefs may be true or false, and that their truth or falsity does not, in most cases, depend on the person who has them. Aside from the starting point I share with Descartes, however, my epistemology, if that is the right word for what I am doing, is almost totally non-Cartesian, for I do not assume, as Descartes and endless idealists, empiricists, and rationalists have, that empirical knowledge depends on indubitable beliefs, or something given to the mind which is impervious to doubt, nor that the contents of our beliefs may in principle be independent of what lies outside us. In other words, I am an anti-foundationalist, and I have left the door open for some form of externalism.

So far, however, I have done little to show that skepticism is untenable or unintelligible. For even if you were to agree that to have a thought, any thought at all, one must have many true beliefs, it does not follow that any of these beliefs directly concern the nature of the world around us. I have suggested that if, for example, you have a thought that you are seeing a snake, then you must believe many true things about snakes: you must know what a snake is like. But such truths are *general*, and general truths like these do not imply that any snakes exist, but only that if there were a snake, it would be without legs or arms, etc. So I have not shown why it is absurd to doubt that the external world in which we all believe actually exists.

Nor, to return to my central question, have I suggested what accounts for, or makes possible, our command of the concept of objective truth. So even though no one can doubt that he or she is capable of judgment or thought, the capacity for judgment remains mysterious. We all have the concept of objective truth; but we can discover only on reflection what makes this possible.

Summary

Since Descartes, epistemology has been based on first person knowledge. We must begin, according to the usual story, with what is most certain: knowledge of our own sensations and thoughts. In one way or another we then progress, if we can, to knowledge of an objective external world. There is then the final, tenuous, step to knowledge of other minds.

I argue for a total revision of this picture. All propositional thought, whether positive or skeptical, whether of the inner or of the outer, requires possession of the concept of objective truth, and this concept is accessible only to those creatures that are in communication with others. Knowledge of other minds is thus basic to all thought. But such knowledge requires and assumes knowledge of a shared world of objects in a common time and space. Thus the acquisition of knowledge is not based on a progression from the subjective to the objective; it emerges holistically, and is interpersonal from the start.

2 *Expressing Evaluations*

This essay explores some basic connections between evaluations and language. The subject as viewed here has barely been touched by philosophers, and much of what is said will concern matters seldom discussed in connection with moral philosophy. So I must ask for a degree of indulgence when we come to some mildly technical material from decision theory and the theory of meaning.

The first part of the essay stresses a negative point: we can learn relatively little about ethics and values generally by concentrating on explicitly evaluative language. But (and this is the subsequent and positive point) there is a connection between evaluative attitudes and meaning, a connection that is fundamental to the understanding of both. I find for a thoroughgoing holism, not only with respect to meanings and beliefs, but also with respect to the relations between the cognitive and the evaluative attitudes. The key to the understanding of all these mental phenomena is to see them from the point of view of an interpreter. Seeing them in this perspective will lead us to appreciate the ineluctably objective and intersubjective elements not only in language and belief but also in evaluation.

The connection between language and evaluation is more fundamental than the study of explicitly evaluative terms suggests. In many branches of philosophy, the study of language has yielded important insights and opened new leads: one thinks for example of many problems in epistemology and ontology, of the theory of action, the study of induction, of causality, essentialism, belief, necessity, and so on. It is a striking fact that the same cannot be said for moral theory. Not that a serious attempt to provide a satisfactory semantics for the natural language uses of words like 'good', 'right', 'ought', 'obligatory', and the sentences containing them might not be rewarding; I believe it would be. But little good work has been done in this area. We do not even have a satisfactory theory of the logical form of most evaluative sentences. There are of course the various special 'logics': deontic logic, the logic of preference, and the like. But these lack a convincing interpretation.

I am not now going to pursue the promising study of the semantics of the language of morals. The present essay is concerned with something more general, and inherently less susceptible of precision, the relation between language (mainly ordinary, non-evaluative, descriptive language) and evaluative attitudes.

Here a word about terminology may help prevent misunderstanding. By 'evaluations' I mean any evaluative attitudes like wanting, desiring, cherishing, holding to be right or to be obligatory, and the negative and comparative versions of these attitudes. I do not want the word to suggest an act, though an evaluation may, of course, be the result of an act of judgment. In particular, an evaluation, as I mean it here, is not a verbal act. I am, however, as my title suggests, concerned with how evaluative attitudes (evaluations) are expressed in language.

How *are* evaluative attitudes expressed in language? Well, of course we often do use explicitly evaluative terms. We say someone ought to be more generous with his time, that the new vice president of the firm has done a good job of winning customers, that butter is better than margarine for sautéing squid, that it was right to lower the age for voting. We also may express our good opinion of a chisel by saying it holds an edge, of a Camembert by saying it is ripe, of an act by saying it was prompt, of a person by saying she is nonchalant. In fact we may express approval or disapproval, or any other evaluative attitude, by saying almost anything (given an appropriate context), just as we may express one and the same belief by uttering any of a vast number of sentences.

It would be a mistake to suppose there is something unusual in expressing evaluations through the use of sentences that contain no evaluative words. If we are shopping for a car with a friend who shares our tastes, the effective way of expressing our positive and negative reactions will be by mentioning the compression ratio, the rack and pinion steering, the drum brakes, or the gear ratios. But the point is more global. In a given context, our words normally have a correct interpretation. We depend on our hearers to get the interpretation right, and we supply what we deem to be adequate clues to this end.

The interpretation that we intend to be put on our words does not necessarily, or even regularly, correspond to what we want to assert, maintain, suggest, or convey; our words, with their intended meaning, are a device by means of which we hope to get across our message, but meaning and message may, and typically do, differ widely. If I say to a man, 'You are a bull', I may mistakenly be asserting that he is a bull, I may insultingly be saying he is stubborn, I may jokingly be suggesting he thinks the stock market will go up, or I may be reminding him that I know when his birthday is. My *words* have the same intended interpretation, the same 'literal' meaning, in each case.

The looseness of the tie between what sentences mean and the purposes they are used to promote explains why there is no hope that the former can be interestingly defined in terms of the latter. When we know what a sentence means, that meaning forms part of the explanation of how we intend, by uttering the sentence, to bring off the feats we do. But there is no one thing, or sort of thing, or list of things, that we must be doing, or must be trying to do, by speaking words with a particular meaning.

The attempt to determine the meaning of evaluative words and sentences by studying the range of their uses has been made so often, and in so many ways, that I must elaborate a bit on why I think this approach cannot succeed. Following Austin (at some distance), we may distinguish three basic intentions with which every linguistic utterance is made: (1) in uttering a sentence, the speaker intends to utter words that in the circumstances will be interpreted as having a certain literal meaning; (2) through the recognition of this meaning by an audience, the speaker intends to be understood as making a particular assertion, asking a particular question, issuing a particular command, expressing a certain desire, etc.; (3) by means of uttering words with the intended interpretation and with the intended force (also correctly interpreted), the speaker intends to accomplish some ulterior (non-linguistic) purpose. This last intention may or may not be intended by the speaker to be recognized by the hearer, but the speaker must intend that intentions (1) and (2) be recognized, this recognition being intended to promote his further ends.[1] For example, I say to Ellen, 'This pig is fat', intending her to interpret my words as true if

---

[1] This threefold division of intentions is inspired by, though not identical with, Austin's division of speech acts into locutions, illocutions, and perlocutions. J. L. Austin, *How to Do Things with Words*, Oxford University Press, 1962. I have incorporated an important idea of Paul Grice's, 'Meaning', *The Philosophical Review*, 66 (1957), pp. 377–88.

and only if the pig I point to is fat, with the intention of asserting that the pig I point to is fat, with the intention of getting Ellen to buy my pig. I might have accomplished my purpose just as well by saying 'Look how fat this pig is' or 'Isn't this a fat pig?' where the meaning of the words would have been different, but the force of my utterance and my ulterior purpose is the same. It is clear that there is no rule that relates what the words, in their intended interpretation, mean, and what the speaker intends to assert, ask, question, command, or commend, much less between these intentions and any ulterior purpose.

There is no way, I think, that appeal to a linguistic convention can bridge the gap between what words mean and what the speaker who uses them means (the force of the utterance) or between either of these and the speaker's ulterior purpose. A convention is a custom; if we break it, we operate outside the custom, though of course by doing so we may take advantage of it. But if I use the imperative sentence 'Look how fat this pig is' to assert that a pig is fat, I do not break any convention of language (or any other that I know of). I want my sentence to be imperative in mood, for it is by uttering just that sentence that I intend to make my assertion. Perhaps it is a convention that decrees the literal meaning of the words, but no convention decrees that imperative sentences are to be used for issuing commands only.[2] Analogously, it cannot be a convention that evaluative sentences are tied to particular sorts of illocutionary act such as advising, goading, or guiding, or expressing an evaluative attitude.

It is natural to think that particular sentences are 'made for' a particular use. Thus it may be thought that a sentence like 'It is foggy' is made for asserting that it is foggy (illocutionary force), or for informing people, or getting people to believe, that it is foggy (ulterior purpose). But no one, I think, has succeeded in explaining the relevant sense of 'made for' in this context—explained why it is that we are using the sentence 'It is foggy' for its decreed or conventional or natural purpose when we are trying to get someone to believe it is foggy, but not when we are teasing them, telling a story, making a philosophical point, or trying to bore a neighbor. I think an utterance of the sentence 'It is foggy', when addressed by an English speaker to an English-speaking audience has only one guaranteed purpose: that

---

[2] For further defense and discussion of this point, see my essays 'Moods and Performances' and 'Convention and Communication' in *Inquiries into Truth and Interpretation*, Oxford University Press, 1984.

it (the sentence uttered, not 'what is said') shall be interpreted as true if and only if it is foggy.

There are cases, needless to say, when a sentence is used for what it is 'made for'. In such cases, what the speaker means can be read directly from the meaning of the sentence, given the circumstances of utterance: in uttering the sentence 'It is foggy' the speaker asserts that it is foggy, thus representing himself as believing that it is foggy at the time of utterance and in his vicinity. In uttering the sentence 'Put down that cleaver' the speaker is ordering the person addressed to put down the cleaver in his hand. Or in uttering the sentence 'Do you see an orc?' the speaker is asking his audience if it sees an orc, thus representing himself as wanting to know. (Those who have confidence in the idea of a standard or natural or conventional use of a sentence usually go beyond these claims, which concern only force, and maintain that some ulterior purpose is also standard.) Although I think there are no conventions linking such uses of sentences with their meanings, it is no doubt essential that an interpreter be able to detect such cases fairly often if he is to come to understand a speaker. Or, more generally and more precisely, an interpreter must be able to tell, often enough, when a speaker holds a sentence he speaks to be true or false, or wants it to be true, or intends to make it true. This is, however, a fact about the nature of radical interpretation, and places no constraints on the illocutionary or ulterior intentions of a speaker.

The key relation, then, between language and attitudes like valuing, believing, and intending is not the attitudes that prompt utterances, for these bear no conventional or rule-governed relation to what the words uttered mean or are intended to mean. The key relation is rather the attitudes, for example of belief or desire, that the speaker has towards his sentences. You might say: what is needed for interpretation is not primarily the speaker's attitudes towards his audience, but towards his sentences. Putting the matter this way oversimplifies, of course, since a speaker's attitude towards his hearers must include, as we have seen, the intention to speak words that will be interpreted as having a certain literal meaning, the intention to speak in such a way that his utterance will be taken to have a specific force, and the intention that these intentions be discerned. There is not, however, any requirement to the effect that a speaker must always intend a hearer to know whether or not he holds a sentence he utters to be true on that occasion (or any other), or has any other attitude towards it. My present point is that though this is not required in the case of any particular speech act, or particular sentence, the possibility of interpretation depends on the ability of the interpreter frequently to tell what the speaker's actual attitudes towards the sentences he utters are. Sometimes what insures this is that the interpreter can observe that the speaker is sincere, and literally means what he says: the sentence he utters is 'made for' saying what he is saying. In this case, the speaker holds the sentence he uses to be true. Too much weight should not be put on sincere, literal assertion, however. It is not very common, and there are many other contexts in which a speaker's attitudes towards his sentences can be detected.

We understand a person when we are able to explain his or her actions in terms of intentions, and the intentions in terms of beliefs and evaluative attitudes. When the behavior to be explained is verbal, we must (it follows) be able to understand his or her words. What we as interpreters are able to do, or what we know, can only be made explicit by a theory that assigns correct interpretations to an agent's beliefs, desires, and words. To put this in a familiar, if ontologically misleading, way, we assign propositions to the agent's attitudes and utterances.

Most discussions of radical interpretation (including my own) have concentrated on the relation between belief and meaning; disenchantment with the analytic–synthetic distinction necessarily led to treating belief and meaning as permanently entangled. In this essay I am exploring the relation between evaluative attitudes and meaning. Since meaning is entangled with belief, my subject really is the relations among the three: meaning, belief, and (as we may say for brevity) desire. There will turn out to be a sense in which each of the three must be viewed as dependent on the other two; but also a sense in which desire is the most basic.

It is clear from what has been said that there are two quite different ways in which evaluative attitudes, and evaluations, are related to sentences. On the one hand, we may think of a person who puts a positive value on the eradication of poverty as embracing or accepting the sentence 'It would be good if poverty were eradicated'. Embracing or accepting an evaluative sentence is to valuing what holding a descriptive sentence true is to belief. In fact there seems no reason not to use the words 'embrace' or 'accept' in both cases: to embrace an evaluative sentence is to value a certain proposition; to embrace a descriptive sentence is to believe a certain proposition. (It should be emphasized that embracing, accepting, or holding a sentence true are attitudes towards a sentence or the proposition it expresses; they are not speech acts. Someone who makes an assertion by uttering a descriptive sentence may represent himself as holding the sentence true, i.e. as having a certain belief, but this is not the same as having the belief. Similarly, someone who commends an action may represent himself as holding the action to be desirable without actually thinking it desirable.)

What is the difference between embracing an evaluative sentence and embracing a descriptive sentence? We have already made the obvious observation that embracing the sentence 'It would be good if poverty were eradicated' is closely related to valuing the proposition that poverty is eradicated. But we can also put this by saying: embracing the sentence 'It would be good if poverty were eradicated' is much like wanting or desiring the sentence 'Poverty is eradicated' to be true. Of course this fact does not eliminate the difference between the two sorts of embracing, since believing a sentence to be true neither entails nor is entailed by desiring that sentence to be true. So there is a clear asymmetry between embracing an evaluative sentence and embracing the embedded descriptive sentence, an asymmetry that becomes apparent when a piece of practical reasoning is put into words.

It is possible, however, to represent this asymmetry in quite a different way. We have been considering the contrast between embracing an explicitly evaluative sentence and embracing a descriptive sentence. But we could instead contrast two different attitudes, belief and desire, as directed to the same sentence (or proposition). This comes out as the contrast between wanting 'Poverty is eradicated' to be true, and believing it to be true, or the contrast between wanting poverty to be eradicated and believing it has been. Which of these two contrasts or asymmetries we take as basic will, I suggest, make all the difference to our study of the relation between valuing and language. Most studies of this relation concentrate on the first contrast, which depends on the use of explicitly evaluative sentences—sentences that 'say' that something is desirable or good or obligatory. Such an approach encourages one of two distortions: either desire is seen as a special form of belief, a belief that certain states or events have a moral or other kind of value, or are obligatory, etc.; or evaluative sentences are thought to lack cognitive content. The first of these views makes evaluation too much like cognition; the second bifurcates language in an unacceptable way by leaving the semantics of evaluative sentences unrelated to the semantics of sentences with a truth value.

For this reason, as well as others that will appear, I think we should take as basic the contrast between the attitude of belief and the attitude of desire as directed to the same sentences. This course will permit a considerable simplification at the start, since it will be possible to postpone consideration of explicitly evaluative sentences until the basic connections between language and evaluation have been established. It has often been observed that we could easily get along without interrogative or imperative sentences—they are not needed in order to ask questions or give orders. A similar remark goes for evaluative sentences; we can express our evaluative attitudes without them. By ignoring the role of evaluative sentences at the outset we will be able to connect our present problem with profound questions about the relations among the propositional attitudes, and between these and language.

According to Hume, 'reason is, and ought only to be the slave of the passions'. By this he seems to have meant that the passions (desires) supply the force that moves us to act, while reason (belief) merely directs this force. I doubt that desire can be distinguished from belief in this way; belief and desire seem equally to be causal conditions of action. But there is a sense in which desire can be said to be more basic conceptually. Desire is more basic in that if we know enough about a person's desires, we can work out what he believes, while the reverse does not hold.

This is best seen by glancing at Bayesian decision theory in a version, such as Ramsey's, that treats probabilities as degrees of belief. What is called subjective probability in theories of this sort is simply belief quantified according to its strength. Desire is taken in its fundamental form as a relation between three things: an agent, and two alternatives, one of which is desired more strongly than the other by the agent. Desire thought of in this way is more fundamental than simple non-relative desire, since it is often far clearer that one course of action or state of affairs is preferable to another than that either is desirable. The reason for this is the sturdy connection between preference and choice, which is how preference manifests itself on occasion. Non-relative desire has no such direct connection with behavior, unless we think of simple desire as implicitly relative to a background of assumptions as to what things would be like if the desired option were rejected.

Here is how belief (subjective probability) is embedded in desire (preference). The choice of a course of action, or more generally a preference that one state of affairs be true rather than another, may always be seen as a choice or preference where the alternatives are gambles. For whatever we choose to do, we cannot be certain how things will come out; or if a certain state of affairs were to obtain, we cannot be sure what else would be the case. So our choices or preferences are determined by how likely we think various outcomes are, given that we act in one way or another (or that one or another state of affairs obtains), and the values we set on the various outcomes. Suppose, for example, that I want to see into the next valley, and to do this I must climb one of two mountains. If I climb K1, which is the easier climb, I may or may not have the view I need; if I climb K2, which is harder, I am certain to see what I want. There are two possible choices, three possible outcomes. Obviously the best outcome is that I climb K1 and see into the next valley; the worst is that I climb K1 and am disappointed; climbing K2, with its assured outcome, is somewhere in between. My choice depends in part on the relative values of the outcomes, essentially the ratio of the differences in desirability between climbing K1 and succeeding and climbing K2 on the one hand, and between climbing K2 and futilely climbing K1 on the other. But my choice also depends on my beliefs, in particular how probable I think success and failure are given that I climb K1. Since I rank the outcomes as I do, there is some probability of success on climbing K1 high enough to prompt me to make that ascent, and some probability low enough to make me climb K2. Suppose the values of the three outcomes are evenly spaced for me: climbing K2 is midway in desirability between climbing K1 and failing and climbing K1 and succeeding. Then if I think success more probable than failure, I will climb K1, and if failure looks more likely, I will climb K2. This result may be read in reverse: given the values I put on the outcomes, which mountain I choose to climb shows something about my subjective probabilities, that is, my beliefs. This is the sense in which belief is 'contained' in desire.

If desire is to this extent more basic than belief, how do we come to grasp a person's desires, particularly desires that are measurable in the way we have just assumed? Perhaps desire is not reducible to anything more basic, but it is possible to reduce measurable desire (often called 'cardinal utility') to simple preference of one course of action or state of affairs over another. Frank Ramsey showed how this was possible by outlining a sequence of observations an interpreter could in theory make which would determine both subjective probabilities and cardinal utilities to any degree of precision, depending only on simple preferences.[3] It is not necessary to describe the method here. The point of the method is that it proves that an interpreter who knows enough about the simple preferences of an agent is entitled by the theory to predict all further preferences of that agent, and to explain them in terms of beliefs and desires, with the beliefs assigned a specific strength and the differences in the strengths of desires made comparable.

Ramsey's theory, and others like it, are normative in character: they limit the patterns the preferences of a rational agent can display. The limitations apply solely to the relations among preferences; there are no restrictions on particular preferences. These theories are normative: they purport to define an aspect of rationality. It would be a mistake, though, to think that real people do not approximate to what theory decrees to be reasonable. The explanation for this is not that by luck or divine dispensation each of us has a share of reason; the explanation is rather that it is only in the environment of an at least roughly rational pattern that propositional attitudes can be said to exist. As interpreters, we cannot intelligibly describe or attribute propositional attitudes unless we know or believe they are arranged in an intelligible pattern. Rationality is, of course, a matter of degree. So also are the clarity and precision that interpretation can achieve. The two go together: the more rational we are able to find an agent, the more unequivocal our attributions of attitudes to that agent. As rationality fades, our ability to describe the failure in clear detail fades too. There is no evading the fact that there are normative constraints on correct descriptions of intentional (and intensional) phenomena.

Officially, a Bayesian theory says nothing about subjective probabilities or desires measured on an interval scale. It does no more than describe relations among simple preferences between alternatives. But given that these relations hold, it is possible to prove that the preferences are just those that would result from consistently applied beliefs graded according to strength and desires comparable with respect to differences in strength. Subjective probabilities and quantified desires are thus, from the point of view of Bayesian theories, theoretical

[3] F. P. Ramsey, 'Truth and Probability', in *Foundations of Mathematics*, Routledge and Kegan Paul, 1931.

constructs whose function is to relate and explain simple preferences. In this sense, beliefs and quantified desires are 'reducible' to simple preferences. Clearly enough, such reduction does not show how to eliminate intensional concepts in favor of extensional ones, since simple preferences are still propositional attitudes. The reduction is within the ambit of the intensional, a reduction of the complex to the simple, of belief to desire, of the quantifiable to the qualitative, of that which must be posited to explain action and much more to that which is more open to observation and introspection.

From the point of view of our present concern, Bayesian decision theories have a fatal drawback: they simply assume that an interpreter can tell what propositions an agent is evaluating or choosing between, or which interpreted sentences express the agent's preferences. Yet this assumption covers the very territory in which we are interested: the area where evaluation and language meet. Decision theory begins with simple preferences between propositions; once these have been identified, the theory allows us to extract the beliefs and desires that went into, and explain, the preferences. But it says nothing about what determined the objects of the original simple preferences. Preferences are, of course, manifested in behavior in many ways. But this fact does not tell us how the content of preferences is fixed.

Decision theory allows us to attach significant, but not directly observable, properties to the objects of choice and preference, and the perceived outcomes of choice, and it does this by postulating an observable pattern. We need now to repeat the process on a more primitive level, before the objects of choice and preference are identified as particular propositions. The objects of preference and choice are, of course, propositions, or propositional in nature; the problem is to say what determines which propositions they are. The idea is simple: if postulating a pattern in preferences makes it possible to derive quantified beliefs and desires from knowledge of the propositional objects of preference, then perhaps postulating more structure, a more complicated pattern, will permit the identification of the propositions themselves.

How can we describe preferences without first identifying their propositional content? If the pattern is to be complex enough to permit identifying propositional content, then clearly the uninterpreted preferences must be described as relating objects that can be given a propositional interpretation. We should also require that an agent's preference for one of these objects over another be open to observation (though the objects themselves need not be observable).

The natural way of describing preferences in a way that meets these conditions is to describe them as relating sentences. Sentences are not observable, but their utterances and inscriptions are, and this makes it possible to discover the preferences of an agent without knowing how to specify the propositional objects. Sentences are at least as finely individuated as propositions; indeed, it is only by using sentences that we can identify the objects of beliefs and the other propositional attitudes. What I am suggesting here is that we can use an agent's own sentences to keep track of his propositional attitudes before we are in a position to interpret the sentences or the attitudes.

Let us suppose, then, that the raw data for radical interpretation are facts to the effect that an agent prefers one sentence to be true rather than another. The sentences are, of course, understood by the agent, but not, to begin with, by the interpreter. The task of the interpreter is to decide on the basis of the data what the agent means by his words, what he believes, and what he values. Thus by starting with preferences between sentences whose interpretation is not known, we will not beg the question with which we started, the question of the fundamental relation between language and evaluation. For it is possible for an interpreter to know that a person prefers that one of his sentences be true rather than another without knowing what the sentences mean, and therefore without knowing the propositional contents of the preference.

It remains to show how interpretation can rest on such a narrow base. This cannot be done in any detail here, but it will be possible to describe in outline a sequence of steps that could in theory lead to a comprehensive system of interpretation. First, however, it will be necessary to depart in an important respect from standard versions of decision theory. Theories of decision, such as Ramsey's, take as unanalyzed the notion of a gamble or wager. But a gamble, though it may be presented in the form of a proposition, involves a relation, typically causal, between propositions. So, for example, the gamble incurred by climbing K1 (which may or may not afford a view into the next valley) requires us to understand the relation between climbing the mountain and seeing the view. There seems to be no satisfactory way in which an interpreter could tell that someone had grasped this relation and had incorporated it into his understanding of an option— short, of course, of being able to communicate by language. Such communication is a goal of radical interpretation, and so cannot be assumed before it starts. I turn therefore to a version of decision theory devised by Richard Jeffrey, in which it is not assumed that the interpreter can tell when an agent is entertaining a gamble. In Jeffrey's system, choices or preferences concern propositions, and the pattern of preferences allows the measurement of the subjective probabilities and values that attach to the propositions.[4] The strength of the resulting measurement is not quite as strong as in standard theories, but it is adequate to explain choices and preferences.

In order to apply Jeffrey's theory, it is necessary to decide what the propositions are among which the agent's preferences fall, and this is once more just what radical interpretation aims to discover. As I suggested above, the best we can do at the start is to record preferences as being between sentences. The interpretation of the sentences (attaching propositions to them) is part of the interpreter's job. How is this to be done?

The answer can be given by outlining a series of steps the end product of which is an interpretation of the agent's language. At the same time, values and degrees of belief will be assigned to each sentence, which amounts to attributing beliefs and evaluations to the agent. The sequence in which these steps are described is dictated by logical, not practical, considerations. Its purpose is to provide an informal demonstration that the constraints laid down by the theory are adequate to yield something close to the concepts of belief, desire, and meaning we normally use in understanding, describing, and explaining human behavior. I do not suggest for a moment that the story I am about to tell bears a direct relation to the way we actually go about learning language, or coming to understand people. At best, the defense of the theory shows how the structural features of the propositional attitudes make the understanding of human action possible.

Since interpretation begins at a point where the interpreter does not understand the sentences of an agent, let us now think of desire and preference as concerned entirely with the truth and falsity of sentences—sentences the agent understands but the interpreter does not. Desire has no application to sentences that are known for certain to be true or false, though other attitudes, such as wishing and regretting, do. It makes no sense to prefer that yesterday had been sunny

---

[4] R. Jeffrey, *The Logic of Decision*, 2nd edition, The University of Chicago Press, 1983.

rather than rainy, or to desire to have been born in ancient Rome. For the same reason, we are indifferent to the truth of tautologies: the news that tomorrow it will snow or it won't leaves us neither cold nor warm. The principle is more general. The more certain we are that something is the case, the less we value it, whether positively or negatively. This may seem to be false; for example, I may be quite certain that I shall not be struck by a meteor before I finish this paragraph, but don't I highly value living that long? I think not. Learning that 'I am not struck by a meteor before I finish this paragraph' is true would give me little satisfaction; I'm already practically certain of its truth. What one may mistake for a high evaluation of truth may instead be a great negative evaluation of falsity: I greatly disvalue the truth of 'I am struck by a meteor before I finish this paragraph'.[5] What these considerations show is that the desirability of a sentence being true depends, as one might expect, on the value we would assign to its truth if we thought it was false, reduced by the probability we assign to its actual truth. The desirability of its truth is thus a measure of the price we would be willing to pay to be certain of its truth. No matter how much we would hate to see it false, we would pay nothing for its truth if its truth is already assured. (I would not have paid to have it so, but I am glad to have finished this paragraph.)

Because the desirability of the truth or falsity of a sentence depends in part on how likely we think it is to be true, it is possible to derive subjective probabilities from preferences. Ramsey did this by using gambles; Jeffrey gets much the same result by measuring how much the subjective probabilities of propositions (sentences for us) affect the desirabilities of those same propositions (sentences). Suppose we find the truth of two sentences, S and T, equally desirable, and both of them more desirable than a tautology (to the truth of which we are indifferent). It's clear that the negations of S and T can't be preferred to a tautology, but the negations may not be equally disvalued because of differences in probability. For example, I may desire the truth of 'There is no nuclear war tomorrow' and 'I find a quarter in the street tomorrow' equally, but I disvalue the falsity of the first enormously more than the falsity of the second. The reason is that I think the first is almost certainly true and the second almost certainly false (these probabilities and relative strengths of desire could radically change). Thus it is possible to compare degrees of belief in sentences on the

---

[5] R. Jeffrey, *The Logic of Decision*, 2nd edition, The University of Chicago Press, 1983, pp. 62–3. I am indebted to Jeffrey for convincing me of this.

basis of simple comparisons of desirability of truth. Additional steps make possible the construction of measures of degrees of belief and strengths of desire.

The determination of the subjective probabilities and desirabilities of the truth of sentences has, it seems, been accomplished without knowledge of what those sentences mean. But this is not quite the case. We have had to depend upon being able to recognize the negation of a sentence, and to recognize at least one tautology. In effect, then, we have illegitimately been assuming that the truth functional sentential connectives could be interpreted. Can this be done on the basis simply of preferences that one sentence rather than another be true? It can, as follows. Suppose we find an operation O on pairs of sentences that has these properties: first, it is symmetrical. This can be shown by discovering that for any two sentences S and T the agent is indifferent between SOT and TOS. Second, it satisfies the condition that for any three sentences, S, T, and U, whenever the agent prefers S to $(TOU)O((TOU)O(TOU))$ he does not prefer $(TOU)O((TOU)O(TOU))$ to SOS, and whenever he prefers SOS to $(TOU)O((TOU)O(TOU))$ he does not prefer $(TOU)O((TOU)O(TOU))$ to S. The operation O can only be the Sheffer stroke—the operation 'not both'. SOS turns out to be the negation of S, and $(TOU)O((TOU)O(TOU))$ is a tautology. (This device depends on the fact that a sentence and its negation cannot both be preferred to a tautology.) Of course if this is right, it will turn out that the tautology has a subjective probability of 1 and its negation a subjective probability of 0.

Since all the truth functional connectives can be defined in terms of the Sheffer stroke, these can now be interpreted. And so in fact can the rest of the speaker's language, using methods that have often been described elsewhere.[6] Briefly outlined, here are the steps. The patterns of inferences from which there is seldom a clear deviation should suffice to uncover the logical constants needed for quantificational structure (including the truth functional sentential connectives when these connect open sentences). Grammatical categories can now be assigned to words: predicates, singular terms, quantifiers, functional expressions will be identifiable. Interpretation of these expressions will then depend primarily on connecting words to the world by way

[6] For further discussion of the nature of radical interpretation, and its connections with Quine's notion of radical translation, see the essays on radical interpretation in my *Inquiries into Truth and Interpretation*.

of their function in sentences. It will be found, for example, that the agent is caused to award a high probability to some sentence when and only when it is raining in his vicinity: the interpreter will then enter as a hypothesis (possibly to be abandoned when more structure becomes apparent) that this is a sentence that means that it is raining. More evidence for this interpretation will come from the probabilities; rain perceived under poor conditions for observation will cause lower probabilities; a downpour experienced in the open a probability of 1, or something close. More evidence still will accumulate as further sentences are given tentative interpretations. Thus a sentence interpreted as meaning that there is a patter on the roof, if held true (given a high probability) ought to increase the probability of the sentence interpreted as meaning that it is raining. In this way, by marking what the speaker takes as evidence for the truth of a sentence, it is possible to interpret sentences and words of an increasingly abstract and theoretical nature.

The interpretation of language has, in this account, been made to rest on beliefs and desires. But the beliefs and desires were seen as directed to sentences whose interpretations were not known at the start. Once the sentences are understood, however, it is easy to specify the propositional contents of the various beliefs and desires, since to understand the sentences a person desires or believes to be true is to know what he desires and believes.

I have sketched in broad outline how I think a person's values are related to his beliefs and the meanings he gives his words. The approach has been foundational in the sense that I have assumed that a radical interpreter is not, at the beginning of his study, informed about any of the basic propositional attitudes of his subject. The idea has been that the pattern of uninterpreted responses of a certain sort is enough to allow the assignment of meanings to words, the attribution of beliefs, and the determination of the objects of desire. The responses are uninterpreted only in that the ordinary propositional contents are not known; the basic data for interpretation are still intensional in character, since they involve the concept of desiring sentences to be true. The relation between a person and a sentence he desires to be true is purely extensional, since it holds however the person and the sentence are described. This does not suggest that the words expressing the relation can somehow be reduced to purely extensional concepts; I'm sure they cannot be.

Our approach to interpretation has been holistic. Holism is forced on us by the fact that what can fairly be treated as evidence for any one of the propositional attitudes can count as evidence only if untested assumptions are made about the others. This is clear from the fact that in the logical sequence leading to interpretation, propositional contents for beliefs, sentences, and desires emerged only at the end, and then simultaneously for language and the attitudes. There was of course a starting place, and that place concerned values or desires. It would not be wrong to say that the evaluative attitudes, and the actions that reveal them, form the foundation of our understanding of the speech and behavior of others.

It should be emphasized again that the sequence I have outlined for arriving at a coherent picture of the thoughts and meanings of a speaker and agent is not meant to be a realistic account of how anyone actually achieves such a picture. For one thing, the role of ordinary social arrangements has been totally neglected; the method assumes a society of two. But the fact that we do not generally come to understand a speaker's words by interacting with him alone does not discredit the method. For if it were not possible to come to understand a speaker by interacting with him alone, neither would it be possible to do it through the intercession of others. Sketching a method shows not only *that* radical interpretation is possible—which of course we knew—but also *how*. Given the number of unknowns for which we must simultaneously solve, this was by no means obvious. More important, outlining a procedure that could in theory lead to successful interpretation has forced us to describe the main features of the pattern of propositional attitudes that make interpretation possible. It is this we wanted to study, particularly the relation between evaluations and language.

Let us come back to that starting point. The key to the solution for simultaneously identifying the meanings, beliefs, and values of an agent is a policy of rational accommodation, or a principle that Quine and I, following Neil Wilson, have called in the past the principle of charity. This policy calls on us to fit our own propositions (or our own sentences) to the other person's words and attitudes in such a way as to render their speech and other behavior intelligible. This necessarily requires us to see others as much like ourselves in point of overall coherence and correctness—that we see them as more or less rational creatures mentally inhabiting a world much like our own. Rationality is a matter of degree; but insofar as people think, reason, and act at all, there must be enough rationality in the complete pattern for us to judge particular beliefs as foolish or false, or particular acts as confused or misguided. For only in a largely coherent scheme can propositional contents find a lodging.

The policy of rational accommodation or charity in interpretation is not a policy in the sense of being one among many possible successful policies. It is the only policy available if we want to understand other people. So instead of calling it a policy, we might do better to think of it as a way of expressing the fact that creatures with thoughts, values, and speech must be rational creatures, are necessarily inhabitants of the same objective world as ourselves, and necessarily share their leading values with us. We should not think of this as some sort of lucky accident, but as something built into the concepts of belief, desire, and meaning.

In the case of belief, what insures that our general picture of the world is one we share with other thinking creatures, and one that is, in its main commonsense features, correct, is that sentences, and the thoughts they may be used to express, are causally tied to what they are about. For in the plainest cases we can do no better than to interpret a sentence that a person is selectively caused to hold true by the presence of rain as meaning that it is raining. This rule can accommodate many exceptions, and its application is subtle and complicated, but to ignore it is simply to abandon interpretation. It follows that in the plainest and simplest matters good interpretation will generally put interpreter and interpreted in agreement. It will also make most of our plainest beliefs true. Clearly, this arrangement leaves no room for a concept of relativized truth.

As with belief, so with desire or evaluation. Just as in coming to the best understanding I can of your beliefs I must find you coherent and correct, so I must also match up your values with mine; not, of course, in all matters, but in enough to give point to our differences. This is not, I must stress, to pretend or assume we agree. Rather, since the objects of your beliefs and values are what cause them, the only way for me to determine what those objects are is to identify objects common to us both, and take what you are caused to think and want as basically similar to what I am caused to think and want by the same objects. As with belief, there is no room left for relativizing values, or for asking whether interpersonal comparisons of value are possible. The only way we have of knowing what someone else's values are is one that (as in the case of belief) builds on a common framework.

Aside from some remarks at the start, I have said almost nothing about explicitly evaluative language. The focus has been, as I said it would be, on the attitudes of belief and preference (or evaluation) as directed to non-evaluative sentences.

But what about explicitly evaluative sentences, sentences about what is good, desirable, useful, obligatory, or our duty? The simplest view would be, as mentioned before, to identify desiring a sentence to be true with judging that it would be desirable if it were true—in other words, to identify desiring that 'Poverty is eradicated' be true with embracing the sentence 'It is desirable that poverty be eradicated'. And it is in fact hard to see how these two attitudes can be allowed to take entirely independent directions. On the other hand, there is a point to having a rich supply of evaluative words to distinguish the various evaluative attitudes clearly from one another: judging an act good is not the same as judging that it ought to be performed, and certainly judging that there is an obligation to make some sentence true is not the same as judging that it is desirable to make it true. For these and further reasons, there is no simple detailed connection between our basic preferences for the truth of various sentences and our judgments about the moral or other values that would be realized if they were true. The full story here is obviously very complicated, and touches on many much disputed matters. But no matter what the subtleties, interpreting evaluative judgments rests on the same foundation as interpreting the evaluative attitudes: everything depends on our ability to find common ground. Given enough common ground, we can understand and explain differences; we can criticize, compare, and persuade. The central point is that finding the common ground is not subsequent to understanding, but a condition of it. This fact may be hidden from us because we usually more or less understand someone's language before we talk with them. This promotes the impression that we can then, using our mutually understood language, discover whether we share their view of the world and their basic values. This is an illusion. If we understand their words, a common ground exists, a shared 'way of life'. A creature that cannot in principle be understood in terms of our own beliefs, values, and mode of communication is not a creature that may have thoughts radically different from our own: it is a creature without what we mean by 'thoughts'.

3 *The Objectivity of Values*

In our unguarded moments we all tend to be objectivists about values. We see ourselves as arguing with others who maintain values opposed to ours. In the heat of dispute it does not seem that we are expressing attitudes with which our opponents are at liberty to differ, nor do we think we are merely trying to bring them to share our goals. We are convinced that we are right and they are wrong, not just in the sense that our values are better than theirs, or more enlightened, but that we are *objectively* correct and they are not. We assume, and assert, that our judgments of what is good, right, or just are true, and that those who disagree with us hold false views.

These are our unguarded moments. On second thought we are apt to grant that others may be as entitled to their opinions as we are to ours. Judgments of value are not, we generously allow, objectively true or false, though some values may be admirable or despicable. We may even be brought to feel ashamed of speaking and acting as though we thought there were truths about the right or the worthwhile. It is politically correct to welcome the diversity of ultimate goals and aims; it smacks of cultural imperialism, we are told, to embrace the objectivity of values.

But should we rest with this second thought? It is impossible, I think, to rest content with it, for it clashes with some of the most powerful intuitions we have: the very intuitions that come with the first, unguarded, thought. Despite the manifest difficulties, no satisfactory theory of morality (or value generally) can fail to accommodate our lively conviction that moral claims are objectively either valid or not.

The denial that value judgments are objective, that they have truth values just as our ordinary judgments about the physical world do, is not to be confused with relativism. The relativist does not question the objective validity of value judgments; he merely insists that what is valuable or right is relative to time, place, person, culture, tribe, or legal system. We are all moral relativists to some degree; any sane person must be. We acknowledge that it is morally wrong to kill someone in order to inherit their money, but that killing may be permitted, or even right, under certain other conditions. We do not blame children for actions for which we would hold an adult responsible. It may (as Plato remarked) be right to hand a man beset by thieves a weapon, but wrong to give the same weapon to a deranged would-be suicide. Relativism becomes progressively more plausible, but also less interesting, the more pervasive the relevant conditions are made, and the more willing we become to recognize that our judgments are valid only as relativized.

Nevertheless, the relativist cannot in consistency deny the objectivity of values. The relativist holds that an individual act has its value objectively, though an act similar in many ways might have a different, though equally objective, value. The relativist about values is no more skeptical about the objectivity of values than the linguist is skeptical about the truth of an utterance just because the same sentence uttered in another context may be false. ("It's raining".)

There are, of course, familiar ethical theories which make evaluative judgments objective: the two best known are the Kantian and the utilitarian. Kant held that there are moral laws or principles or maxims which admit of no exceptions. They tell us that acts of certain sorts are obligatory or forbidden in every circumstance, in the sense that no action falls under more than one principle. Such imperatives are categorical. As Kant put it, categorical imperatives are unconditional, meaning that from the point of view of practical reason the agent either must or must not perform the relevant acts. There can, of course, be disputes as to what the unconditional principles are, and what particular actions fall under them. But the question whether some principle is a valid moral principle is independent of our judgment, and so also is the question what actions fall under a particular principle. Thus for a Kantian, the objectivity of moral judgments follows directly from the nature of principles. It also follows that, in any genuine moral dispute, at least one party must be wrong.

Many utilitarian theories also have the obvious consequence that questions of good and bad, right and wrong, reduce to questions about the relative amounts of pleasure or pain, satisfaction or dissatisfaction, utility or disutility, a state produces or an act brings about; such views make judgments of value as objective as any matter of fact can be.

Like many other philosophers, I can accept neither the Kantian imperative nor utilitarian consequentialism. It is harder to make a convincing case for the objectivity of moral judgments if, unlike the Kantian or the utilitarian, you hold that there are legitimate moral conflicts. I am convinced of the objectivity of many moral principles, but I believe such principles can come into genuine conflict; it can happen that we ought to perform some act and also ought to refrain from performing it. We are all familiar with what are taken to be examples: we have innocently promised to perform an act which, it turns out, will result in untold misery; we are obliged both to stay home with our ailing mother and to join the resistance; we ought to save the lives of our children if we can, but are placed in a situation in which we can save either of two children, but cannot save both; we have made two promises which no amount of foresight could have led us to suspect could not both be honored. The last two examples show that moral dilemmas do not necessarily require two principles which collide in application, for a single principle can apply to the same situation in conflicting ways.

Some philosophers have reasoned from the existence of conflicting principles to the conclusion that moral (or evaluative) judgments cannot have truth values, cannot be true or false. Thus both Bernard Williams and Philippa Foot have argued, in rather different ways, that since we feel genuine regret when we know or believe that we have foregone a genuine value, or contravened a genuine obligation, we must admit the legitimacy of both the value or obligation served and the one foregone. But if obligations which are opposed may nevertheless both be legitimate, they argue, then neither obligation can be called objectively valid at the expense of the other, since to accept opposed obligations as valid would be to accept a contradiction. In this way, the existence of conflicts in the personal domain becomes an argument against the idea that interpersonal or inter-cultural, as well as personal, conflicts have an objective solution.

Persuasive as some find this argument, I do not think the case against the objectivity of moral judgments has been conclusively made. Regret that the course followed entails losing something valuable, or neglecting a real obligation, does not necessarily show that the course followed was not the objectively correct course. We can, however, accept conflicts in particular cases, and so also the principles that lead to the clash, only if such claims are not absolute, not exceptionless, not, in Kant's word, categorical. We must be prepared to allow that though it may be an objectively correct principle that we should honor our debts, there may be cases where it would be objectively wrong to do so. It would be trivial to take this to mean only that the maxim, "It is wrong not to pay one's debts", has a finite list of exceptions it is too boring to enumerate, for this would bring us back to the idea of exceptionless (but complicated) principles we are too lazy or ignorant to state explicitly. The interesting cases arise when there is no such list, when the exceptions are not really exceptions, but rather cases where the obligation to honor one's debts, though never inapplicable, is rather *overruled* by some obligation or value which, under the circumstances, is more pressing. I cannot hope to give this view its due here; I have tried elsewhere. My present interest is in making plausible the objective correctness of evaluative judgments on the assumption that objectively correct principles may lead to conflicts in application to particular cases.

Let me begin by making an obvious point which it is easy to forget when arguing about objectivity generally. A judgment is objective if it is true or false, or possibly neither, but its truth value (true, false or neither) is fixed: its truth value is independent of who makes the judgment, and of the society or period in which the thinker lives. The truth value of a judgment depends on just two things: the facts, and the contents of the judgment, the proposition being judged. If people throw rocks or shout or shoot at each other, there is not necessarily, or perhaps even often, any proposition the truth of which is in dispute. A dispute requires that there be some proposition, its content shared by the disputants, about which opinions differ. If you are one of those who are skeptical about the clarity or usefulness of the concept of a proposition or content (and I am such a skeptic), this formulation of the concept of a dispute will need reworking. The same goes for formulations that depend on the notion of incompatible beliefs or judgments, for such formulations depend for their clarity on our understanding what it is for two people to have the same belief or to consider the same judgment. Appeal to language will not directly help, since two people can agree on the truth of a sentence while not agreeing on what the sentence means. The concept of two people meaning the same thing by a sentence is as much in need of further analysis as the question of the identity conditions of propositions, beliefs, or judgments. But progress here is possible, and, as we shall see, promises to throw light on our central problem.

The question of the objectivity of moral judgments, or the nature of moral disputes is, then, as much a question about how the *content* of moral judgments is determined as it is a question about the nature and source of moral values. Here I am concerned only with the first, with why the facts that determine the content of moral judgments give reason to suppose both that such judgments are true or false, and that there is more agreement on moral and other values than it might at first seem.

Discussions of the objectivity of value are frequently—and perennially—infected by the inherently unintelligible question *where* values are. Hume puts it this way:

Examine the crime of *ingratitude* ... Enquire then where is the matter of fact which we here call *crime*; point it out; determine the time of its existence; describe its essence or nature; explain the sense or faculty to which it discovers itself ... the crime of ingratitude is not any particular *fact*; but arises from a complication of circumstances, which, being presented to the spectator, excites the *sentiment* of blame ... The vice entirely escapes you ... till you turn your reflection into your own breast.[1]

John Mackie, in his attractively plain-spoken book, *Ethics: Inventing Right and Wrong*, says that for the objectivist "... there is something that backs up and validates some of the subjective concern which people have for things." And he adds, "If there were something in the fabric of the world that validated certain kinds of concern, then it would be possible to acquire these merely by finding something out, by letting one's thinking be controlled by how things were." Mackie then asks,

What is the connection between the natural fact that an action is a piece of deliberate cruelty—say, causing pain just for fun—and the moral fact that it is wrong? ... it is wrong because it is a piece of deliberate cruelty. But just what *in the world* is signified by this 'because'? It is not ... sufficient to postulate a faculty which 'sees' the wrongness: something must be postulated which can see at once the natural features that constitute the cruelty, and the wrongness, and the mysterious consequential link between the two.[2]

It is strange to speak of values as being, or not being, "out there". The things and events to which we attach values are certainly out there (for

---

[1] *An Enquiry Concerning the Principles of Morals*, ed. L. A. Selby-Bigge, Oxford University Press, 1957, pp. 287–8.

[2] John Mackie, *Ethics: Inventing Right and Wrong*, Penguin Books, 1977, p. 41.

the most part, anyway); the properties we predicate of such things are neither here nor there, for properties have no location. When we speak of values, we don't even *seem* to be referring to entities of some odd sort, and so objectivity or realism with respect to values can't sensibly be construed as an ontological issue. The same is true of weights, colors, and shapes. These aren't "out there"—or anywhere else.

I want, then, to separate two issues. It seems to me that close attention to the nature of evaluation can throw light on the question whether such reasons can intelligibly be judged as correct or incorrect without settling the question whether values are real or exist "in the world". So I plan to concentrate on what might be called the epistemological problem and let the ontological problem, if there is one, take care of itself. For I think that if we were to solve the epistemological problem we would lose interest in the supposed ontological problem.

I sympathize here with Hare, who asks us to

... think of one world into whose fabric values are objectively built; and think of another in which those values have been annihilated. And remember that in both worlds the people in them go on being concerned about the same things—there is no difference in the 'subjective' value. Now I ask, 'What is the difference between the states of affairs in these two worlds?' Can any answer be given except 'None whatever'?[3]

Mackie quotes this passage only to chide Hare for overlooking the distinction between moral judgments and a metaethical account of the nature of moral judgments. Mackie allows that the difference would not matter to our everyday evaluations; but he thinks it does matter to philosophy. It matters so much, in fact, that in his opinion all our everyday value judgments are false, since all of them suppose, falsely, that there are values "in the world". I am skeptical about the ethics–metaethics distinction, at least in this case. It seems to me that if it matters to the philosopher that all value judgments are false, it should matter to everyone else too. So, agreeing with Hare and Mackie that it doesn't matter to everyone else, I conclude, with the satisfaction only an application of *modus tollendo tollens* can give, that it does not matter philosophically.

I also take comfort from the words of another anti-objectivist, Simon Blackburn. He writes,

... the extra ingredients the realist adds (the values or obligations which, in addition to normal features of things, are cognized ...) are pulling no

[3] R. M. Hare, *Applications of Moral Philosophy*, Macmillan, 1972.

explanatory weight: they just sit on top of the story which tells how our sentiments relate to the natural features of things.[4]

I agree with Hare and Blackburn that it adds nothing to an account of values to insist that they are real, part of the furniture of the world, something to be found or discovered. But I do not think that this settles the issue whether there are evaluations the correctness of which is as independent of our judgment as our beliefs about what Blackburn calls the "natural" features of things.

Blackburn argues that if values were in the world they would explain nothing; they just "sit on top" of the natural features of the world, natural features that happen to turn us on or off. (This argument is also used by Gilbert Harman.) But plenty of real features of the world just "sit on top" of others, are supervenient on them, without this counting against the objectivity of attributions of these features to objects that are certainly in the world. Being green, for example, sits on top of more fundamental properties of objects, though in a very complicated way, and so in one sense the greenness of objects explains nothing. Colors (and the other so-called secondary qualities) supervene on the properties a really finished physics needs. Our perceivings and thoughts supervene on the physical properties of our bodies. But of course thoughts and colors do explain things, not in the way physics does, but in other ways. Colors and thoughts aren't *definable* in physical terms—that's why they can explain what physics can't. But explanatory power is not in this case related to ontology. It is true—objectively true—that some things are green and people have certain thoughts. This doesn't require that there be objects or events in addition to physical events and objects, but it does empower and require explanations of a different order.

There is an argument for objectivity which seems to me caught up in the same confusion; it is to be found in the work of John McDowell and David Wiggins. They claim that there is a variety of reaction-dependence which values share with secondary qualities, but which does not make values any the less objective. I think this thesis is misleading because I see it as an attempt to answer a bad question.

John Mackie says, "... my thesis is ... specifically the denial that there are values not contingent on any present desire of the agent".[5]

[4] Simon Blackburn, "Errors and the Phenomenology of Value", in *Morality and Objectivity*, ed. Ted Honderich, Routledge and Kegan Paul, 1985, p. 8.
[5] *Op. cit.*, p. 29.

The bad question to which this is supposed to be an "answer" is: are values in any sense contingent on the desires of agents? David Wiggins and John McDowell agree with Mackie that values are in some sense contingent on the desires (or other evaluative attitudes) of agents, but unlike Mackie they think that this does not bring the objectivity of values into question. For, they maintain, secondary qualities also are conceptually tied to how they are perceived by human agents, and yet such qualities are objective. I quote Wiggins:

... pillar-boxes, painted as they are, count as red only because there actually exists a perceptual apparatus (e.g., our own) that discriminates, and learns on the direct basis of experience to group together, all and only the actually red things ... But this in no way impugns the idea that redness is an external, monadic property of a postbox.[6]

I think that unless redness is defined as the property something has if it causes us to see the thing as red (under the right conditions, and all that), and this is an idea Wiggins quite properly disavows, it is false that things would not count as red unless someone had the right equipment to see them as red. I say this on the assumption, of course, that things count as red if and only if they are red—that is, that they count as red whether or not they are so counted. (Of course, things would not be *called* "red" unless speakers were caused to use this word when confronted with red things.)

McDowell puts the position this way:

[To] ascribe a value to something is to represent it as having a property which (although it is there in the object) is essentially subjective in much the same way as the property that an object is represented as having by an experience of redness—that is, understood adequately only in terms of the appropriate modifications of human ... sensibility ... [E]valuative 'attitudes' ... are like ... color experience in being unintelligible except as modifications of a sensibility like ours.[7]

These remarks seem to me to be mistaken or confused because, as I just said, they are addressed to the pointless question *where* such properties as rightness and redness reside. Wiggins says that redness is "external" (it is in or on the pillar-box), McDowell that it is "there in the object"; Mackie thinks values are "not in the world". Well, Mackie is right, but not because values are elsewhere—or that any

---

[6] David Wiggins, "Truth, Invention, and the Meaning of Life", *Proceedings of the British Academy*, 62 (1976), pp. 348–9.

[7] John McDowell, "Values and Secondary Qualities", in *Morality and Objectivity*, ed. Ted Honderich, Routledge and Kegan Paul, 1985, p. 118.

other properties are "in the world", for they are nowhere. The question whether these properties, whether primary, secondary, or evaluative, are contingent on the existence of human sensibilities or sense organs is equally misleading. Some properties are relational in the sense that nothing could have them unless something else existed: examples are the properties of being a mother, a murderer, or sunburned. But neither the secondary qualities nor the evaluative properties are like this; they are not defined or understood in terms of a relation. Wiggins agrees that red is not a relational property, but says "it is in one interesting sense a *relative* property", in that color is a category that "corresponds to an interest that can only take root in creatures with something approaching our own sensory apparatus".[8] It seems to me that in this sense all perceptual properties are relative.

This is not to say, of course, that there are no interesting correlations between the properties objects have and our perceptions of those objects. Red objects tend to cause us to believe the objects are red, square objects tend to cause us to believe the objects are square, and precious objects tend to cause us to prize them. It is because the objects and events have the properties they do that they cause us to have the attitudes we do. So far, nothing in these platitudes points to a distinction between primary and secondary qualities, or to a distinction between these and the properties for which we value things. Any genuine question about objectivity must lie elsewhere. Objectivity depends not on the location of an attributed property, or its supposed conceptual tie to human sensibilities; it depends on there being a systematic relationship between the attitude-causing properties of things and events, and the attitudes they cause. What makes our judgments of the "descriptive" properties of things true or false is the fact that the same properties tend to cause the same beliefs in different observers, and when observers differ, we assume there is an explanation. This is not just a platitude, it's a tautology, one whose truth is ensured by how we interpret people's beliefs. My thesis is that the same holds for moral values. Before we can say that two people disagree about the worth of an action or an object, we must be sure it is the same action or object and the same aspects of those actions and objects that they have in mind. The considerations that prove the dispute genuine—the considerations that lead to correct interpretation—will also reveal the shared criteria that determine where the truth lies.

---

[8] David Wiggins, "Truth, Invention, and the Meaning of Life", *Proceedings of the British Academy*, 62 (1976), p. 349.

Basic to the understanding of the utterances of another speaker is observation of the circumstances in which the speaker, sincerely as far as we can tell, applies a predicate. The application of a predicate represents a judgment, and therefore is expressed by a sentence such as "This is a nose", "That is lavender", "It's warm in here". Sometimes a word does the work of a sentence: "Rain!", "Lion!", "Gavagai!". We learn to understand what is meant by evaluative expressions in the same way: "Good!", "Bad!", "That was wrong", "This is silly", "How brave". These expressions, we learn, apply to actions and objects of the sorts to which we find them applied. With time, we grasp the concept, and can make our own applications. Once we have grasped a concept, we sort out for ourselves where we think others are right and where wrong in applying it, and we are in a position to appreciate that we can make mistakes. If we find that some speakers deviate wildly from our usage, it is open to us, as always, to decide they do not mean what we do by the same words.

If, instead of asking where values are, we turn to the problem of understanding what it is like to judge that an act or object or institution is morally desirable or ought to exist or is obligatory, we realize that we must be attributing some property or other to an entity or group of entities. The semantic nature of such judgments is clear: we are *classifying* one or more things as having a certain property. The thing or things must either have that property or not (assuming the things exist). There is no coherent way to avoid this conclusion. We say, and think, for example, "I ought to visit my sick friend and I will". No one doubts that the second conjunct is true or false. But then what does "and" mean here? No one has explained the role of conjunction except by saying: a conjunction is true if and only if each conjunct is. It follows that the first conjunct is true if the sentence as a whole is. (Alan Gibbard is an honorable exception to the rule that philosophers who deny that moral judgments have truth values seldom make a serious attempt to explain the semantics of such sentences. I judge Gibbard's attempt to be clearly inadequate.)

The central issue remains: how do we tell what the content of a particular moral judgment is? This is a question of interpretation, of the understanding by one person of the utterances of another, since there is no other context in which the content of a judgment can be agreed to or disputed. To take up the position of an interpreter is consciously to assume the status anyone with thoughts and attitudes must be in, for the attitudes of a person have a content—are interpretable—only if that person is in communication with others; only interpreters can be interpreted. Thus by explicitly introducing the interpreter we complete in microcosm the social situation which alone gives content to the idea of being right or wrong about a shared public world. An interpreter is not an idle bystander; he is an essential player in a performance that requires complex causal interactions between people and the world.

An interpreter cannot hope to determine the contents of a person's desires, without also determining what the person believes; and there is no way to determine the contents of either of these attitudes in a sufficiently detailed way without linguistic communication, which requires interpretation of the person's speech. The problem is due to the holism of the mental: it is, so to speak, all or nothing: if we fully understand anything of another person's propositional attitudes, we understand a great deal (see Essay 2).

To what extent do these considerations apply to the evaluative attitudes? It is possible, I think, to show that the justified attribution of values to someone else provides a basis for judgments of comparisons of value, what is called the interpersonal comparison of values. But the comparability of values does not in itself imply agreed-on standards, much less that we can legitimately treat value judgments as true or false. Now I want to go on to suggest that we should expect enlightened values—the reasons we would have for valuing and acting if we had all the (non-evaluative) facts straight—to converge; we should expect people who are enlightened *and fully understand one another* to agree on their basic values. An appreciation of what makes for such convergence or agreement also shows that value judgments are true or false in much the way our factual judgments are.

Let me survey the considerations that make for this conclusion. First, there are the norms or values of rationality. It is a necessary feature of interpretation that the successful interpreter tends to match his own norms of rationality to those of the person he or she is interpreting. This is obvious in the case of elementary logic. Our primary evidence for identifying and interpreting the logical constants of a speaker (such as "and", "or", "if and only if", etc.) has to be the patterns, fixed or shifting, of the speaker's attitudes to his sentences. So if I find a connective that creates a sentence out of two sentences, and such that the speaker always (or almost always) assents to the compound sentence when and only when he assents to each sentence taken alone, I can do no better than treat that connective as the speaker's sign for conjunction. Of course, I say this on the assumption that this is how *I* understand conjunction; someone else may not mean what I do by the words "and" or "conjunction". The point is that by interpreting by the only standards of interpretation available to me, I have, on a primitive level, made the speaker I am interpreting a good logician (by my own norms of reasoning, it should go without saying; I have no others). For I have so fixed things (i.e., interpreted him) that he "infers" each conjunct from a conjunction. With respect to the simplest and plainest logical matters, a sharing of norms of rationality is an inescapable artifact of interpretation.

Needless to say, no one is a perfect logician. Having made a start by assuming consistency, finding it where we can, we prepare the ground for making the fallings off from rationality in others intelligible. We expect failures in reasoning when memory plays an important role, when sentences become complex, when distractions and temptations are part of the picture. Such deviations make interpretation difficult, and can easily put the interpreter in the position of having to choose between equally plausible, but different, total interpretive schemes; there can be trade-offs calling on us to decide whether a speaker means what he usually means (or we usually mean) by certain words, or is confused in his reasoning, or has made an egregious error of fact. In such cases there is not necessarily just one correct theory.

I do not say that there can be no real differences in norms among those who understand each other. There can be, as long as the differences can be seen to be real because placed within a common framework. The common framework is the area of overlap, of norms one person correctly interprets another as sharing. Putting these considerations together, the principle that emerges is: the more basic a norm is to our making sense of an agent, the less content we can give to the idea that we disagree with respect to that norm.

Good interpretation makes for convergence then, and on values in particular, and explains failure of convergence by appeal to the gap between apparent values and real values (just as we explain failure to agree on ordinary descriptive facts by appeal to the distinction between appearance and reality). Thus there is a basis for the claim that evaluations are correct or incorrect by interpersonal—that is, impersonal, or objective—standards. For if I am right, disputes over values (as in the case of other disputes) can be genuine only when there are shared criteria in the light of which there is an answer to the question who is right. Of course, genuine disputes must concern the values of the very same objects, acts, or states of affairs. When we find a difference inexplicable, that is, not due to ignorance or confusion, the difference is not genuine; put from the point of view of an interpreter, finding a difference inexplicable is a sign of bad interpretation. I am not saying that values are objective because there is more agreement than meets the eye, and I certainly am not saying that what we agree on is therefore true. The importance of a background of shared beliefs and values is that such a background allows us to make sense of the idea of a common standard of right and wrong, true and false.

Dummett at one point suggests that an attribution of courage to a person who has died without ever being placed in a situation requiring courage has no truth value. Dummett's reason for saying this is that there is no way anyone will ever be able to tell whether the person was brave. I agree that such an attribution may have no truth value, but the reason is not that verification is lacking, but that we simply haven't had to make up our minds about such cases. I think the same applies to many of the puzzles philosophers raise about split brains, multiple personalities, or, more to the present point, very difficult or unusual moral problems. It is consistent with objectivity that there should be no clear answers about what is right or obligatory in such cases. It may be no accident that not one of the Socratic dialogues which starts as an attempt to define some moral concept ends up with an answer.

But no matter what the subtleties involved, interpreting evaluative judgments rests on the same foundation as interpreting the evaluative attitudes: understanding depends on finding common ground. Given enough common ground, we can understand and explain differences, we can criticize, compare, and persuade. The main thing is that finding the common ground is not subsequent to understanding, but a condition of it. This fact may be hidden from us because we usually more or less understand someone's language before we talk with them. This invites the impression that we can then, using our mutually understood language, discover whether we share their view of the world and their basic values. This is an illusion. If we understand their words, a common ground exists, we already share their way of life.

Darwin considered the natives of Patagonia simple brutes, their language a series of grunts. Bruce Chatwin tells us, however, about Thomas Bridges, a missionary to Patagonia in the 1880s. Bridges, according to Chatwin, "uncovered a complexity of construction and a vocabulary no one had suspected in a 'primitive' people". Chatwin warms to his theme:

Finding in 'primitive' languages a dearth of words for moral ideas, many people assumed these ideas did not exist. But the concepts of 'good' or 'beautiful', so essential to Western thought, are meaningless unless they are rooted to things.[9]

I agree: values are rooted to things. That has been the theme of this paper. I have argued that values are objective, that they are rooted to things, and I have tried to say, as clearly as I could, what this entails. I wish I were able to declare that I know of a way to decide, in those cases where a decision is called for, what the right decision is, what we ought to do. This would be a foolish thought, a foolish hope. But perhaps it will be agreed that the thesis of the objectivity of values is not only worth discussing, but that discussing it may be one way of bringing about agreement on what is now disputed.

APPENDIX

One part of the brain, the amygdala, is responsible for emotional or evaluative responses to perceived facts. Another part of the brain, the hippocampus, assigns to those same facts a degree of belief or subjective probability. In other words, beliefs and desires, the main explainers of action and intention, employ quite different bits of gray matter. So striking is the effect that if the amygdala of a human adult is severely damaged, the emotive response to normally disagreeable stimuli (say a sudden loud noise) is suppressed, though the existence of the stimulus is accurately noted, while an adult whose hippocampus is damaged displays the appropriate emotion in response to the same stimulus, but fails to record its cause.[10]

It is somewhat surprising that a person can respond positively or negatively to a stimulus he or she apparently does not know to be present; it is more surprising that a person can know he or she is experiencing a normally painful stimulus and yet fail to respond appropriately. But however separable they may be as responses, the onset of belief and the onset of desire in such cases have a common cause, the stimulus itself. Furthermore, both beliefs and desires are, as we like

[Editor's note: These pages were the opening pages of another essay entitled 'Objectivity and Practical Reason' that was published in *Reasoning Practically*, edited by E. Ullmann-Margalit (Oxford University Press, 2000), 17–26. This essay contained much material that duplicated word for word material in essays 2 and 3 and I have therefore deleted it.]

[9] Bruce Chatwin, *In Patagonia*, Summit Books, 1977, pp. 135–6.

[10] A. Bechara, *et al.*, "Double Dissociation of Conditioning and Declarative Knowledge Relative to the Amygdala and Hippocampus in Humans", *Science*, 269 (1995), pp. 1115–18.

to say, propositional, that is, they have the sort of content we attribute to declarative sentences. We desire it to be true *that* the loud sound stops (without necessarily believing there is a loud sound); we believe *that* there is a loud sound (without necessarily wanting it to stop). Or, to take a more normal example, we desire it to be true *that* we learn the meaning of the word "amygdala"; we believe *that* we will find out what "amygdala" means by looking in the O.E.D. Given this desire and belief, we may be prompted to take the appropriate volume of the O.E.D down from the shelf. (We will be disappointed: the word is not in the O.E.D. Better look in Webster's Third.)

Philosophers interested in morality and action hardly need to appeal to the anatomy of the brain and ingenious experiments on subjects who have been seriously brain damaged to be persuaded that there is a basic difference between motivational states like desires and cognitive states like beliefs. Much of the history of moral philosophy, ancient and modern, concerns the question how the distinction is to be drawn. How should it be drawn? Richard Jeffrey's ingenious version of decision theory sees it as I have just set it up: two attitudes towards items in the same set of propositions.[11] The distinction then emerges almost automatically: the natural constraints on a rational set of beliefs and desires induce quite different forms of measurement on the two attitudes: beliefs support a ratio scale, desires support an interval scale. The reason for this formal difference springs from an intuitively clear distinction. Beliefs have inherent positive and negative limits, certainty and total disbelief. Some propositions we are certain are true, some we are certain are false. All other degrees of belief fall between these end points. Zero degree of belief is fixed; tradition and convenience put certainty at One. Desire is not like this. No matter how much we want some proposition to be true, we can imagine that there may be some other proposition we would prefer were true. Similarly for those propositions we would detest to find true. The scale of better and worse has no natural limits.

But hasn't this analysis of the difference between cognitive and evaluative attitudes left something out? The contrast between the attitudes is perhaps clear enough in an elementary way, but how about the linguistic *expression* of the attitudes? Well, couldn't we say, "I want it to rain" (that is, "I want it to be the case that it rains"),

---

[11] Richard Jeffrey, *The Logic of Decision*, 2nd edition, University of Chicago Press, 1983.

or "I believe that it will rain"? We do in fact often express our attitudes by saying such things. When we talk this way, though, we are
not literally expressing our attitudes, we are *describing* them. This can
be appreciated by noting that if such self-describing sentences really
did express our values and beliefs, there would be nothing to argue
over with others, and it would be impossible to discover or decide that
some judgment of our own was mistaken or wrong-headed.

Judgments have a propositional content, so if judgments are different, if they have a different subject matter, then the propositional
content of those judgments must be different. Here a little care is
needed. Sentences and propositions don't, strictly speaking, express
attitudes. People do, for example by uttering sentences in specific circumstances. In such cases we can also say their utterances express
attitudes. But there is no form of sentence that is reserved for any
particular use. We may feel that declarative sentences are "made for"
giving information or making claims or expressing beliefs or stating
theories, but there is no rule of language that makes such uses "normal" and others not. There is not even a moral constraint that points in
this direction, except, of course, in specific situations. Imperative sentences are not reserved for commands, nor interrogative sentences for
questions. Given this independence of meaning from specific ulterior
uses (this is what I have elsewhere called the autonomy of meaning),
it is not hard to imagine that we could manage without the imperative
and interrogative moods.

What we cannot imagine is that we might lack a way of stating
our disagreements with others about the moral and other values of
acts, institutions, policies, and just about everything else. It is not
imaginable that we would not have words for the irreducible and various properties we ascribe to objects, persons, and events when we
want to classify them as good, bad, moral, blameworthy, right, cour-
ageous, courteous, trustworthy, loyal, kind, obedient, cheerful, etc.
Creatures anything like us, creatures capable of thought and action,
have concepts of the evaluative properties, and employ these concepts in making judgments. I belabor these thunderously obvious facts
because I think many philosophers have in effect denied them, or at
least have evaded their consequences.

Perhaps the simplest observation with which to start is this: predicates like "good", "right", "honorable", and "cruel" stand for concepts.
For a creature to have a concept it is not sufficient that it react differentially to things that fall under the concept: it requires that the

creature be able to classify things it *believes* fall under the concept while aware that it may be making a mistake. To apply a concept is to make a judgment, and judgments may be true or false according to the creature's own understanding of the concept. If I judge that some act is immoral, I assign it to a class whose membership is determined by whatever criteria I have, but it is my criteria that determine whether the act belongs in that class, not my assignment in any particular case. Evaluative concepts no doubt differ in many ways from other concepts, but if they are concepts at all, if they are eligible for employment in judgments and can form part of the content of meaningful sentences, then they must allow the distinction between what actually falls under the concept (as understood by its user) and what the user judges in particular cases to fall under the concept.

There is a closely related consideration that conspires with these features of judgment to support the thesis that evaluative attitudes have as their objects propositions that have a truth value. This is their role in practical reasoning. When we reason about what to do or try to do, or about the value or morality of the actions of others, we must combine factual judgments with our values. We *conclude*, as I remarked a few minutes ago, from our desire to know what the word "amygdala" means, and our belief (false as it happens) that we will find out what it means by looking in the O.E.D., that we would do well to look there. Such reasoning, if properly laid out, is surely valid. But validity is defined as a truth preserving mode of reasoning. If practical reasoning can be shown to be (in some cases) valid, the premises and conclusion must have truth values. Our understanding of the logical constants brings out the same point. We say, *if* it is desirable that my jetlag be cured *and* taking Melatonin will cure it, *then* it is desirable that I take Melatonin. But what do "and" and "if . . . then" mean here? "And" is usually defined as yielding a true sentence if and only if each conjunct is true, and "if . . . then" is similarly defined as a truth functional connective. If we abandon these definitions, what should we put in their place?

Is there some way we can tinker with the notion of validity to avoid this outcome? It is no help to look to standard types of imperative and deontic logics. Such logics often suggest *rules* of valid infer-ence. But it is one thing to set down intuitively attractive rules and another to show that the rules are valid, which requires a demonstra-tion based on semantics, and this is typically lacking. Attempts have been made to supply an appropriate semantics for logics that eschew the concept of truth, but study reveals that no serious and complete semantic theory lies behind those proposals, at least those with which I am familiar.

We should then face the fact that it is difficult, if not impossible, to avoid the conclusion that evaluative judgments have truth values, that is, are objectively true or false.[12] Perhaps evaluations sometimes are neither, as may happen with ordinary declarative sentences and judgments; but even when neither, they have truth *conditions*.

Simon Blackburn has seen the power of some of these arguments, and he accepts the idea that evaluations have truth values, but he holds that accepting this idea does not commit him to the objectivity of values. He reconciles his "projectionist" view with the idea that evaluations are true or false by treating talk about truth in evaluative contexts as purely performative: when we say a judgment is true, we merely endorse it, give it the nod. He writes, "Granted that it is correct to reply to a moral utterance by saying 'That's true' or 'That's not true', the question remains of what sort of assessment is indicated by these responses," and he answers,

But isn't the theory saying that there is really no such thing as moral truth, and nothing to be known, believed, entailed—only the appearance of such things? Not at all. It is a complete mistake to think that the notion of moral truth and the associated notions of moral attributes and propositions disappear when the realistic theory is refuted. To think that a moral proposition is true is to concur in an attitude to its subject: this is the answer to the question with which I began the essay. To identify this attitude further is a task beyond the scope of this essay, but it is the central remaining task for the metaphysic of ethics. To think, however, that the anti-realist results show that there is no such thing as moral truth is quite wrong. To think there are no moral truths is to think that nothing should be morally endorsed, that is, to endorse the endorsement of nothing, and this attitude of indifference is one that it would be wrong to recommend, and silly to practice.[13]

There is indeed an endorsing *use* of the word "true", as we should expect, given its meaning. But this use does not determine what the word means. How could it, given the word's relation to valid inference or to an orderly account of the semantics of speech generally? Truth, the serious concept we employ when we allow that what we

---

[12] "Objectively true" = "true".

[13] Simon Blackburn, "Moral Realism", in *Morality and Moral Reasoning*, ed. John Casey, London: Methuen, 1971, pp. 101–24. I have quoted the opening sentence and final paragraph.

say and what we think may or may not be true, is, by dint of this very characteristic, necessarily objective: whether an utterance or belief is true is not, in general, up to us.

Hume, Bentham, Hare, Blackburn, and a host of others have emphasized the intrinsically motivational, subjective, emotive, or projective character of value judgments. They are surely right. But it is a mistake to suppose that the nature of the attitude that is revealed or expressed by evaluative judgments rules out objectivity. If we judge some act better than any other act open to us, we are motivated to perform it. If we deem an act cruel, we dislike or detest it. If we say a practice is immoral, we are (if we are sincere) expressing disapproval. Whether these connections are as simple as these remarks imply is not my present concern. My point now is simply that one can believe in these connections without questioning the objectivity of moral and other evaluative judgments.

4 *The Interpersonal Comparison of Values*

We constantly make judgments comparing the interests of two or more people. Sometimes such judgments provide reasons for action, sometimes they serve to explain or excuse the actions of the judge or of the agent whose interests are at stake. It is remarkable that we seldom find arriving at such judgments particularly difficult. Some cases are hard, of course; the same can be said concerning some decisions which affect one person only. But on the whole we do not experience the problem of comparing the interests of different people as harder in kind or degree than comparing conflicting interests of our own. Naturally we are more apt to be ignorant of the interests of others than of our own; but this is a variable we have no trouble accounting for.

Given how often we make judgments involving interpersonal comparisons of interest, and our general intuition that our moral principles and standards of rationality apply in much the same ways to such judgments as to personal decisions, it is strange that we find it difficult to explain how we make the interpersonal judgments. It is not a psychological explanation the absence of which is surprising; it is lacking, but not surprisingly. What is surprising is that we have no satisfactory view of the basis for our interpersonal comparisons. In this paper I argue that we have a basis for interpersonal comparisons, one that is actively and unavoidably at work when we consider the competing interests of more than one person. The existence and nature of this basis are not necessarily obvious, though the facts to which I shall appeal are in some sense known to us all. I should perhaps say at the outset that it is not my aim to present a method or formula for deciding hard cases. Indeed, if my main thesis is correct, we should not expect to find a general method. At best what I am vaguely calling "the basis" serves to give a point to discussions of alternative methods.

It is not clear what the basis for our interpersonal comparisons is; neither is there a settled opinion as to the nature of such judgments. Some utilitarians believed that interpersonal comparisons were factual in character, and this is a position again gaining supporters. Others hold that judgments of interpersonal value are essentially normative.[1] Obviously the question of the basis for interpersonal comparisons is not independent of the normative–descriptive issue.

Some of the difficulty is no doubt due to differences about what are to count as judgments of interpersonal comparisons, what form they are to take, and what the elements of comparison are to be. Up to a point these matters may be settled by fiat, a task to which I now turn. In the end, however, deciding what the question is and addressing the question will turn out to be related in ways that defy dividing the discussion neatly into two parts.

I plan to concentrate on judgments made by a third party ("the judge") comparing the interests of two or more others. It will not do, of course, to rule that the values of the judge are not to enter into her judgment, since that would be to decide in advance of understanding the nature of such judgments that they are not to be normative— whatever exactly that means. But we can decide without prejudice to central matters that the judgments shall not be *about* the interests of the judge. Of course we often do compare our interests with those of others; but these cases may introduce our own interests in two ways that are easy to confuse, once as part of what is judged and once as a determinant of the judgment. To keep these elements separate as far as possible, the judge, A, is to compare the interests of B and C, where A, B, and C are three different people. I take for granted that A's judgments may depend, perhaps legitimately, on her own values or interests.

What are these interests or values the judge is to compare? The judge may be concerned, not with what B and C are interested in, or what they value or prefer, but with their "true" or impersonal interests, what would in some way be best for them, or perhaps best for society, or best from the point of view of justice, quite apart from their apparent, or even enlightened, interests. Such comparisons, however, conspicuously and directly involve what the judge values or deems good or just, and these are factors from which I want to

[1] For a useful commentary on contemporary opinions, see A. K. Sen, "Interpersonal Comparisons of Welfare", in M. Boskin (ed.), *Economics and Human Welfare*, New York: Academic Press, 1979.

insulate the judgment as far as possible. So I choose to consider only those judgments that compare the preferences, desires, or evaluations whether apparent or enlightened, of those concerned. Let us say that both B and C want to buy the same house. Each is prepared to buy it if he can. A makes judgments of these sorts: "B wants the house more than C does", "According to their own values, B will gain more by getting the house than C will", "Considering their own evaluations, B will end up better off than C would if B rather than C gets the house". These judgments are different in important ways, and what might serve as a basis for one might not serve as the basis for another. But they are together in that they compare, in various ways, the preferences, desires, or evaluations of B and C. It is such judgments that I wish to discuss.

I am aware of the dangers of lumping desires, evaluations, and preferences together, or of assuming that because they all enter into decisions and the formation of intentions they form a homogeneous group of motivational forces. But given the general nature of the problem with which I am concerned, it is not essential to take account of the distinctions among the evaluative attitudes. So I shall take no account in this essay of the differences, and shall use "desire", "evaluative judgment", and "preference", as I have in an earlier essay, to refer to the same broad set of attitudes. I shall say something about the differences in another essay.

Now suppose that our judge owns the house coveted by B and C and that she has decided to sell it to one of them. We can imagine that there are three distinct steps in her reasoning, insofar as it involves the desires of B and C. First, she determines what she can of their preferences, their value rankings, perhaps on an interval scale. Second, she *compares* these preferences, her judgment or judgments being of the kind just mentioned. Finally she weighs these and any other factors she considers relevant, and makes a decision. If these steps really could be kept distinct in principle, then it would be clear that it is the second step with which we are concerned. It will turn out, however, that the first two steps are interdependent in a surprising way. Once this interdependence is described, it will be possible to improve the distinction between the last two steps, that is, to separate interpersonal comparisons from the evaluations or decisions based in whole or in part on them.

First, however, I want to point to an obvious difficulty in making the distinction. The difficulty is not superficial since once made it tends to undermine a number of current theories about interpersonal comparisons. Let us ask the judge on what ground she judges that *B* values having the house more than *C* does. The judge answers that although both would-be buyers have similar incomes and financial responsibilities, *B* is willing to pay more than *C*. (Obviously more subtle and perhaps convincing answers are possible.) The evidence or grounds of the judgment that *B* values the house more than *A* does are then plainly factual and descriptive. But how about the judgment itself? If the judge goes on to use the judgments of comparative strengths of desire as a reason in favor of a decision to sell to *B* rather than to *C*, it is difficult not to count the judgment of interpersonal interests as a normative judgment belonging to the final evaluative step of deciding what course of action is best or most desirable. What the judge has done is use the fact that *B* is willing to pay more as a reason for increasing the value she sets on selling to *B*; the reference to strengths of desire merely acts as a middle term in getting from valued fact to valued action. The valued fact is that *B* is willing, under the circumstances, to pay more than *C*. Given the role in decision that the interpersonal comparison played, we are bound to say that when the judge held that *B*'s desire was stronger than *C*'s she was already making a value judgment, for she accepted the fact that *B* was willing to pay more than *C* as a *reason* to sell to *B* rather than to *C*.

The point does not depend on a connection with a decision or action of such importance. Perhaps the judge merely expresses her view of the competing desires of *B* and *C* by way of a recommendation, an endorsement, or praise for a past act. If the judge supports these evaluative judgments by reference to her comparison of interpersonal interests, that comparison is infused with the explicitly normative character of the final evaluation. It may be suggested that to escape this problem we should consider cases where the judge performs no action in response to her interpersonal comparison. I will return to this idea in a moment.

Some writers insist, or acknowledge, that all interpersonal comparisons are normative. Amartya Sen quotes Robbins to this effect.[2] Fredrick Schick suggests that we "assimilate" one utility scale to another by giving the same weights to the items highest and lowest on the individual scales, that is, normalize the scales on the basis

2 Ibid., p. 190.

of two chosen points much as we might normalize temperature scales at freezing and boiling by insisting that all scales assign the same numbers to those points.[3] (Centigrade and Fahrenheit have yet to be normalized.) Since Schick assumes interval measurement of individual preferences, his method would yield not only interpersonal comparisons of differences, but also absolute comparisons.[4] He sees this as a just or moral way of treating people alike. Richard Jeffrey has a somewhat more elastic proposal, which he also sees as normative from the start, though he believes it is essentially the method we actually use in judging what is just or best.[5] I shall return to Jeffrey's proposal later. (I think he is basically right, but gives no reason for thinking so.)

These suggestions are not without interest, but they do not touch my problem. What I call a "basis" for interpersonal comparisons cannot be something that is freely chosen, something that may be accepted by one person or society, but not by another. Schick's and Jeffrey's proposals concern what is just or fair, or (as it is popular to say these days) what it is to treat someone as a person. If the concept of interpersonal comparison enters independently, it can only be if there is some further, non-arbitrary way of characterizing it; and no such way is yet in sight. Otherwise, these methods concern judgments of interpersonal strengths of preference only in that they tell us how we *ought* to judge conflicting claims—conspicuously normative judgments.

John Harsanyi has shown that if individual preferences and the social welfare function satisfy the von Neumann and Morgenstern axioms, and if social preferences are related to individual preferences in certain intuitively natural ways (Pareto optimality, etc.), then the weights the social welfare function assigns to various social states will be the sums of the individual preferences when the individual utility functions have been adjusted for origin and unit.[6] Jeffrey takes this to be a normative justification of a certain way of making interpersonal comparisons: our normative judgments that certain solutions to

[3] F. Schick, "Beyond Utilitarianism", *Journal of Philosophy*, 68 (1971), pp. 657–66.

[4] In his typescript Davidson had noted to himself here that in his final draft he would briefly explain what he meant by "absolute comparisons"—MC.

[5] R. C. Jeffrey, "On Interpersonal Utility Theory", *Journal of Philosophy*, 68 (1971), pp. 647–56, and "Remarks on Interpersonal Utility Theory", in S. Stenlund (ed.), *Logical Theory and Semantic Analysis*, Dordrecht: D. Reidel Publishing Co., 1974 pp. 35–44.

[6] J. C. Harsanyi, "Cardinal Welfare, Individualistic Ethics and Interpersonal Comparisons of Utility", *Journal of Political Economy*, 63 (1955), pp. 309–21. Reprinted in E. S. Phelps (ed.), *Economic Justice*, Harmondsworth: Penguin, 1973, pp. 266–85.

problems involving the interests of two or more people are fair shows that we have used this method of making interpersonal comparisons. This interpretation of Harsanyi's result seems to me unexceptionable, though subject to the doubts I have already expressed if it is taken to provide a non-arbitrary basis for interpersonal comparisons. However, Harsanyi himself has quite a different view of interpersonal comparisons. He says, "... interpersonal comparisons of utility are not value judgments based on some ethical or political postulates but rather are factual propositions based on certain principles of inductive logic".[7]

Much simplified, but not, I think, distorted, here is Harsanyi's argument. It is in principle perfectly possible to make sound, justified, attributions of attitudes and beliefs to others. We do this on the basis of what can be observed of their behavior, verbal and otherwise, perhaps along the lines I have suggested elsewhere. Not being skeptics about the possibility of knowing what is in the minds of others, we have to allow that what can be observed is often adequate for knowledge of the interests, desires, intentions, worries, and beliefs of others. But then, Harsanyi says, it does not make sense to say that two people are alike in all relevant observable respects but have different thoughts and feelings. Or perhaps it makes sense, but it is bad science. To quote Harsanyi,

If two objects or human beings show similar behavior in *all* their relevant aspects open to observation, the assumption of some unobservable hidden difference between them must be regarded as a completely gratuitous hypothesis and one contrary to sound scientific method ... Thus in the case of persons with similar preferences and expressive reactions we are fully entitled to assume that they derive the same utilities from similar situations.[8]

In the last step, we determine the variables on which changes in mental states and attitudes depend, and so can compare the utilities of people who differ in taste, sensitivity, and training. There is in effect one grand, empirical law of utility which relates the cardinal utilities of any individual to all the relevant variables. Though utilities will, as ever, be unique only up to a linear transformation, this will not matter to interpersonal comparisons, since everyone is on the same (interval)

[7] J. C. Harsanyi, "Cardinal Welfare, Individualistic Ethics and Interpersonal Comparisons of Utility", *Journal of Political Economy*, 63 (1955), pp. 309–21. Reprinted in E. S. Phelps (ed.), *Economic Justice*, Harmondsworth: Penguin, 1973, p. 282.

[8] Ibid., p. 279.

scale. There is a very similar argument in some publications of Ilmar Waldner.[9] I'll come to Waldner in a minute.

This argument is appealing, mainly because of the strong analogy with legitimate arguments. There is, for example, G. E. Moore's observation that it would be absurd to say of two apples that one was good and the other not but that there was no other difference. And it is certainly true that we do often know what others think and intend and want, and this knowledge must be based on what can be observed. It would be a mistake to deride this claim on the grounds that it is a form of behaviorism. Behaviorism is objectionable only if it maintains that mental states are *nothing but* the phenomena we normally take to be evidence for them; or that mental concepts can be explicitly defined in terms of the behavioral concepts. No such doctrine is involved here, as I tried to show in a previous essay. But there is, I think, something wrong in Harsanyi's *argument* to show that interpersonal comparisons are "factual propositions". (I am not at this point questioning the conclusion.)

Let us accept as clear and correct the principle that if all possible evidence for two unobservables is the same, we should identify the unobservables. Questions could be raised about this principle, but they are not relevant to Harsanyi's argument. The question I want to raise concerns the application of the principle. Clearly the principle applies only to unobservables for which there is evidence. But is there any evidence for interpersonal comparisons? Since that is the issue to be settled, the answer can hardly be assumed as a premise of the argument. Harsanyi's argument seemed plausible because interpersonal comparisons are made (we are told) on the basis of the same sort of evidence we use for attributions of mental states generally. Since attributions of belief and desire to individuals are justified by the evidence, so must the interpersonal comparisons be. The cases are not in fact parallel. We do have evidence for legitimate attributions of belief, say. We can see this in a standard way by noting that a belief helps explain what is evidence for it. We use choice behavior under certain circumstances as evidence for a belief. If the belief were different, it would not explain the same choice behavior.

But now consider one of Harsanyi's examples. Suppose we want to explain why one person is willing to work for lower wages than

---

[9] Ilmar Waldner, "The Empirical Meaningfulness of Interpersonal Utility Comparisons", *Journal of Philosophy*, 69 (1972), pp. 87–103.

another at the same job. We might do this by saying, he has a smaller disutility for labor because his physique is more robust than the other person's and there is no difference in their economic needs. Would this explanation suffer from an arbitrary linear transformation of one utility scale of one of the people involved? Clearly it would not. There is on the one hand the available evidence for each worker concerning relative strengths of preference for work at various wages. Enough such evidence would permit a prediction for each worker, and hence a comparison of the wages at which each worker would choose to work. We could *call* this an interpersonal comparison of utility if we pleased, but doing so would add no new information. If we discover a correlation between physiques and individual utility functions, that of course adds information that preferences alone do not yield. But the extra information yields exactly the same prediction, and explains the same behavior, if the utility functions are transformed in permissible ways. Why, Harsanyi asks, should we choose different absolute utilities for two people when the circumstances are the same in all relevant respects? The question is misleading. There is no motive for making any choice at all. Unless of course, we want to make judgments of merit or fairness or to suggest social policy; and then, I have urged, a normative judgment is involved.

Waldner points out, in effect, that there are other ways of obtaining interval scales of preference than by the von Neumann and Morgenstern method. (It would be better called the Ramsey method, since Ramsey came first, and unlike von Neumann and Morgenstern he did not assume that there are, or that people act on, objective probabilities.) One suggestion, at least as old as Bentham,[10] is to use least noticeable differences as a measure of equal differences in preferential strength. It is an empirical question whether, if one found satisfactory ways of determining utility by both the Ramsey method and the least noticeable differences approach, one of the two utility functions for a given individual would be a linear transformation of the other. Suppose that it turned out to be the case that for each individual the functions were so related.[11] Would this, as Waldner thinks, justify us in making

---

[10] See Appendix IV, p. 555, in D. Baumgardt, *Bentham and the Ethics of Today*, Princeton: Princeton University Press, 1952.

[11] For a report on an experiment that tested a closely related hypothesis, see D. Davidson and J. Marschak, "Experimental Tests of a Stochastic Decision Theory", in C.W. Churchman and P. Ratoosh (eds.), *Measurement: Definitions and Theories*, New York: Wiley, 1959, pp. 223–69.

interpersonal comparisons of differences in utility? We would have an empirical way of making certain social choices, provided we decided to use least noticeable differences in making such choices. And we would have some general facts to which we could appeal to justify the choice. But the idea is this: if alternatives differ in value by the smallest appreciable amount, then no matter who the valuer is, those alternatives differ in value for that valuer by the same amount. This is not an *empirical* claim, since no evidence has been produced in its favor. What is clear is that nothing new or different would be explained by normalizing utility functions by reference to a common unit based on least noticeable differences. Waldner says, "... the principle of not postulating any differences unless there is some reason to do so is hardly a matter under dispute".[12] Perhaps so; but in the present case we have been given no reason to postulate anything at all.

I have argued that normative theories do not provide a basis for interpersonal comparisons on the ground that such theories are really decisions to use certain facts in the evaluation of social arrangements or decisions. This is not a complaint against such proposals, but a way of partially defining what I mean by a "basis" for comparisons. A basis would be non-arbitrary, at least in that it would not be chosen with an eye to subsequent value judgments. I have rejected a range of descriptive interpretations of interpersonal comparisons because comparisons interpreted in these ways add nothing to the descriptive or explanatory power of the theories to which they are added. So we seem to have rejected both of the two possibilities: the basis is normative or descriptive; it is neither, so there is no basis. Should we then give up on the attempt to found interpersonal comparisons? I think not. I think interpersonal comparisons have a basis in the following sense: in the process of attributing propositional attitudes like beliefs, desires, and preferences to others, interpersonal comparisons are necessarily made. The values that get compared are those of the person who attributes preferences or desires to someone else, and of the person to whom the attributions are made. I do not mean that in attributing a value to another the attributer consciously or unconsciously makes a comparison, but that in the process of attribution the attributer necessarily uses his own values in a way that provides a basis for comparison; a comparison is implied in the attribution.

---

[12] Waldner, *op. cit.*

Let me recall some features of what I have said previously about how beliefs are attributed. Normal attributions of single beliefs are made against a background of knowledge or assumptions concerning the general character of a person's further beliefs, desires, and intentions, and a way of interpreting his speech. Under these favorable, though not unusual, circumstances, we often learn what someone believes through his assertions. Indeed, if we know that an assertion is sincere, and what the words, as spoken on that occasion, mean, we almost always will be right in supposing that the speaker believes what he has asserted. (The only exceptions will be cases where the speaker himself is wrong about what he believes.) Suppose someone asserts, and we deem him sincere, that pollux is a dread disease and castor is its cure. If we conclude that he believes this, we will also conclude, without necessarily giving it a separate thought, that he believes that pollux is a dread disease; that there exists at least one dread disease; that there is at least one curable disease; that something is either a cure or a poison; and so on. These further conclusions or assumings take no further time on our part; they come along with the first conclusion. Yet they are separable from the first, since it is possible for a person to believe something and fail to believe a logical consequence. Evidence might come along that would push us in the direction of attributing a contradictory belief to a person. The more striking the contradiction, the harder it would be to be certain we were right; a flat enough contradiction in the beliefs as we interpreted them is sure to throw the interpretation in doubt. So if we are certain someone made two sincere assertions, and those assertions contradict one another, we must wonder whether we are right about what was asserted. The doubt could easily go back to the question what the words used by the speaker meant.

Blatant logical error will tend to dissolve under good interpretation, but so will other errors to lesser degrees. If someone has a belief, whether true or false, about disease, this can only be because he has some views of what disease is that are true; otherwise there would be no reason to suppose that it was disease he was thinking about. These other views in turn depend for their identity on further beliefs; and again, many of these must be true if some are to be false. Many of the beliefs that give identity to some one belief are bound to be related as matters of degree: the degree of belief one has in one proposition will vary as the strength of belief in other propositions varies. Looked at from the point of view of the interpreter, it would be the best reason to count an interpretation wrong to find that nothing the interpreter counted as evidence for a certain belief was counted as evidence by a person to whom he assigned the same belief.

Similar remarks apply to more particular beliefs. In general it must be part of what makes a belief a belief that a dog is before me that it is the presence and absence of dogs that causes the belief to wax and wane. As an interpreter, I can do no better at the start than to suppose that a belief someone else is caused to have is the same as a belief of mine that has the same cause. This is, of course, the crude outline of a policy for interpretation, and will necessarily be modified in many ways. The modifications depend on a large variety of matters: how well placed observers are, the condition of their sense organs, and the other relevant beliefs we have found reason to attribute to them. Someone who, unlike me, does not believe that dogs bark, may well fail to be caused to believe a dog is before him when I would be, given a dark night. The easiest errors to allow for in others are those we realize we might have made if we had been in their shoes.

The kind of explanation and understanding that flows from knowledge of the propositional attitudes of others involves, of course, the semantic properties of the propositions involved, and of the sentences that express them. This is why an interpreter in general cannot assign a certain attitude to someone else while supposing that the attitude plays a role in the thoughts of the other radically different from the role it would play in his own thoughts were he to share the attitude. Thus it would be a mistake to suppose that the accommodating policies I have been urging on interpreters are nothing but a matter of helping interpreters discover truths whose character owes nothing to the thoughts of the interpreter. It is a tautology that we use our own concepts in understanding anything. What is not quite as easy to appreciate is that when it is the propositional attitudes of others we are trying to understand, two systems of thought must be made to mesh. This is not to suggest that the systems might be all that different; on the contrary, we see that comparisons with respect to similarities or differences depend on a large degree of similarity.

The process of making the beliefs and other propositional attitudes of others intelligible to ourselves necessarily involves our fitting others into our own scheme to a degree. There is no good sense, though, in thinking this makes our attributions of attitudes less than objective, or that we are distorting the thoughts of others in the process of identifying them. Such doubts would be appropriate only if we had another concept of what beliefs and desires and so forth are "really" like to contrast with the ones we apply in the ways I describe. Failing such an alternative, we ought to accept the fact that the strategies we must follow in making others intelligible are nothing but the process of determining what is true about them. The best interpretation an interpreter can devise, though it reads his own beliefs and standards of rationality into the minds of others, is as objectively correct as can be.

Appreciation of the source of this objectivity can perhaps be encouraged by dwelling briefly on an aspect of the relation between communication and belief. If someone aims to accomplish some purpose through saying something that is understood by a hearer, she must speak on the assumption that the hearer knows, or can learn, enough to interpret the speech as the speaker intends. This is impossible, however, unless the interpreter knows, with respect to many sentences of the speaker, that she holds them true (whether or not she utters them). The reason for this, put all too simply, is that the meanings of words are determined by the sentences containing those words that are held true. But then a successful interpreter of the utterances of a speaker knows both what the speaker's sentences mean, and, with respect to many sentences, that the speaker holds them true (or the degree to which she holds them true). Thus the interpreter knows, for each of these sentences, that the speaker has a particular belief.

A speaker's beliefs must (in important and relevant matters) be known to an interpreter; many must also be *shared* by him. The sharing takes two forms. First, as I have argued, there is no alternative to treating someone whose beliefs and meanings and other attitudes we wish to understand as being logically coherent. There can be intelligible exceptions, of course, given a general background of coherence, but exception can't be the rule. Thus, interpretation takes on a normative tone. In understanding others, in attributing propositional attitudes to them, I have no choice but to consider what inconsistencies do least harm to intelligibility; inconsistency here being inconsistency as I see it. My own standards of rationality necessarily enters into the process of interpretation.

So do my views of what is true, both in general matters (what is the nature of disease) and in matters of what is most plainly evident on occasion. For as we have seen, it is only by treating or interpreting another as often or in strategically important ways agreeing with me that I make sense of (correctly interpret) her propositional attitudes.

Should we say that in interpreting others we "compare" their logic and beliefs with our own? To put it this way would seem to argue for two separate stages: first we learn what they believe, and then we compare. This separation cannot, I have argued, be maintained until a general basis for interpretation has been laid. Before conscious comparison is possible, our own standards of consistency and views of the general character of the world have entered essentially into the process of determining what others think. A meaningful comparison depends on first having placed both minds in nearly enough the same realm of reason and the same material realm. So let us say that the attribution of propositional attitudes, while it involves a collating of beliefs, does not amount to a comparative judgment. It establishes a basis for comparative judgments.

What has been said of beliefs applies with modifications to the evaluative attitudes. We make others intelligible by interpreting their beliefs and other attitudes; interpreting means assigning propositions (our own sentences) to their propositional attitudes. Since the sentences we have available for assignment are identified by their role in our own economies, a correct interpretation of someone else must make the objects of his or her attitudes the objects of corresponding attitudes of our own. This "must" is one of degree. The match must be good enough in important respects to give a point to the failures of fit, these being the interesting cases where we disagree in what we hold true or in what we cherish. And there is the question of what it means to say two attitudes correspond.

The same sentences are the objects of both belief and desire: this reinforces the claim that the interpretation of the evaluative attitudes proceeds along the same general lines as the interpretation of the cognitive attitudes. At the same time, it guarantees that there will be multiple, and often conflicting, considerations in assigning an interpretation. We might know, for example, that a particular sentence apparently stands in certain logical relations to others for a given speaker; that he would prefer it true rather than some others; that his faith in its truth was modified to various degrees by observed changes in the world and by changes in his faith in the truth of other sentences. All of these considerations bear on the interpretation of the sentence, for on deciding it expresses a certain proposition, one has also decided on something believed and something desired, and the interpretation of related beliefs, sentences, and desires has been restricted. Given the multiplicity of considerations, it is inevitable that different considerations will often favor different interpretations. Remembering that the underlying policy of interpretation requires us to choose an interpretation that matches the other's beliefs and desires to our own as far as possible, the conflict in considerations means that we have come across a recalcitrant case. Making a fair fit elsewhere perhaps forces us here to interpret a sentence the other holds true and wants true by one we hold true while hating that we must.

In the case of belief, two quite different pressures operate to form the beliefs of those we interpret into comprehensible patterns: a pressure in the direction of truth (also, of course, as the interpreter sees it) and a pressure toward consistency. Two similar pressures are easy to recognize when it comes to identifying preferences or desires. We find it hard to credit straightforward examples of intransitivity of preference; we tend to explain apparent cases by changes in preference over time, or to suspect the propositions being compared are larger in number than we had supposed. In fact all the constraints that a Bayesian theory of preference places on the pattern of beliefs and evaluations exert a prima facie claim on interpretation; consistency of preferences with one another and with beliefs is a constitutive pressure on interpretation simply because we cannot easily rationalize (i.e., explain or understand) deviations from it. Deviations, especially if obvious, require complex and often far-fetched explanations, though such explanations are sometimes available, or are assumed to be available.

The other pressure is toward agreement in preference. Perhaps preference can accommodate larger deviations than belief from what we count as rationality, but again there are limits. As with belief, the limits do not pick out particular attitudes where deviations are necessarily unintelligible; the limits are vague, just as degree of intelligibility can vary, and what they concern is the amount and kind of deviation that we can understand and explain. Disagreements on some general principles of evaluation are much harder to accommodate than others, and disagreement on general principles is usually harder to make intelligible than disagreement on the value of particular acts and individual events. Nevertheless, with desire as with belief, there is a presumption (often overridden by other considerations) that similar causes beget similar evaluations in interpreter and interpreted. This is not, I repeat, either an empirical claim or an assumption for the sake of science. It is a necessary condition of correct interpretation.

There should be no temptation to confuse the methodological need to interpret others as sharing our beliefs and values in important respects with the moral, or moralistic, advice to view the opinions and attitudes of others with imaginative sympathy, or to hunt for generous interpretations of the motives of others. These are policies we can follow or not, and following them depends on our having already largely made sense of what others believe and want. Nor is the method I claim we must follow in correct interpretation a matter of asking ourselves whether we would prefer to be in someone else's shoes, along with his ideas and preferences; I hope not, since I find such questions unintelligible. Equally unintelligible is the question what I would prefer if I were you, since we can imagine as answers: what I now prefer, and, what you now prefer. (Counter-identicals have this character, as Nelson Goodman remarked some time ago. If I were Mozart, would I have written the *Magic Flute*—or have been a philosopher?) One might, in a metaphorical mood, describe my method for understanding someone else as putting him in my shoes; but this would certainly be a misleading metaphor if taken seriously. While plenty of imagination is called for in a good interpretation, I am not asking anyone to imagine he is playing another's part. I simply call attention to the fact that the propositions I must use to interpret the attitudes of another are defined by the roles they play in my thoughts and feelings and behavior; therefore in interpretation they must play appropriately similar roles. It is a consequence of this fact that correct interpretation makes interpreter and interpreted share many strategically important beliefs and values.

Once we have decided what someone else believes or wants, and what his utterances mean, we can explain much of his behavior. Would our explanations be as good if we were to make an arbitrary linear transformation of his utility (reference) function? Of course they would: this we have already seen. It is not explanatory power that causes us to put the preferences of others into relation with our own, but the process of deciding what the other's preferences are in the first place.

The "basis" of interpersonal comparisons is then provided for each of us by his own central values, both his norms of consistency and of what is valuable in itself. These norms we do not choose, at least in any ordinary sense; they are what direct and explain our choices. So no judgment is involved in having one basis or another, much less a normative judgment.

Early in this essay I criticized a standard picture of how decisions are made concerning the interests of two or more people. According to this picture, we first decide what the interests of each person are;

then we compare those interests in strength; then we judge or decide what should be done. I argued at the start that given this picture it was often difficult to separate the last two steps, and as a consequence the character of the interpersonal comparison was hard to determine. I have urged in the sequel that there is something fundamentally wrong with the idea that interpersonal comparisons are implicit in such attributions. But of course what is implicit can be made explicit. There is no reason we cannot judge the relative strengths of our own interests and those of others, or compare the interests of two others. My point has been that we do not have to establish, argue for, or opt for, a basis for such judgments. We already have it.

If it is true that the basis of interpersonal comparison already exists when we attribute desires to others, then we can, after all, make a fairly clear distinction between interpersonal comparisons and the normative judgments based on them. For issues of fairness, justice, and social welfare play no favored role in our attributions of evaluative attitudes and preferences to others.

PROBLEMS AND
PROPOSALS

5 *Turing's Test*

In the October 1950 issue of *Mind* A. M. Turing predicted that by the year 2000 it will be possible to build a computer that will have at least a 30 per cent chance of fooling an average interrogator into thinking it is a person.[1] Given that Turing allowed his interrogator only a five-minute interview, and given the further conditions he placed on the test, he was probably right. But the interest of the article lies not in this prediction; it lies in the test itself, for the test is designed to throw light on the nature of thought. I propose in this paper to consider how good Turing's test (or Turing's Test, as I shall call it) is. Some, but not all, of the issues to be raised were discussed by Turing.

Turing starts with the question 'Can machines think?' but immediately abandons this question in favor of the rather different question whether a digital computer can pass a certain test. It is fairly clear that Turing did not believe anything of philosophical importance would be lost by the substitution. He argued that limiting machines to digital computers would cause no loss of generality because a digital computer, given enough memory, can mimic any discrete state machine. He brushed aside the possibility that an analog, or partly analog, device might do better, and did not consider parallel processing. Nothing I shall say depends on the restriction to digital computers except for the fact that certain aspects of their operation can be described in purely formal terms (the 'program').

Turing specified that the machines to be tested be digital computers partly because he was familiar with them and believed a correctly designed digital computer could pass his test. He also wished to avoid a problem in giving a general definition of a machine. The problem

---

[1] *Mind*, 59 (1950), p. 442. All further references to this article are in parentheses in the text.

was that he wanted to allow his designer a free hand with 'engineering techniques', but thought this might allow the production of a biological object, particularly if the engineering team included both sexes. Even with a restriction to teams of one sex, he thinks it might be possible to 'rear a complete individual from a single cell of the skin of a person'. We would not, he says, be inclined to regard this as 'constructing a thinking machine'. It seems to me he ought also to have worried that it might be possible to rig things so that the circuitry of the nervous system of a person would be reproduced in a digital computer by a method that required no insight into how or why the resulting program of the computer gave the computer what were, or passed for, thoughts. This (theoretical) possibility shows, I think, that Turing was not quite clear about his reasons for restricting the test to digital computers. But it does not matter so far as evaluating his test is concerned, for the Test itself can be applied to any object whatever.

The design of the Test shows this immediately. The Test places an interrogator before two teleprinters (or computer terminals), one connected to a terminal operated by a woman, the other connected to a computer. Woman and computer are hidden from the interrogator. The interrogator types out questions addressed to the two objects in the attempt to determine which is which; the woman tries to help the interrogator, while the computer is programmed to try to deceive him. A trial concludes when the interrogator specifies which terminal the interrogator believes is connected to the woman and which to the computer. The computer's score is the per cent of trials in which the computer is thought to be the woman.[2] Clearly any object can be given this test. Even a pebble, connected so as to give no response, would get a score (and perhaps not a poor one; it might be thought to be an especially truculent woman). Turing does not say what he would make of a computer that was consistently chosen over the woman to be the woman; it seems that he would have to count this as a case of the computer 'winning', but one might also consider it a failure on the part of the computer successfully to simulate human (female) thinking.

The sexist aspect of the Test is obviously adventitious, and just as obviously it can be eliminated by making the choice one between a person and a machine. Let us suppose this change has been made. But a

[2] Turing's actual test is different. First he finds how well the interrogator does when trying to tell a helpful woman from a deceitful man. Then he asks whether the interrogator does any *better* when choosing between the woman and the computer.

difficulty remains, for Turing is never quite explicit about an essential feature of the experimental design: the instructions to be given the interrogator. Should the instructions read, 'One of these terminals is connected to a person, the other to a machine. You have x minutes to interrogate them through these terminals and to decide which terminal is connected to the person.' One trouble is that the answer will be affected by what the interrogator takes the word 'machine' to include. The same will be true if 'digital computer' is substituted for 'machine'. It would be worse to ask which of the terminals is connected to something that thinks, since Turing believes a properly constructed computer could think.

More carefully put: Turing is not sure whether standard or ordinary usage allows the word 'think' to be correctly or even meaningfully applied to machines; indeed, he says the question 'Can machines think?' is 'too meaningless to deserve discussion' (p. 442). Turing's Test is designed to separate what he considers the meaningful or interesting aspects of thought from the less interesting. It does this by denying the interrogator knowledge of the 'uninteresting' aspects. Turing thinks there are other features that distinguish people from machines which might affect the judgment of the interrogator though they should not matter, such features as having a voice, or shining in a beauty contest; the Test removes these features from consideration.

It is hard not to sympathize with Turing in all this; how an object is produced and the materials from which it is constructed, even if not obviously unrelated to how we use the word 'think', seem to raise questions a philosopher or psychologist might well wish to separate from 'deeper' issues. If I were to discover that my best friend had been born by hatching from an egg, or had been conceived by a process that required the active collaboration of three creatures of different sexes, it would probably not influence my opinion that he or she could think. And it is hard to see how the materials matter. Of course we believe, with good reason, that only creatures with a certain biological make-up actually do think; but if my friend turned out (after all these years) to be made of silicon, I'd change my mind about what materials a person might be made of, not my judgment that he was a person. So it appears to be appropriate on Turing's part to arrange his test in a way that leaves the interrogator ignorant of most of the physical traits of the object ranged against the person being tested.

Of course the interrogator must know at least one thing about the physical aspects of the objects he is judging; the observer must know it is they that are physically responsible for the observable clues. So the interrogator must know that each of the objects has the causal capacity to produce the available evidence.

This restriction of evidence has suggested to some critics that Turing's Test assumes the validity of behaviorism. If behaviorism entails no more than that the evidence shall be available to others besides the person or device to be tested, Turing's Test is behavioristic. Turing does not insist that thought (or 'consciousness' as he tends to call it in this context) must in principle be detectable, but points out that unless the presence of thought can be determined on the basis of external evidence, the question whether a machine can think has no special interest, since the same question will apply equally to everyone (else). So unless the issue is solipsism, behaviorism in the broadest sense must be assumed. Turing's Test is not behavioristic in any other familiar way. There is no suggestion that mentalistic terms should be eliminated or defined on the basis of what is immediately observable; the point of the Test is to see whether, and on what basis, normal human judges are able or willing to assign mental attributes to machines. Equally clearly, Turing does not specify in what terms the evidence is to be described. The terminals display letters (let's say). Whether this should be described as 'behavior' is up to the interrogator. I conclude that Turing's Test is not behavioristic in a way that limits its interest.

It does not follow that the Test is adequate to determine the presence of thought in an object. If it is inadequate, this can only be because the evidence has been shorn of elements vital to the detection of thought.

Turing's Test eliminates the possibility of telling *whether* a creature or machine thinks without determining *what* it thinks. Under normal conditions we frequently can determine that an object thinks without needing to discover anything in particular that it thinks. We can usually tell that a creature thinks just by looking at it, or if we can't see it, by being told, or knowing in some other way that it is a man or woman. These are fallible ways of knowing, but any way of telling will be that. All such ways, however, are eliminated by the Test. So in the Test, any evidence that thinking is going on will have to be evidence that particular thoughts are present.

Turing has limited the information the interrogator has to knowledge of his own (verbal) input to each terminal, and the (apparently resulting, apparently verbal) output of each terminal, an output caused by the person or computer at the other end. (A condition of the Test is the interrogator's knowledge that the output is so caused.) Of course if a response has any linguistic meaning at all, there must be a thoughtful cause. But the computer is the thoughtful cause of a response only if *it* means something by the words it produces. The interrogator can tell that it means something only if he can tell what it means.

The Test makes meaningful verbal responses the essential mark of thought. The conditions of the Test make this an appropriate mark, and of course the production of meaningful verbal responses would satisfy us that thought was present. It may be, however, that there are other sufficient criteria for thought. I do not believe so, but in the absence of an argument to this effect we should say that Turing's Test aims to discover whether a sufficient condition for thought is satisfied; the condition is not claimed to be necessary.

In order to fire our imaginations, Turing has his computer produce what seem to be English sentences. But of course the computer might not be speaking English. Those sentences might have entirely different meanings for the computer than they have in English; or they might have no meaning at all. That is for the interrogator to find out. How is this to be done?

At this point it seems wise to drop Turing's 'control' from consideration. Asking the interrogator to distinguish the computer from the person may make for a better experimental design, but it distracts from the underlying problem in several ways. First, it places an undue emphasis on strategy; in the short run all sorts of tricks may fool even the shrewdest interrogator. Second, too much depends on how clever or intelligent or informed the person is. But, and this is the important point, what we are interested in is the nature of thought, and we might count an object as thinking even if it were easily distinguishable from a person. It will improve our ability to concentrate on the question of thought if we simplify the Test by having a single object under study; the interrogator will now be asked to decide whether or not the object is thinking. It must be allowed at once that this is not the same test as Turing's. It is a better test if what we want to know is what our (the interrogator's) criteria for thought are. It is not as good if what we want to know is how well a given computer can mimic the verbal responses of a person. Since I am interested here in the first question, I shall henceforth consider the Modified Test instead of Turing's Test.

Let us suppose the object under test produces what seem to be sentences in English in response to questions couched in English.

How can the interrogator tell that the object understands English, that is, is 'speaking' English? One sort of evidence is simply that the answers exactly resemble English sentences; it has the syntax right. Another sort of evidence is that the relations between questions and answers, and between answers, seem appropriate; the answers show an apparent knowledge of the world. It would be too much to suppose all this is an accident. Knowledge of English and of the world must be responsible for the productions of the object. It would be inappropriate to complain that this conclusion is not forced by the evidence; we could have no better evidence if the object were an English-speaking person.

We should accept, then, that there is adequate reason to suppose thought is responsible for the object's replies. What is uncertain is whether the object is thinking. It would not be, for example, if a person were monitoring the interrogator's questions and then typing replies into the circuits of a machine. This possibility can be ruled out by (truthfully) informing the interrogator that the object is autonomous: the answers are not mediated by a person.

The interrogator still cannot tell whether the object thinks; cannot tell, in other words, what the object means by anything it causes to be presented to the interrogator. The reason the interrogator cannot tell is simple: he has no clue to the semantics of the object. There is no way he can determine the connection between the words that appear on the object's screen and events and things in the world. Of course there must be some connection; there is no other way to account for the intelligibility of the object's English. It is the nature of the connection that is in doubt. It is perfectly possible that the connection between words and things was established by someone who programmed the object, and then provided purely syntactic connections between words for the object to wield. In this case it is the programmer who has supplied the semantics, who has understood English, and has given meaning to the words produced by the object. The interrogator is quite right to take the productions of the object as having a meaning, but the object doesn't mean anything, and there is no reason to take it to be thinking.

In order to discover whether the object has any semantics, the interrogator must learn more about the connections between the output of the object and the world. The Test, whether Turing's original test, or the Modified Test, prevents the interrogator from obtaining the information he needs concerning these semantic connections. In the normal course of affairs we have two ways of learning what people mean by what they say. Merely by observing that they are people we (legitimately) infer that they have learned their language through the usual conditioning processes, which connect things and events with words. The connections are, of course, ultimately causal. By learning the person's language, we learn (usually indirectly) the general nature of the connections between the person's words and the world. Or we can discover these connections directly, through observing relevant causal interactions between the speaker, the world, and the speaker's audience. If we do not understand the speaker's language to begin with, and no translator is available, the direct method is the only method available.

Turing's Test, and its modified version, are inadequate, then, to discover whether or not an autonomous object thinks. The reason for this, it should be remarked, is not because the Test restricts the available evidence to what can be observed from the outside but because it does not allow enough of what is outside to be observed. The Test is inadequate because the interrogator cannot assume that he understands what the object means (if anything) and no translator is available.

What is needed is evidence that the object uses its words to refer to things in the world, that its predicates are true of things in the world, that it knows the truth conditions of its sentences. Evidence for this can come only from further knowledge of the nature of the object, knowledge of how some of its verbal responses are keyed to events in and aspects of the world, events and aspects also known to the interrogator. The easiest way to make this information available is to allow the interrogator to watch the object interact with the world. The interrogator wants to know not only how the object responds to his questions, but also how those responses depend on mutually observed events, changes, and objects.

It is clear, then, that the physical characteristics of the object will matter a great deal. We have already noticed that one physical characteristic was essential: the object had to be causally responsible for the 'messages' observed by the interrogator. But now we see that the object's 'body' matters for further reasons, since the object must be able to respond to many of the same features of the world that can be noted by the interrogator, and it must be possible for the interrogator to see or otherwise learn that the object is responding to those features. For the object to have a semantics, it must operate in the world in a certain way, and for someone else to grasp those semantics, there must be a three-way interaction among object, interrogator, and a shared world. How much like a person an object must be to be intelligible—to have thoughts—is unclear; indeed, it makes the most sense to think of thoughtfulness as a matter of degree, as it surely is with a developing child. Too much difference in what can be perceived will put limits on the possibility of communication and of thought, as will great differences in mobility, size, and the ability to reveal emotions and thoughts by movement and expression. But the ability to perceive things does not depend on the details of the sense organs (the blind can perceive the same things the sighted perceive), and emotions can be expressed in many ways.

It is now evident that Turing's Test is radically flawed: it cannot provide an interrogator with enough information to decide what an object means or thinks, and so whether it thinks. Turing wanted his test to draw '. . . a fairly sharp line between the physical and the intellectual capacities of man' (p. 434). There is no such line. Turing went on, 'No engineer or chemist claims to be able to produce a material which is indistinguishable from the human skin. It is possible that at some time this might be done, but even supposing this invention available we should feel there was little point in trying to make a 'thinking machine' more human by dressing it up in such artificial flesh' (p. 434). Turing may be right about the skin; but it is more of a question than he thought.

The Test must be modified once more. The object must be brought into the open so that its causal connections with the rest of the world as well as with the interrogator can be observed by the interrogator. (If it seems desirable to restore the comparative aspect of Turing's 'imitation game', then the object must be made indistinguishable from a person from the interrogator's point of view.)

Can the interrogator now tell what the object thinks? The answer is that it depends on how long the interrogator can question and observe the object. Let us suppose the interrogator finds that the object uses words just as he does: the connections with the world are, as far as he can tell, what the semantics of English require. The interrogator infers (let us suppose correctly) that the object's linguistic dispositions are similar to his own in relevant ways.[3] In the case of a person, the interrogator would be justified in assuming that these dispositions

---

[3] This does not mean that the object and the interrogator must be disposed to utter the same words under the same conditions, but that they are disposed to hold the same sentences true under the same conditions.

were acquired in the usual way: in the basic cases, by past causal intercourse with things and circumstances of the sort to which the person is now disposed to respond. We justifiably assume that a person who is now disposed to hold that 'is a dog' is true of dogs came by that disposition through experiences of dogs. But the assumption is not justified in the case of a computer: it may have been provided with a program and sensing devices that cause it to respond 'That's a dog' when asked and there is a dog in range. Somewhere in the history of the computer (it is safe to suppose) a knowledge of dogs played a role, but that role may not justify the idea that the computer knows anything about dogs, or means anything when it produces the sentence 'That's a dog.'

The point is sometimes made by imagining a person who says 'That's a dog' when faced with a dog, not because the person has ever seen or heard about dogs, but because he has experienced creatures that are not dogs, but are to every appearance the same as dogs. Call these creatures 'cogs'. The speaker, though his linguistic dispositions are the same as those of someone who means what we do by the word 'dog', doesn't mean what we do by the word. His word 'dog' applies to cogs, not dogs. He made a mistake in calling a dog a 'dog'.[4] The computer which has never experienced a dog and has no memory of dogs can't mean dog by the word 'dog'; there is no reason to think it means anything at all. Thought and meaning require a history of a particular sort. We know a lot, in a general way, about the histories of people (of course we can be wrong about them), but unless we are told, or can observe it in action over time, we have no basis for guessing how a computer came to have the dispositions it has.

It is unclear exactly what kind of history is necessary for various kinds of thinking or meaning, just as there was uncertainty about the sort of causal interaction necessary to provide present evidence for an object's semantics. But our intuitions are clear enough in many cases. You can't remember the Civil War if you were born long after it ended, no matter how much you have heard about it. You don't know a person you have never seen or talked to or corresponded with; and you don't understand a language if there are not numerous connections between your use of words and experiences like such knowings and rememberings.

---

[4] This argument is in Hilary Putnam, 'The Meaning of "Meaning," ' in *Philosophical Papers*, Vol. II: *Mind, Language, and Reality*, Cambridge University Press, 1975.

It may seem that minds are, after all, inscrutable if no present observation of their operation can reveal what they are thinking. But of course this does not follow. In the case of people, a very little present observation usually tells us a great deal about their history; in the case of an artefact, this may not be true. But even the mind of an artefact can, if it has one, be understood; it just takes longer, long enough for some history to be observed, since it cannot be inferred.

Nothing in these reflections suggests that an artefact, a computer, for example, might not think. But if I am right, it thinks only if its thinking can be understood by a human interpreter, and this is possible only if the artefact physically resembles a person in important ways, and has an appropriate history.[5] Turing's Test is inadequate because it deprives the human interrogator—the interpreter—of knowledge he must have to decide what the object thinks and means. Behind this inadequacy lies the mistaken thought that the physical realization of a program makes very little difference to its mental powers. On the other hand Turing was right, in my opinion, in taking as the only test for the presence of thought and meaning the interpretive powers and abilities of a human interpreter.

[5] Turing considers the idea of programming a computer to be like giving the mind of a child adequate sense organs, and letting it learn as a child does (pp. 454–60). But he views this simply as an economical way of producing a device with mature thoughts; he does not see it as the only way.

6 *Representation and Interpretation*

A person is a physical object which in detail and as a whole functions according to physical laws. So there can be no reason why an object indistinguishable in every way from a natural person should not be designed and built by people. It follows that there is no reason why an artificial object could not think, reason, make decisions, act, have beliefs, desires and intentions. But how much like us must an artifact be, and in what ways, to qualify as having thoughts?

I plan to start by following what might be called the method of addition and detachment: what must we add to the most thoughtful objects we know—computers—before we can say that they have thoughts; what could we detach from a person and still count him or her as a thinking creature? To begin with the 'detachable':

1. **Origin.** Does it matter to the possibility of thought and genuine intelligence whether an object was conceived and born in more or less the way people are conceived and born? Those who are clear about the boundaries between kinds of objects will no doubt count artifacts as belonging to no natural kind, and so to a very different kind than women and men. Perhaps it would be a mistake to call an artifact a person, simply on the grounds that no artifact could be a person. This is a verbal matter which has no connection, so far as I can see, with the question whether an artifact can think, act, and feel like a person. (Many believe everything was created by a divine designer; to hold this is to hold that everything is an artifact. This does not usually seem to prevent believers from viewing their neighbors as persons.)

In thinking about the matter, we might also consider what we would say if an object physically identical with a person were to be created by accident; lightning strikes a rotten log in a swamp, let us suppose, and entirely by chance an object exactly like me in all physical respects results: it apparently has my memories, seems to recognize my friends, and responds to questions in what sounds like English. Although the object wouldn't be me, and we might refuse to call it a person, it would be hard to say why it wouldn't have thoughts and feelings. (However, it wouldn't, for reasons to be mentioned in a moment; see 4. below. The point is that this failure would not be due to its origin.)

I conclude that the origin of a natural person is a detachable property so far as cognitive and conative matters are concerned.

2. **Building Materials.** Being made of one material or another also seems to be a detachable property. If silicon, or reconstituted orange juice, could perform in the same ways as the materials from which we are actually constructed, it would make no difference to the possibilities for thought if we were made of silicon or reconstituted orange juice. If I were to discover that Daniel Dennett is made of silicon chips I would not change my mind about his mental powers, his feelings, or his intentions. Nor would I be greatly surprised. Similarly (to take an example that has exercised some philosophers), it would not affect my estimate of people's thoughts, emotions, and actions if I were to learn that on a scale too small to have been detected until now each of us contains billions of intelligent creatures the sum of whose actions adds up to ours. Needless to say, the indifference of intelligence and feeling and intention to the material in which it is realized is in principle. It may well be that only the materials of which we are actually constructed can work in just the way they do.

3. **Size and Shape.** Must an object look like a person in order to be counted intelligent? A first reaction is apt to be that appearance does not matter: this was certainly assumed by Turing. We may even feel that our moral perception is at stake in giving this answer. But size and shape could matter if they sufficiently inhibited the ability to communicate not only beliefs but also feelings and intentions. Thoughts, desires, and other attitudes are in their nature states we are equipped to interpret; what we could not interpret is not thought.

4. **History.** Thoughts require a history. Not only must an object capable of thought be capable of learning: it must have learned a great deal. A creature or object cannot have a thought about stars or squid or sawdust unless that thought somehow traces back causally to appropriate samples. There cannot be a memory of an event or person unless there has been causal commerce with the event or person. A brain, or brain-like object, whatever its other powers, could not be said to have any ordinary thoughts about ordinary objects unless there was a history of causal interactions with objects of the same sorts. This

does not show, of course, that such an object cannot be an artifact. It does show that an artifact cannot have thoughts unless it can learn and has learned from causal interactions with the world.

Now I come to the much harder questions of addition: what must be added to computers as they now exist (and I speak only of those I know about) to insure that they are capable of thought?

The important general point is this: it is not enough for a computer, or a robot under its direction, to be good at a single task, such as playing chess, making change, solving equations, or finding proofs of theorems. An enormous supporting repertoire is necessary. I have allowed myself to speak as if computers could actually perform such tasks as playing chess; we do talk this way, but such talk is metaphorical. Think what it takes to play chess. In order to play chess, it is necessary to want to win, or at least to understand the concept of winning. To understand the concept of winning, it is not enough to know what it is to win at chess; it is necessary to have a general conception of what it means to win in any activity. This involves in turn an understanding of the concept of a rule or convention, an idea of activities that may be ends in themselves, and an ability to classify certain activities as games.

In order to move a piece as part of a chess game the move must be intentional, and be done for a reason; any intentional action requires a reason in the form of an end or desired outcome and a belief that the action may achieve that end. A chess playing computer may in some sense be said to have the aim of winning. But does it really satisfy the most ordinary conditions for having a desire, of wanting something? Doesn't this require the possibility of having other desires? Ordinary desires like wanting to win at chess compete with further values, they are conditioned by experience, and grow stale with repeated frustration. In other words, to have one desire, it is necessary to have many.

A similar point applies in the case of beliefs. Alitalia Flight 19 leaves Turin for London on Tuesdays at 8:30 in the morning. We can learn this by consulting a computer; but does the computer know what we learn by consulting it? The answer is that it does not because it does not know what a flight is, where Turin is, or even that Tuesday is a day of the week. It would be easy enough to add this information to the computer's memory, and in principle to add anything else that might flesh out the claim that the computer knows what it is talking about. The point is not that a computer couldn't have thoughts: the point is only that to have even one thought—one belief or desire—a computer would have to have a very great many other thoughts and desires. Beliefs and desires can exist only in the context of a very rich conceptual system. Before anything in such a system can intelligibly be interpreted as a belief or desire—as a thought of any kind—the system must contain much of the basic information that people have. Until that point is reached, we can say that various pieces of information, even ends and strategies, are represented in the system, but the system can't be interpreted as having the information, ends, or strategies.

There is no certain reason in principle, I conclude, why an artifact—a computer for example—could not think, hope, desire, intend, and act like a person. There may of course be technical impossibilities. Perhaps nothing could be even roughly the size of the brain and work as fast, or learn as fast, unless it was made of organic materials. Perhaps what the brain does when it reasons irreducibly requires analog devices. Since these (perfectly real) possibilities do not seem to me of any philosophical interest, I shall ignore them here.

It may seem obvious that if an artificial object thinks and acts enough like a person, someone who knows how the object was designed and built would be able to describe and explain the mental states and actions of the object. But this does not follow, for there is no reason to suppose that there are definitional or nomological connections between the concepts used by the designer and the psychological concepts to be described and explained. This should be clear if we imagine that the builder has simply copied, molecule by molecule, some real person. The builder may know everything about the neurological, biological, and physical characteristics of his artifact, and yet be quite ignorant of what or how his creation thinks or feels. So one sort of 'complete' understanding does not necessarily imply another.

Let us suppose, however, that the artifact contains as its most important element the physical realization of a program of a kind suitable for running on a computer, and the program, as well as the details of its realization, is known. The designer intends certain formal elements of the program, when realized, to be like thoughts; both the formal elements and their physical realizations are to be representations of objects in and facts about the world. The program itself is, of course, specified entirely in syntactic terms: the program does not say what its elements represent. The semantic aspects of representation—reference, naming, describing, and truth—are not themselves represented in the program.

The fact that a program specified entirely in syntactical terms cannot contain its own semantics does not prove that a device that realizes that program can't have a semantics; it merely shows that knowing and understanding a program realized by the device does not in itself make the device intelligible as a thinking object. What, in the program, is a representation of an object or a fact for someone who designed the program cannot automatically be interpreted as a representation of that object or fact for the device that realizes the program. Understanding its program will not, then, necessarily reveal what a physical realization of the program thinks, or even whether it thinks.

The reason, as I have just suggested, has to do with the nature of explanation. We are imagining a device, a physical device, the workings of which can be described, explained, and, to some extent at least, predicted in terms of two different theories and vocabularies. One theory is that of physics, or biology, or neurophysiology, or is the theory implicit in a specified program (I do not mean to suggest there are not basic differences between such theories); the other theory is the more or less everyday common-sense theory that explains the thoughts and actions of human agents in terms of their motives, personalities, their habits, beliefs and desires. The question is how closely these theories could be related to each other; whether, in particular, theories of the first sort may differ from theories of the second sort mainly in being more precise and detailed, or whether the differences are fundamental.

Explanations require classifying concepts, a vocabulary that has the resources for sorting objects and events in ways that allow the formulation of useful generalizations. Suppose we want an explanation of the collapse of the Tacoma–Seattle bridge. Although I have just used a complex system of classification—geographical, political, and structural—to pick out the event to be explained, the description is nearly useless for explanatory purposes: there are no general laws governing collapses of bridges in certain areas. If we want an explanation, we need to describe the collapse in quite different terms, perhaps (as a start) as the collapse of a structure with a certain strength and design that occurred with a wind of a certain strength blowing from a certain direction. (Obviously the vocabulary in which such a description was couched would still fall far short of inviting a really detailed explanation—one good enough, for example, to explain why the very similar Throg's Neck bridge did not collapse.)

A particular physical event, state, or disposition is one that can be picked out—described uniquely—using a vocabulary drawn from some physical science. A particular mental event, state, or disposition is one that can be picked out—described uniquely—in the vocabulary we reserve for the intentional. So if mental events and states are identical with physical events and states, the very same events and states must have descriptions in both the mental and physical vocabularies. But this does not mean that the classificatory concepts utilized by one of these vocabularies will serve for the formulation of laws, and hence for giving nomological explanations, relevant to phenomena described in the other vocabulary. The mental and the physical share ontologies, but not, if I am right, classificatory concepts.

Since this distinction is essential to understanding my further argument, let me offer a simple analogy which I have used before. Suppose, following folk advice, I am attempting to go to sleep by counting sheep. Every now and then, at random, a goat slips into the file. In my drowsy state I find I cannot remember the classificatory words 'sheep' and 'goat'. Nevertheless I have no trouble identifying each animal: there is animal number one, animal number two, and so on. In my necessarily finite list, I can specify the class of sheep and the class of goats: the sheep are animals 1, 2, 4, 5, 6, 7, 8, and 12; the goats are animals 3, 9, 10, and 11. But these classifications are no help if I want to frame interesting laws or hypotheses that go beyond the observed cases, for example, that goats have horns. I can pick out any particular sheep or goat in my animal numbering system, but I cannot, through conceptual poverty, tell the sheep from the goats generally. So it may be with the mental and the physical. Each mental event, taken singly, may have (must have, if I am right) a physical description, but the mental classifications may elude the physical vocabularies. If so, no physical or non-mental science could be expected to explain thinking, the formation of intentions, or the states of belief, desire, hope, and fear that characterize our mental lives and explain our actions.

That is how things might be: the mental, though identical with part of the physical world, might not be caught in the explanatory nomological schemes of physics, neurology, biology, or computer design—might not be caught, that is, as long as it was described in mentalistic terms. Is there reason to think this is actually the case? I think there is.

First, though, I want to qualify the character of the claim to follow. The explanatory power of a theory or discipline relative to a given range of phenomena can be judged according to many criteria: accuracy of prediction, robustness, simplicity, sensitivity to confirmation or disconfirmation, and so on. Our ordinary knowledge often suffices for rough explanations of mental phenomena in terms of the physical. To take a case, much is known about the effects on thought, alertness, frame of mind, and attention of a multitude of chemical substances. It would be foolish not to suppose that as the mechanisms of the brain are better understood, we will be able to explain with greater precision why we think, reason, and act as we do. Nothing I say can be interpreted as suggesting that such explanations are not full of interest and may not have vastly important applications.

But the question remains whether there are theoretical limits to the extent to which, say, computer simulation of aspects of the mental can explain the simulated aspects; whether, that is, there is a permanent conceptual divide between the psychology of the mental and various other explanatory systems.

We have agreed to ignore the question whether there are physical obstacles to the creation of a thinking digital computer; so let us suppose that one exists, and that we know the program it realizes. Why wouldn't knowledge of the design and program of this computer tell us what it is thinking and explain its actions?

The shortfall may be put in terms of the distinction between syntax and semantics. A program is characterized entirely by its formal, that is, syntactical, properties: the formal properties of what it will accept as input and produce as output, and the formal aspects of the processes that mediate between input and output. Insofar as one's understanding of the device that realizes the program is based on knowledge of the program, then, one's understanding is limited to formal or syntactical matters. It is just this restriction to the formal, of course, that makes a computer and its program in its way so totally explicable, so amenable to clear treatment. But this same feature constrains what can be explained. Knowing the program is enough to explain why the device produces the marks or sounds or pictures it does given an input described in similarly abstract terms. This knowledge does not touch on questions of meaning, of reference to the outside world, of truth conditions, for these are semantic concepts. The conceptual gap between syntax and semantics was made completely clear for the first time by Alfred Tarski when he proved that although resources adequate to formulate the syntax of a language are available in languages with anything like the expressive power of a natural language, the resources needed to define the basic semantic concepts for a language cannot, on pain of contradiction, be present in the language itself. It seems evident enough that there is a fundamental difference between semantics, which relates words to the world, and syntax, which does not; but Tarski has clinched the matter.

It's the sheep and the goats again. There is the language in which each animal can be picked out, but which lacks the concepts needed for classifying the animals as sheep or goats; similarly, syntax can provide a unique description of each true sentence, since it can provide a unique description of every sentence, but it can't classify sentences as true or false.

Roughly speaking, then, the understanding that can come from knowing the program of a device is limited to understanding why and how the device processes and stores 'information'; it goes beyond this to say what the information is, or even that it is information. If we knew no more than the program, we would have no reason to say the device had any information, or that any aspect of or event in the device represented anything outside the device.

The sophisticated response at this point is to grant the conclusion and claim it as a virtue. Men and women, it may (and has) been said, just are processing devices, and that is how a serious science of their behavior must describe them. It is true (the response continues) that in our ordinary descriptions of mental states we identify those states by their contents, their relations to the outside world. In our careless way we may say that Columbus believed the world is round, that he wanted to reach the East Indies by the easiest route, and for these and further reasons he intentionally sailed west to reach the East. A science of psychology that attempts to be as comprehensive and potentially precise as, say, molecular biology, will not describe inner states in such partly outward terms. This is, I think, true. It does not follow that there is another way of describing such states which would throw light on thought and action.

There can be no doubt that it is a salient feature of our usual ways of describing and identifying mental states that we relate the inner to the outer, the mind to the public world outside. Columbus could have believed the world was round and have been wrong; but he could not have believed this if there had been no world. The contents of beliefs and other mental attitudes are specified by mentioning objects, or kinds of objects, with which the subject of those attitudes must have come into causal contact of one sort or another. (This is naturally not always true, but it must be so in the most basic cases.) The causal element is even more obvious when it comes to perception and memory. If Jones sees that there is a bird in the bush, a bird in the bush must be causing him to believe there is a bird in the bush. If Smith remembers that he drank a pint of ale at lunch, his drinking a pint of ale at lunch must have caused him to believe he drank a pint of ale at lunch. In the case of perception and memory, truth is directly at stake; what is believed must be true. The logical dependence of the contents of thoughts on causal connections with the objects of thought is not usually so direct or easily timed, and is not generally such as to insure veridicality.

Talk of intentional action often makes causal reference both to the past and to the future of the action: thus if Cain killed Abel, he must have done something that caused Abel's death, and if he killed Abel intentionally, he must have been caused to act by a desire for Abel's death. Beliefs, desires, and intentions are themselves causal dispositions. A desire for Abel's death is (no doubt among other things) a disposition to be caused to cause Abel's death given appropriate beliefs, the opportunity, etc.; a belief that a stone can be lethal will, when combined with certain desires, cause an intention to kill Abel; and the intention includes a disposition to cause Abel's death.

These built-in causal aspects of our normal talk of mental states and events militate against the use of these concepts in a precise science. To appreciate why, we need only think of causal and dispositional concepts in the everyday explanation of non-mental events. Something is frangible if it would be caused to break by certain events; something is biodegradable if it would be decomposed by natural biological processes. Since this is what 'frangible' and 'biodegradable' mean, a mature science will not be satisfied to explain why something broke by referring to its frangibility, just as it is only a little help to be told a pill put someone to sleep because of its soporific quality. Such explanations can be completely empty: provided we know what sunburn is, we learn nothing by being told someone is sunburned because he was exposed to the sun. But more often such explanations are merely incomplete. The claim that a pill put someone to sleep because of its soporific quality has content, since the pill might have put the person to sleep not because it was soporific but because under the special circumstances that obtained it acted as a placebo. Similarly, if we explain why someone ate by pointing out that he was hungry we do explain the eating by adverting to a state that is partly understood as a causal disposition to eat; but the explanation is not empty, since eating can easily have other causes.

It is often thought that scientific explanations are causal, while explanations of actions and mental affairs are not. I think almost exactly the reverse is the case: ordinary explanations of action, perception, memory, and reasoning, as well as the attribution of thoughts, intentions, and desires, is riddled with causal concepts; whereas it is a sign of progress in a science that it rids itself of causal concepts. The dissolving of some salt is explained, up to a point, by saying that salt is soluble and this salt was placed in water; but one could predict the dissolving on the basis of far more general knowledge if one knew the mechanism, what it is about the constitution of the salt that accounts for its dissolving. When the mechanism is known, the explanation will not call on the causal concept of solubility. (I do not mean to suggest that such explanations are not in some sense causal, nor that the laws of physics are not causal laws; the point is rather that in an advanced science the explanations and laws will not employ causal concepts.)

The deeply causal character of the concepts we use in describing and explaining mental phenomena is not unrelated to the distinction between syntax and semantics mentioned some pages back. When the causal nature of memory forces us, in specifying the contents of a memory, to refer to causes normally outside the person, not only are we part way to a causal explanation of a belief, but we have also given a semantic interpretation of it. Though our beliefs, intentions, fears, and other feelings are private and subjective if anything is, they cannot be identified or explained except by tying them from the start to external objects and events.

Most of the time most of us are necessarily content to describe and explain ordinary phenomena by appeal to causal powers. But we know, or trust, that in the case of the physical sciences a better explanation is available, or ultimately will be. I may have to explain why a prism causes white light to show the spectrum by appeal to the dispersive character of the prism. But I know that science can do better, and in doing better will do without the causal disposition.

Why then shouldn't we hope that a scientific account of the workings of the brain, or, for that matter, knowledge of the program of a device that successfully mimics the workings of the mind, will explain the mechanisms that support or constitute thought in the same way that the mechanisms behind the dispersion of light or biodegradation have explained what lay hidden when all we could do was use causal concepts like being biodegradable or dispersive? There is a reason not to expect any such explanation to allow the elimination without loss of our usual mental and psychological concepts.

The reason has to do with the irreducibly normative character of the concepts we use to describe and explain thought.

It is obvious enough that there are norms of rationality that apply to thoughts. If we believe certain things, logic tells us there are other things we ought or ought not to believe at the same time; decision theory gives us an idea of how the beliefs and values of a rational man must be related to each other; the principles of probability theory set limits to how we may rationally adjust our faith in a hypothesis given that we accept certain evidence; and so forth. These simple reflections suggest how we use norms to criticize and advise others, or to modify our own beliefs and choices. But there is a more subtle, and more basic, way in which these same norms necessarily enter into our descriptions and explanations of mental phenomena. If someone believes Tahiti is east of Honolulu, then she should believe Honolulu is west of Tahiti. For this very reason, if we are certain she believes Honolulu is west of Tahiti, it is probably a mistake to interpret something she says as showing she also believes Tahiti is west of Honolulu. It is probably a mistake, not because it is an empirical fact that people seldom hold contradictory views, but because beliefs (and other attitudes) are largely identified by their logical and other relations to each other; change the relations, and you change the identity of the thought. Simple, easy to grasp logical relations can't be widely or often offended by a thinker and the workings of that thinker's mind still be identified as thoughts.

The issue is not whether we all agree on exactly what the norms of rationality are; the point is rather that we all have such norms, and that we cannot recognize as thought phenomena that are too far out of line. Better say: what is too far out of line is not thought. It is only when we can see a creature (or 'object') as largely rational by our own lights that we can intelligibly ascribe thoughts to it at all, or explain its behavior by reference to its ends and convictions.

This means that when anyone, scientist or layman, ascribes thoughts to others, he necessarily employs his own norms in making the ascriptions. There is no way he can check whether his norms are shared by someone else without first assuming that in large part they are; to the extent that he successfully interprets someone else, he will have discovered his own norms (nearly enough) in that person. This 'discovery' is an artifact of interpretation, of course, and not an empirical finding. But if the subject under study is to remain thought and intelligence, a normative methodology cannot be avoided.

Does the prominence of normative elements really distinguish the explanation of cognitive phenomena from other forms of explanation? After all, norms enter in the human study of any subject. Standards of elegance, simplicity, and explanatory power are norms that are involved in any choice of theory, and observations are made, rejected, and evaluated in the light of theory and further norms.

All this is true, of course, but it does not touch the crucial point. The crucial point isn't that norms enter in the one case and not in the other, but that they enter in a special and additional way in the study of mental phenomena. Whatever is studied, the norms of the observer will be involved. But when what is studied is the mental, then the norms of the thing observed also enter. When thought takes thought as subject matter, the observer can only identify what he is studying by finding it rational—that is, in accord with his own standards of rationality. The astronomer and physicist are under no compulsion to find black holes or quarks to be rational entities.

Here we find the hint of an explanation of the irreducibly causal character of the concepts we apply to thinking and acting. In general, as I said, appeal to causal powers and dispositions reveals ignorance of detailed explanatory mechanisms and structures. If a substance is soluble, there is something about its composition—an unspecified something—that causes it to dissolve under the right conditions. Science can say what that something is, and so dispense with solubility as an explanatory concept. But beliefs, which are also causal dispositions, are specified in terms of their relations to one another and to events and objects in the world, and in judging the relevance of these relations to the identification of particular beliefs, norms are necessarily employed. In order to keep intact the normative features that help define beliefs and other thoughts, a degree of looseness in their connections with events as described in non-cognitive terms is required. The 'unscientific' concept of cause takes up the slack. This slack is not the slack of ignorance: it is the slack that must exist between two schemes of description and explanation, one, the mental, being essentially normative, the other not.

Given the normative and causal character of reason explanations, and hence of thought, the only way to tell if an artificial device, whatever its design, material, or program, has beliefs, intentions, desires, and the ability to perceive and interact with the world as a person does, is to attempt to interpret the behavior of the device in the same way we do the behavior of a person. A consideration of the nature of interpretation has shown why understanding the program and physics of a device, even though that device is capable of genuine thought, speech, and action, is not the same as understanding the thought and speech and action of that device. The most important argument for this conclusion has been that interpretation involves the use of normative concepts like consistency, reasonableness, and plausibility, and these concepts have no role in the understanding of a syntactically specified program.

7 *Problems in the Explanation of Action*

I hold that there is an irreducible difference between psychological explanations that involve the propositional attitudes and explanations in sciences like physics and physiology. In a volume of essays on my work, J. J. C. Smart questioned how conclusive my reasons for this view are. He concluded his comments by saying,

I find [Davidson's] argument congenial but have given some reason for thinking that it may be found to have a sort of circularity by some of those against whom it is presumably directed. This is not surprising. I do not think that there are any really knock-down arguments in philosophy: we need to fall back somewhere on considerations of relative plausibility.[1]

I agreed with this judgment at the time, and I am now if anything even more convinced that Smart was right. The following essay makes no attempt to improve on the reply I gave at the time.[2] My aim here is to provide a larger setting for that reply, and to respond to some related issues that have been raised by others.

Let me begin by answering Wittgenstein's famous question: what must be added to my arm going up to make it my raising my arm? The answer is, I think, nothing. In those cases where I do raise my arm, and my arm therefore goes up, nothing has been added to the event of my arm going up that makes it a case of my raising my arm. Just possibly, however, something must be subtracted from my arm going up to make it a case of my raising my arm; I'll come to this possibility presently.

When I say nothing has to be added to my arm going up to make it a case of my raising my arm, I don't mean no further conditions have

[1] The quotation is from p. 182 of Smart's "Davidson's Minimal Materialism" in *Essays on Davidson: Actions and Events*, ed. Bruce Vermazen and Merrill B. Hintikka, Oxford University Press, 1985.   [2] Ibid., pp. 244–7.

to be satisfied to insure that the rising of my arm is a particular case of my raising my arm; this much is obvious, since it can easily happen that my arm goes up without my raising it. But this addition is an addition to the description we give of the event, not an addition to the event itself. So what my claim comes to is this: of the many individual events that are risings of my arm, some are cases of my raising my arm; and none of the cases of my raising my arm are events that include more than my arm going up. Nothing is added to the event itself that makes it into an action.

Why should we think otherwise? No one believes something must be added to a tree to make it an oak; some trees just are oaks. One reason we may be inclined to think mere arm risings can't be arm raisings is that we want to maintain the distinction between what an agent undergoes—what happens to him or her—and what the agent does, and we think of arm risings as something that happens to us, while raising an arm is something we do. But the distinction between doings and sufferings is not endangered if we allow that some arm risings are arm raisings, since we remain free to distinguish between arm risings that are deeds and arm risings in which agency plays no direct part.

Still, if we ask what makes a particular case of an arm going up a case of an arm being raised, a natural answer is that the agent made his arm go up. This way of putting it suggests that what the agent did can't be identical with his arm going up; the cause can't be identical with the effect. The effect is the arm going up; the cause is what made it go up. Perhaps this "making" is the thing that must be added to the arm going up to make it the raising of an arm.

There are good reasons for resisting this line. The most obvious is that if what marks the difference between something an agent does and what happens to that agent is a prior act of the agent—a making happen—then for the prior act to be something the agent does, another antecedent is required, etc. It also will not help to suggest that to do something an agent must do something else, such as try to perform the desired act, for trying is itself an act, and so would require a prior trying, etc.

It seems clear that it must in general be a mistake to suppose that whenever an event is caused there must be something called a causing. Dropping an egg may cause it to break. Here we have one event (dropping the egg) which causes another (the breaking). But there is not a third event which is the causing of the second event by the first.

If such a third event were required to relate the original cause and effect, two more events would presumably be needed to relate the original cause and effect with the causing. The difficulty, so far as there is one, is an artifact of grammar. In the sentence "Smith kicked Jones", the verb conceals reference to an event: the logical form of such a sentence is made more nearly manifest, in my opinion, by something like "There was a kicking of which Smith was the agent and Jones the victim". This makes us think "caused", as it appears between phrases referring to events, must also conceal reference to still another event. But "caused" relates events, as do the words "before" and "after"; it does not introduce an event itself. Similarly, to say someone made his arm go up (or caused his arm to go up) does not necessarily introduce an event in addition to the arm going up.

However, it may. If I rig up a pulley and rope, I can raise my paralyzed left arm by pulling on the rope with my right arm, and in this case I do, of course, raise my left arm by doing something else. So all we can say for sure is that not everything we do is done by doing something else, or nothing would ever get done. Raising an arm is usually done without doing anything else, but not always.

Suppose that I am right that in the usual case, if my arm went up because I raised it nothing must be added to my arm going up to make it a case where I raised my arm. To put this slightly less awkwardly: if I raise my arm, then my raising my arm and my arm rising are one and the same event. But how about the less usual case where I raise my arm by doing something else? If I raise my left arm by pulling on a rope with my right arm, has something been added to my left arm going up to make it a case where I raised my arm? The answer to this question has been much debated. This may seem surprising, since it is obvious that I would not have raised my arm at all if an event clearly separable from my arm going up had not occurred, namely, my pulling on the rope. But all this shows is that my pulling on the rope is not identical with my arm going up; it does not show that something was added to my arm going up that made it a raising of my arm.

The issue is this. We can agree that my pulling the rope and my arm going up are two different events, and one caused the other. We can also agree that given this causal relation, I raised my arm. The debate concerns the relation between my pulling the rope and my raising my arm. One answer is that these are two separate events, and that therefore I performed two actions: one action involved just the pulling of the rope, while the other includes my paralyzed left arm going up.

If this is the right answer, then something has indeed been added to my left arm going up that makes it a case of my raising my arm. What has been added is my pulling the rope. My raising my arm is thus the sum of two events, one the cause of the other.

I reject this answer, mainly because it seems to me clear that though I do, of course, perform two sorts of action, a pulling and a raising, there is only one act I perform, one act which belongs to two (and no doubt many more) sorts. The single action, the pulling of the rope, is, on my view, the very same action as my raising my arm (by pulling on the rope). If this is right, then the answer to Wittgenstein's question for a case like this is that nothing is added to the rising of my arm that makes it a case of my raising my arm because the rising of my arm is not part of my action at all. So once again, though in a very different way, the answer to Wittgenstein's question is "nothing".

It is no objection to my "identity" thesis that I might have pulled on the rope without raising my arm. The two descriptions of what I did are not logically equivalent, and so one description might have applied to my action and the other not; the point is that in this case both descriptions do apply. There is, however, a more serious difficulty with the identity thesis; it concerns times and places. In the story we have been telling, my pulling the rope and my raising my arm occur at the same time and in (almost) the same place. But suppose I thank someone for a pleasant evening by telephoning and leaving a message on her answering machine. Then my act of phoning and her getting thanked take place at different times and places. If my acts of phoning and thanking her are one and the same, I must have finished thanking her long before she was thanked. How can this be? My reply (which I have made at greater length elsewhere) comes in two parts. First, we need to notice that the verb to thank, like very many others, is a causal verb: x thanks y if and only if there are two events, call them e and e′, such that x is the agent of e, e′ is a being thanked by y, and e caused e′. In words, x did something that caused y to be thanked. So the time lapse between my phoning my friend and her being thanked does not show I performed two actions; what it shows is that the one action I performed did not have its desired consequence until later. This leads to the second point. To say I thanked my friend entails that I did something that caused her to be thanked. But while what I did could correctly be described as my phoning and leaving the message at the time I performed this action, that same action could not be described as thanking my friend until she received the message. So although my telephoning and my thanking her were the same action, what I did can't be described in both ways until long after the performance. In the same way my great-great-grandfather in the paternal line could not have been described in just these terms during his lifetime. That does not show he was not the same person as Clarence Herbert Davidson of Inverness.[3]

The topic of this paper is the explanation of action; it may seem that the discussion so far is only remotely connected with explanation. But this appearance is misleading. In fact the causal character of the concepts used in talking about action is an essential part of what must be grasped in coming to a clear view of the nature of action explanation. What I have emphasized so far is the way we very often identify actions by referring to their consequences. Thus thanking someone is doing something that causes that person to be thanked; killing someone is doing something that causes that person's death; building a house is doing something that causes a house to be built; and so on.

One form the explanation of action can take is what we may call explanation by redescription. So if you ask me why I am pulling on the rope or telephoning, I can answer by saying I am raising my paralyzed arm or thanking my friend. Not any redescription will serve. If I had no idea that the rope was tied to my arm, but thought it was tied to a bag of groceries, then my pulling the rope would still be my raising my arm, but this fact would not explain my pulling the rope. The difference between explanatory and non-explanatory redescriptions is that the explanatory redescriptions supply a purpose with which the agent acted, an intention. Though the redescription characterizes the action in terms of a consequence of the action, that consequence is seen as intended when the redescription is offered as an answer to the question "Why did you do that?"

Perhaps it will now seem that after all something is added to an event to make it an action, namely an intention. Certainly it is true that if some event, say my arm going up, is an action, then there must also be an intention. But in my view, the intention is not part of the action, but a cause of it. Just as nothing is added to my telephoning my friend when that act becomes a thanking, so nothing is added to my arm going up if that event is caused by an intention.

---

[3] I discuss this issue at greater length in "Adverbs of Action" in *Essays on Davidson*, pp. 230–41.

At one time (about twenty-five years ago, when I wrote "Actions, Reasons and Causes") I thought there were no such states as intending; there were just intentional actions. This was, I now believe, an error. This is clear in the case where an intention is formed long before the intended action is performed, and even clearer in the case where the intended action is never performed. Intentions are also required to explain how complex actions are monitored and controlled.[4]

Although intentional actions are caused by intentions, it is not enough to insure that an action was performed with a certain intention that it was caused by that intention. For example, I might intend to meet my daughter at a certain restaurant on her birthday. Believing her birthday is tomorrow, I go to the restaurant today to make a reservation, and there I meet my daughter. Her birthday, it turns out, is today. So my intention to meet her at the restaurant on her birthday has caused me to do that very thing—but by lucky accident, and therefore not intentionally. Deviant causal chains of this kind present a problem in the explanation of action, since we would like to be able to say what the conditions are that must be satisfied if an action is to be intentional. Several clever philosophers have tried to show how to eliminate the deviant causal chains,[5] but I remain convinced that the concepts of event, cause, and intention are inadequate to account for intentional action.

I come now to a delicate issue about which I have no firm conviction: another problem area. The issue concerns the stages in the emergence of an intention. An intention to act (or to refrain from acting) requires both a belief and a desire or pro-attitude: a desire or pro-attitude toward outcomes or situations with certain properties, and a belief that acting in a certain way will promote such an outcome or situation. The emergence of an intention requires two transformations on the belief–desire couple. The first is obvious. The belief and the desire must be brought together; a course of action must be seen by the agent as attractive in the light of the fact that it promises to bring a desired state of affairs about. This transformation is what is usually thought of as "practical reasoning", reasoning from the perceived

---

[4] This change of mind and the reasons for it are recorded in "Intending", reprinted in *Essays on Actions and Events*, Oxford University Press, 1980.

[5] For examples, see David Armstrong, "Acting and Trying", *Philosophical Papers*, 2 (1973), pp. 1–15, and "Beliefs and Desires as Causes of Actions: A Reply to Donald Davidson", *Philosophical Papers*, 4 (1975), pp. 1–8; Christopher Peacocke, "Deviant Causal Chains", in *Midwest Studies in Philosophy*, Volume IV, ed. Peter French, Theodore Uehling, Jr., and Howard Wettstein, University of Minnesota Press, 1979.

value of the end to the value of the means. But this is not enough; we do not perform every action that we believe would promote some good or satisfy some obligation. We don't if for no other reason than that we can't, since acting to promote one good will often prevent our acting to promote some other good. And of course many actions that we know would promote some good we also know would produce much greater evils. When an intention is formed we go from a stage in which we perceive, or imagine that we perceive, the attractions and drawbacks of a course of action to a stage in which we commit ourselves to act. This may be just another pro-attitude, but an intention, unlike other desires or pro-attitudes, is not merely conditional or prima facie. If it is to produce an action, it can't be simply an appreciation that some good would come of acting in a certain way.

This story about how beliefs and desires cause an action is arrived at not by introspecting a process of which agents are generally aware, but by reflecting on the nature of beliefs and pro-attitudes on the one hand, and on the nature of action on the other. As a result, it is easy to question the claim that these "steps", which logic seems to demand, correspond to anything in the actual psychology of action. It is clear that most of our actions are not preceded by any conscious reasoning or deliberation. We don't usually "form" intentions, we just come to have them. And it is striking that in explaining why we did something we usually say nothing about the attractions of the alternatives we passed up, or the drawbacks that were outweighed by the positive feature or features we mention in giving our reasons. One is attracted by the simplicity of Aristotle's account of action done for a reason, which corresponds exactly to the explanations we most commonly give of actions; he treats the contents of a belief and a desire as providing the premises of an argument, and performing the action as drawing the conclusion. Aristotle is right, I think, in treating the explanation of an action as the retracing of a course of reasoning on the part of the actor. But I do not see how the "reasoning" can be as simple as Aristotle wants it to be. And the more complex we find the logic of the reasoning, the more strain we put on the idea that the causality of action corresponds to the reconstructed logical steps.

Doubts have often been expressed (for example by Philippa Foot and Thomas Nagel) about the need for a pro-attitude or desire in explaining action. The suggestion is that belief alone is often adequate to spark an action. Thus, someone may perform a disagreeable task simply because he promised to, while finding nothing desirable or attractive about the task. It is true that in explaining an action there is usually no need to mention both the belief and the pro-attitude. If it is asked why someone put his foot down, the answer may be that he believed that by putting his foot down he would crush a snail; if this is the answer, it is obviously assumed that he wanted to crush the snail. But in the same way one could mention only the desire; the belief would then be obvious. A more important issue is involved, for to deny the need for a pro-attitude in the etiology of action is to lose an important explanatory aid. If a person is constituted in such a way that if he believes that by acting in a certain way he will crush a snail he has a tendency to act in that way, then in this respect he differs from most other people, and this difference will help explain why he acts as he does. The special fact about how he is constituted is one of his causal powers, a disposition to act under specified conditions in specific ways. Such a disposition is what I mean by a pro-attitude.

Intentional actions are, then, by their most common descriptions seen as sandwiched between cause and effect. If we know that someone intentionally crushed a snail, we know some action of his was caused by a desire to crush a snail, and a belief that by performing the action he would promote the crushing of a snail; and we also know that the action so caused itself caused a snail to be crushed.

The way explanation is built into the concepts of action, belief, and desire has understandably raised doubts, both about how truly explanatory reason-explanations are, and about whether they are genuinely causal. The first doubt is engendered by the Molière factor. How can the appropriate belief and desire explain an action if we already know, from the description of the action, that it must have been caused by such a belief–desire pair, and we know that such an action is just what such a belief–desire pair is suited to cause? A small part of the answer is that Molière was wrong; it may explain why a pill put someone to sleep to advert to its dormative power, since a pill without such a power might put someone to sleep (it might have acted as a placebo). But we also realize that we learn little about why someone crushed a snail by being told he wanted to crush a snail and believed, etc.—we learn little more than that the action was intentional under the given description. However, most reason-explanations do not take this form. It may be far from obvious that the reason someone put his foot down was to crush a snail. The more interesting point involves the cause. It is true that someone who has a desire that he believes he can realize by acting in a certain way will have a tendency to act in that way.

But as we noticed, most such tendencies are not realized. Much of the explanatory force of reason-explanations comes from the fact that they specify which pair, from among the vast number of belief–desire pairs that were suited to cause the action, actually did cause it.

There can be no doubt, however, that reason-explanations, by virtue of the features we have been depicting, are in some sense low-grade; they explain less than the best explanations in the hard sciences because of their heavy dependence on causal propensities. The fact that beliefs and desires explain actions only when they are described in such a way as to reveal their suitability for causing the action reduces the power of the explanation, and so does the fact that the explanation provides no reason for saying that one suitable belief–desire pair rather than another (which may well also have been present in the agent) did the causing. These two facts are connected, for both are due to the unavailability of accurate laws for reason-explanations.

If laws were available to back up reason-explanations, reason-explanations would consist in a specification of the law and naming the relevant belief and desire; the condition would automatically be satisfied that the belief and desire caused the action. Lacking a law of the right kind, it is essential to advert to the causal relation, since the belief and the desire might be present, and the action take place, and yet the belief and the desire not explain the action. If adequate laws were available, there would be no need to describe the cause in terms of the effects it tends to produce, just as, when sophisticated laws are in hand, we can dispense with reference to such dispositions as being soluble or frangible in explaining why an object dissolved or broke.

At one time it was widely thought that just because there are no serious laws linking reasons with actions, the relation between reasons and actions could not be causal, whereas I have been suggesting that appeal to causal concepts is appropriate to the explanation of action in part just because strict laws are not available. The two apparently opposed views can be reconciled if we hold that causal relations obtain between events however the events are described, while laws deal with types of event, and hence with particular events only as they have the properties that earn them membership in a type. One can then maintain that cause and effect must in principle be describable in terms that instantiate a law, but can be mentioned in explanatory contexts in other terms. Thus beliefs and desires may really cause actions, even though the actions, beliefs, and desires are not types that lend themselves to treatment by serious laws.

This view, which I have developed over the years in a number of papers,[6] has seemed unsatisfactory to a number of philosophers, and I would like to discuss some of the difficulties they have found, or thought they have found.

A difficulty which unites many critics concerns explanation. How, they wonder, can beliefs and desires explain an action if no law is invoked? It is one thing to say that singular causal statements ("this event caused that event") are extensional, and so remain true no matter how the events are described; it is quite another thing to accord such statements explanatory force no matter how things are described, for explanation is intentional. Of course, reason-explanations don't explain no matter how cause and effect are described; there is the very strong requirement that the belief and desire be described in terms of their semantic contents, and that these contents imply the desirability of the action as seen by the agent. So, the complaint continues, the explanation copes with the reasons insofar as they show how the action was reasonable for the agent, but it fails to explain the causality.

Carl Hempel, proponent of the "covering law" theory of explanation, has proposed a solution.[7] He suggests that the laws of action state what a rational agent will do. The rational agent will do what, in the light of his beliefs and desires, is his optimal course of action. To explain the agent's actions, we describe his attitudes in terms of their contents, we refer to laws that specify how any rational agent acts in various circumstances, and add as a premise that the agent was rational. To deal with the problem that even a rational agent often has reasons for doing incompatible things, Hempel proposes to accept some version of decision theory, which supplies a way of weighing competing claims. I shall pass over, in this paper, the question how adequate decision theory is, and the related problem of giving such a theory a clear empirical interpretation. There remains this oddity in Hempel's proposal; the "laws", so called, of decision theory (or any other theory of rationality) are not empirical generalizations about all agents. What they do is define what is meant (or what someone means) by being rational. Application of Hempel's scheme

---

[6] Particularly in essays 6–10 in *Essays on Actions and Events*.

[7] Carl Hempel, "Rational Action", in *Proceedings and Addresses of the American Philosophical Association*, The Antioch Press, 1962, pp. 5–24, and *Aspects of Scientific Explanation*, Free Press, 1965, pp. 463–89. I have discussed this suggestion further in "Hempel on Explaining Action" in *Essays on Actions and Events*.

depends on knowing that the agent is rational, but there is no way of determining this except by establishing that the "laws" fit the agent. The "explanation" in terms of rationality therefore lacks explanatory force.

Dagfinn Føllesdal has written that he agrees with Hempel that explanation requires laws, and complains of my account of reason-explanation that it divorces such explanation from laws that would make it truly illuminating.[8] He agrees that explanation often succeeds although strict laws covering the case are not known, and so the descriptions of cause and effect that would instantiate the laws are not known, but he insists that "To say that A is a cause of B does not contribute to an explanation of the occurrence of B unless there is a law which is instantiated by A and B under approximately these descriptions."[9] In my opinion, though I think not in Føllesdal's, the difference between us here is largely terminological; but when terminology is adjusted, an important difference may be discovered in the background.

First, what is to count as a law? Since I was interested in the question whether reason-explanations are or ever could be just like the best explanations for which physics strives, I set very high standards for what I called "strict" laws; they were to be "closed" in the sense of requiring no ceteris paribus clauses; they were to come as close to allowing the unconditional prediction of the event to be explained as the perhaps irreducibly probabilistic character of physics allows. I was also prepared to interpret the concept of law as strictly as had all those philosophers who claimed there were no laws to back up reason-explanations. Føllesdal takes a slacker view of laws; for him it is a law that "Any severely dehydrated person who drinks water will improve". He then points out that a person might instantiate several such "laws" at the same time, and these laws might predict contradictory results; we would then have to "balance the laws against one another".[10] I had assumed that laws had to be true, and so couldn't lead to contradictions. But as I say, this is just a matter of terminology. Many philosophers of science consider the ascriptions of tendencies, propensities, and causal powers to involve laws, and the laws they involve, while perhaps not properly stated in the form that Føllesdal

[8] Føllesdal's comments appear in "Causation and Explanation: A Problem in Davidson's View on Action and Mind" in *Actions and Events: Perspectives on the Philosophy of Donald Davidson*, ed. Ernie LePore and Brian McLaughlin, Blackwell, 1985.

[9] Ibid., p. 315.   [10] Ibid., pp. 318–19.

suggests, certainly provide most of our everyday understanding of the world and of people. As I already pointed out, beliefs and desires have causal powers, and that is why they explain actions. If "Someone who wants to crush a snail has a tendency to do what he believes will result in crushing a snail" is a law, I agree that reason-explanations require, and appeal to, laws. But I wonder whether or not Føllesdal agrees with me that this "law" adds nothing to what we already understand if we know what a want or desire is; and whether he agrees that the relevant belief and desire explain the action only if the belief–desire pair caused the action in the right way.

The interesting matter on which Føllesdal and I differ concerns the question whether reason-explanations and explanations in physics constitute two different kinds of explanation, neither being reducible to the other (which is my view), or whether "our theory of the mental and our theory of nature are both parts of one comprehensive theory..." (p. 321). Of course explanations of mental events must include reference to physical causes (as in perception, etc.), and as we have seen, actions are typically characterized in terms of their physically described consequences. So any "theory" of the mental must cover interactions between the mental events (i.e., events described in mentalistic ways) and physical events (events characterized in physical ways). The basic difference that I think exists between reason-explanations and the explanations of an ultimate physics can therefore be put this way: laws relating the mental and the physical are not like the laws of physics, and cannot be reduced to them. Since action explanations require such laws, action explanations are not like explanations in physics, and cannot be reduced to them. The laws of many physical sciences are also not like the laws of physics, but I do not know of important theoretical (as opposed to practical) reasons they cannot be reduced to the laws of physics. But there is a reason why psychological concepts like belief, desire, and intentional action, and the laws containing them, cannot be reduced to physical concepts and laws. I shall come back to this point in a moment.

Ted Honderich has raised a related question about my account of action explanations.[11] His complaint is that one event causes another only in virtue of certain properties, and these are the properties that

---

[11] See Ted Honderich, "The Argument for Anomalous Monism", *Analysis*, 42 (1982), pp. 59–64; "Psychophysical Lawlike Connections and Their Problem", *Inquiry*, 24 (1981), pp. 277–303; "Nomological Dualism: Reply to Four Critics", *Inquiry*, 24 (1981), pp. 419–38.

instantiate a law. Therefore, he argues, if the only real laws are physical, mental events and states cannot cause or be caused by physical events and states. The conclusion Honderich seems to draw is that either there are strict psychophysical laws or mental events are not identical with physical events. In my opinion Honderich has failed to note the difference between events described in terms that allow the application of laws without ceteris paribus clauses, laws that make no use of causal tendencies, potentialities, or dispositions, and laws that, by using such devices, allow us to choose what we call the cause according to our special explanatory interests. (This distinction can be maintained even if there are no laws altogether free from appeal to such concepts, for there will be laws as free as possible from using such concepts, and laws that do not come close.) Laws of these different sorts all yield explanations, but explanations of different sorts. Explanation in terms of the ultimate physics, though it answers to various interests, is not interest relative: it treats everything without exception as a cause of an event if it lies within physical reach (falls within the light cone leading to the effect). Every event in this area is a cause of the effect no matter how causes and effect are described. Special sciences, or explanatory schemes, take note of more or less precise correlations between effects of certain kinds and far more limited causes of certain kinds. These correlations, of the sort we find in economics, geology, biology, aerodynamics, and the explanation of action, depend on assumptions about other things being more or less equal—assumptions that cannot be made precise. We can agree with Honderich to this extent: depending on the sort of explanation we are interested in, different properties of events are treated as causally efficacious. But interest aside, every property of every event is causally efficacious.

Some have denied this. Lars Bergström, for example, says,

The fact that a system is open (in the sense, I suppose, that some of its components are influenced by factors outside the system) does not prevent the existence of strict laws describing (parts of) the system. For example, consider an electronic calculator: the numerals displayed are strictly determined by the buttons pressed even though factors outside the system determine which buttons are pressed.[12]

[12] The passage is quoted with approval by Føllesdal from p. 16 of Bergström's "Føllesdal and Davidson on Reasons and Causes", in *Tankar och Tankefel: Tillä gnade Zalma Puterman*, ed. Wlodzimierz Rabinowicz, 50 ar, 1. oktober 1981 (Filosofiska Studier utgivna

The quotation emphasizes how easily we disregard factors we are not interested in. For of course the "law" mentioned above fails (to mention one of a thousand possibilities) if the current goes off between button pressing and numerals displayed.

In these remarks, I have made no distinction between a science like geology and the explanatory scheme of "folk psychology"; the big distinction came between physics and the rest. If there is a distinction between reason-explanation and the rest, it must depend on some further feature of reason-explanations. (And of course there may be a significant sense in which geology, etc., cannot be reduced to physics.) Let me say what I think this special feature is that sets reason-explanations, and psychological concepts generally, apart.

Let me first make clear that in my view the mental is not an ontological but a conceptual category. Mental objects and events are at the same time also physical, physiological, biological, and chemical objects and events. To say of an event, for example an intentional action, that it is mental is simply to say that we can describe it in a certain vocabulary—and the mark of that vocabulary is semantic intentionality. Reason-explanations differ from physical explanations because they are couched (in part) in an intentional vocabulary, and the basic concepts of this vocabulary cannot be reduced, or related by strict laws, to the vocabularies of the physical sciences.

The reason mental concepts cannot be reduced to physical concepts is the normative character of mental concepts. Beliefs, desires, intentions, and intentional actions must, as we have seen, be identified by their semantic contents in reason-explanations. The semantic contents of attitudes and beliefs determine their relations to one another and to the world in ways that meet at least rough standards of consistency and correctness. Unless such standards are met to an adequate degree, nothing can count as being a belief, a pro-attitude, or an intention. But these standards are norms, our norms, there being no others.

The point to emphasize is not that we as explainers and observers employ our norms in understanding the actions of others; in some sense we employ our norms whatever we study. The point is rather that in explaining action we are identifying the phenomena to be explained, and the phenomena that do the explaining, as directly answering to our own norms; reason-explanations make others intelligible to us only to the extent that we can recognize something like our own reasoning powers at work. It would be a mistake to suppose that this is merely a sign of lack of imagination, or perhaps of soft-heartedness. It is a central, and irreplaceable, feature of the intentional. We have noticed the obvious fact that a belief and a desire explain an action only if the contents of the belief and desire entail that there is something desirable about the action, given the description under which the action is being explained. This entailment marks a normative element, a primitive aspect of rationality. Similar remarks can be made about the identification of particular beliefs and desires.

There is, I think, a strong tendency on the part of many psychologists today, and perhaps of many philosophers of psychology, to think that rationality itself can somehow be reduced to non-normative, perhaps formal, characteristics. I have in mind some of the work of Jerry Fodor, of Fred Dretske, and even Dagfinn Føllesdal's remarks about a single unitary system for explaining both the physical and the mental. Let me conclude by sketching briefly, and with no attempt at serious argument, where I believe these efforts at reduction, if they were successful, would lead.

Imagine that there were spaces in the universe, persistent over time, but moveable and changeable in shape, spaces within which nothing could be observed from outside, even with the use of the most sophisticated instruments. Let us call these spaces black holes. Obviously our explanations of what goes on in the observable world will be incomplete unless we know something about the black holes. For these holes absorb observable material and energy and spew it out, they move relative to other objects, they change shape, they help mold gravitational fields.

We build up a theory about these black holes. Since the aim of the theory is to complete our explanation of the rest of the world, the theory must be comprehensive—it must deal with every relevant aspect of change and force. It must, in a word, be a physical theory. This theory will aim to describe, on the basis of what goes on outside, what is going on inside a black hole.

Would there then be something we could call a science of black holes? Certainly not, as distinct from physics generally, for all we did to complete our scientific account of the world was to fill in the physical description of what was in the hole. Using our knowledge of what happens outside, we extrapolated in.

As far as I can see, a science of animal behavior that aimed to be continuous with physics would be no different: it would merely substitute black boxes for black holes. It would describe what went into such boxes in physical terms (as it is sometimes said "stimuli" should be described), and it would describe the output in terms of physical motion (as it is sometimes said "responses" should be described). Would this science differ from, or add to, ordinary physics? Not in any way. The laws would be those of physics, and all the phenomena treated would be described in physical terms. But what would such a science tell us about intentional action?

To see this, think of a tribe of monkeys the members of which respond to the threat of danger by emitting a certain cry. Other monkeys, hearing this cry, respond as to danger. The situation has all the components of our story so far. To explain the behavior of the monkeys we do not need to attribute intentions or beliefs to them (I am not arguing that they don't have intentions or beliefs). And so nothing in their behavior as described has to count as making a mistake. Of course it can happen that a monkey lets out the 'danger cry' when danger is not present, and his fellows may react as to danger. From our point of view this may seem a mistake. But unless the monkeys *believe* there is danger when there is not, no error has been committed; they have simply responded to a stimulus that usually, but not always, accompanies danger.

I take it as obvious that linguistic behavior is intentional and so requires belief. It is only where intention and belief are present that the concept of a mistake can be applied. The monkey's responses in our story are not intentional, and so of course cannot be a model for linguistic behavior. But this is only part of the present point. The present point may rather be put this way; whether or not intention is present, not enough is in place to insure that.

8 *Could There Be a Science of Rationality?*

Many philosophers have doubted whether psychology can be made a serious science. Wittgenstein writes,

> The confusion and barrenness of psychology is not to be explained by calling it a 'young science'; its state is not comparable with that of physics, for instance, in its beginnings .... For in psychology there are experimental methods and *conceptual confusion* ....
>   The existence of experimental methods makes us think we have the means of solving the problems which trouble us; though problem and methods pass one another by.[1]

I take this to apply not just to psychology as it existed when Wittgenstein wrote, but to be a judgment *sub specie aeternitatis*. Gilbert Ryle seems to have been of the same mind. When it comes to explaining human behavior, it is pretentious, he thinks, to hope to do better than common sense:

> [W]hen we hear the promise of a new scientific explanation of what we say and do, we expect to hear of some counterparts to those impacts [like those of which physics treats], some forces or agencies of which we should never have dreamed and which we shall certainly never witness at their subterranean work. But when we are in a less impressionable frame of mind, we find something implausible in the promise of discoveries yet to be made of the hidden causes of our own actions and reactions. We know quite well what caused the farmer to return from the market with his pigs unsold. He found that the prices were lower than he had expected. We know quite well why John Doe scowled and slammed the door. He had been insulted.[2]

Where Wittgenstein and Ryle are contemptuous of the idea of a serious science that aims to explain human behavior, Quine is ambivalent.

---

[1] *Philosophical Investigations*, II, xiv.
[2] *The Concept of Mind*, Barnes & Noble, New York, 1949, pp. 324–5.

Does Quine think the concepts of meaning, communication, interpretation, belief, and so on can be worked into a serious science of
behavior? Given the attention Quine has paid to the understanding
of language, and his view that philosophy is continuous with science,
you might think Quine would say yes. And as I shall show in a minute,
there is some reason to think this is Quine's answer. But there is also
reason to think it is not.

J. B. Watson, the originator of modern behaviorism, thought that
concepts like those of belief and desire were 'heritages of a timid
savage past', 'medieval conceptions', of a piece with 'magic and
voodoo'. B. F. Skinner, a longtime friend of Quine's, put it more
mildly: 'The objection (he says of such concepts as those of intention,
belief and desire) is not that these things are mental but that they offer
no real explanation and stand in the way of a more effective analysis'.
He speaks repeatedly of 'an alternative to mentalistic formulations',
and adds 'I would not be involved in this if I did not think that mentalistic ways of thinking about human behavior stand in the way of
much more effective ways.'

Quine seems to agree with Skinner and Watson, as his open
endorsement of behaviorism suggests he would. 'All in all, [he writes]
the propositional attitudes are in a bad way. These are the idioms most
stubbornly at variance with scientific patterns.'[3] Much of the chapter
of *Word and Object* titled 'Flight From Intension' is directed against
those who think we can talk freely of propositions and the propositional attitudes without asking for a basis in behavior. This is consistent
with providing such a basis, that is, legitimatizing these very concepts.
But further remarks put such a possibility in doubt. After accepting Brentano's claim that intentional idioms (those we use to report
propositional attitudes) are not reducible to non-intentional concepts,
Quine remarks, 'One may accept the Brentano thesis either as showing the indispensability of intentional idioms and the importance of
an autonomous science of intention, or as showing the baselessness
of intentional idioms and the emptiness of a science of intention. My
attitude, unlike Brentano's, is the second.'[4]

Perhaps that should settle the matter, but I'm not sure it does.
For what, after all, is the status of Quine's attempt to give a behavioristic account of what is sound in translation? Quine does not

[3] 'Mind and Verbal Dispositions', in *Mind and Language*, ed. Samuel Guttenplan,
Oxford University Press, 1975, p. 92.
[4] *Word and Object*, MIT Press, 1960, p. 221.

attempt to reconstruct the concepts of meaning, analyticity, and the rest as philosophers have thought of them. But what he does provide is intended to make sense not only of speakers, but of what they say. It does this by telling when a translation of the speaker's words is acceptable on behavioristic grounds. My question remains: is this enterprise merely the best we can do, but not even the beginning of a science, or is it the direction we must take if we want to be scientific about verbal behavior? In particular, are even the behaviorally sound substitutes for meaning and analyticity (e.g. stimulus meaning and stimulus analyticity) still irreducible to physiological or physical matters, or may they give way, in the fullness of time and the increase of knowledge, to the more precise sciences? Quine often speaks as if they may.

In 'Mind and Verbal Dispositions' Quine distinguishes three levels of 'purported explanation' of linguistic phenomena: the mental, the behavioral, and the physiological. The mental he dismisses as 'scarcely deserving the name explanation'. But does this mean that transposing to the behavioral level must change the subject? Not at all: 'let us recognize that the semantical study of language is worth pursuing with all the scruples of the natural scientist. We must study language as a system of dispositions to verbal behavior ...' Earlier in the same essay he remarks on the 'conspicuous fact that language is a social enterprise which is keyed to intersubjectively observable objects in the external world', and suggests that this opens the door to getting 'on with a properly physicalistic account of language'.[5]

The first step, then, from the mental to dispositions to behavior, does not change the subject, which is the semantic analysis of language; it just puts it in the way of being more scientific. Dispositions for Quine are physical states—physiological states when the disposition is what we would usually call mental, like gullibility; physical in the case of the dispositions of physical objects, like solubility. And while Quine does not think anyone now knows how to give a physiological account of any behavioral disposition, he seems sure there must be one. (Since for present purposes there is no point in distinguishing physiology from a special domain of physics, I'll talk from here on as if physics were the whole of natural science.) On this point, Quine writes:

A disposition is in my view simply a physical trait, a configuration or mechanism ... Dispositions to behavior, then, are physiological states or

---

[5] The quoted passages are on pages 87–91 and 84.

traits or mechanisms. In citing them dispositionally we are singling them out by behavioral symptoms, behavioral tests. Usually we are in no position to detail them in physiological terms. [However] The deepest explanation, the physiological, would analyze these dispositions in explicit terms of nerve impulses and other anatomically and chemically identified organic processes.[6]

The reasoning seems to be this; if an object has a disposition, this fact must depend on the physical properties of the object. So whatever can be explained by appeal to the disposition must be explicable in physical terms, whether or not we know how to give the relevant physical description. Solubility illustrates the point: at one time we knew there was some unknown physical property of an object that made it soluble; now we know what that property is. Quine also seems to hold that a fair account of the concept of evidence can ultimately be given in physical terms. In *Word and Object* he says, 'Any realistic theory of evidence must be inseparable from the psychology of stimulus and response, applied to sentences,'[7] and in *Roots of Reference* he adds, 'Our liberated epistemologist ends up as an empirical psychologist.' The learning process, he thinks, is accessible to empirical science. 'By exploring it, science can in effect explore the evidential relation.' Since 'The attribution of a behavioral disposition, learned or unlearned, is a physiological hypothesis, however fragmentary,' we may conclude that 'mental entities are unobjectionable if conceived as hypothetical physical mechanisms and posited with a view strictly to the systematizing of physical phenomena.'[8]

Several ideas emerge in these passages. The theme of the irreducibility of the mentalistic vocabulary, when combined with the thesis that there could be a serious—i.e., physiological or physical—account of the evidential relation and other mental concepts, is only consistent with giving up our present talk of propositional attitudes in favor of a vocabulary limited to that of physiology or physics. The claim that 'dispositions to verbal behavior' are physical configurations suggests that far from being irreducible to the physical vocabulary, a sensible reduction is in the offing.

It may be that at one time Quine was uncertain about the relation between the mental and the physical vocabularies, but in more recent writings he has settled for the view that talk of beliefs, desires, actions,

---

[6] 'Mind and Verbal Dispositions', p. 92.   [7] *Word and Object*, p. 17.
[8] The quotations are from *The Roots of Reference*, Open Court, 1973, pp. 3, 36, 12, and 33f.

and meanings is not reducible to something more scientific, but that its usefulness for everyday descriptions and explanations cannot be denied. The relation between the mental and the physical which Quine now seems to accept is what I have called 'anomalous monism', the position that says there are no strictly lawlike correlations between phenomena classified as mental and phenomena classified as physical, though mental entities are identical, taken one at a time, with physical entities.[9] In other words, there is a single ontology, but more than one way of describing and explaining the items in the ontology.

There are several reasons for the irreducibility of the mental to the physical. One reason, appreciated by Quine, is the normative element in interpretation introduced by the necessity of appealing to charity in matching the sentences of others to our own. Such matching forces us to weigh the relative plausibilities of different deviations from coherence and truth (by our own lights). Nothing in physics corresponds to the way in which this feature of the mental shapes its categories.

Another reason, perhaps easier to grasp, lies in the irreducibly causal character of mental concepts. Let me give a non-mental example first. The state of being sunburned is necessarily a state caused by the action of the sun. No completed physics would make use of the concept of sunburn, not only because part of the explanation is already built into the characterization of the state, but also because two states of the skin could be in every intrinsic way identical, and yet one be a case of sunburn and the other not.

The propositional attitudes, the semantics of spoken words, and behavior as we normally understand it, are all like this. The reason, both in the case of the attitudes and in the case of semantics, is the same: what our words mean, and what our thoughts are about, is partly determined by the history of their acquisition. The truth conditions of my sentence 'The moon is gibbous', or of my belief that the moon is gibbous, depend in part on the causal history of my relations to the moon. But it could happen that two people were in relevantly similar physical states (defined just in terms of what is within the skin), and yet one could be speaking or thinking of our moon, and the other not.

When it comes to explaining behavior, as normally conceived, this feature of the propositional attitudes is an asset, for behavior, thought

[9] I introduced the phrase and the idea in 'Mental Events' (1970), reprinted in *Actions and Events*, Oxford University Press, 1980.

of as actions, is also an irreducibly causal concept. This is because actions are typically described not merely as motions but as motions that can be explained by the reasons an agent has—his or her beliefs and desires. Thus if I pay my bill by writing a check, it is necessarily the case that I wrote the check because I wanted to pay my bill and believed that by writing a check I would be paying my bill. Actions are individuated along the same lines as propositional attitudes; this is why the attitudes do as good a job as they do in explaining actions. But this way of individuating and of picking out actions is not going to help create a science of behavior that might in principle become an identifiable province of physiology or physics.

There have been numerous attempts to extract from the propositional attitudes a purely subjective (or 'narrow') content not subject to the difficulties for science introduced by externalism. If this could be done, it would remove a major obstacle to making psychology a science, leaving only the normative aspect of the mental to make trouble. The reason thinkers like Jerry Fodor and Noam Chomsky want to find a purely internal element or aspect of the propositional attitudes is obvious: it is only if mental properties are supervenient on the physical properties of the agent that there can be any hope of identifying the mental properties with physical properties, or of finding lawlike connections between the two. If mental properties are supervenient not only on the physical properties of the agent but in addition on the physical properties of the world outside the agent, there can be no hope of discovering laws that predict and explain behavior solely on the basis of intrinsic features of agents. Both Fodor and Chomsky have made clear that they think an internal variety of the intentional is essential to making psychology a serious study. For related reasons, Fodor has also rejected most forms of holism, at least so far as language is concerned. He gives a number of reasons, but what seems to motivate the rejection is the conviction that unless the meanings of expressions can be tied in lawlike ways to specific neural configurations, there is no hope for a serious account of linguistic phenomena. Such ties would, of course, rule out externalism.

What I think is certain is that holism, externalism, and the normative feature of the mental stand or fall together: if these are features of the mental, and they stand in the way of a serious science of psychology, then Ryle, Wittgenstein, and Quine in his more pessimistic mood are right. There can be no serious science or sciences of the mental. I believe the normative, holistic, and externalist elements in psychological concepts cannot be eliminated without radically changing the subject. I do not want to argue these points in this paper, having done so at length elsewhere.[10] My interest here is rather to ask what follows if I am right. Pretty clearly, it does not follow without argument that there cannot be a scientific psychology: whether this follows depends on what you mean by 'science', and whether the features that I maintain characterize the mental stand in its way. What does follow is that psychology cannot be *reduced* to physics, nor to any other of the natural sciences. But unless we simply legislate science to be what can be reduced to a natural science, the failure of reduction should not in itself be taken to show that what cannot be so reduced does not deserve to be called science.

Since my own approach to the description, analysis (in a rough sense), and explanation of thought, language, and action has, on the one hand, what I take to be some of the characteristics of a science, and has, on the other hand, come under attack by both Fodor and Chomsky as being radically 'unscientific', I plan to examine my theory, if that is the word, to see how or whether it can be defended as science. I should remark at the start that I think the outcome is mixed.

One way to think of the moment when psychology came of age as an empirical science is with the work of Gustav Theodor Fechner, whose life spanned most of the nineteenth century (1801–1887). Fechner began as a physicist, but then drifted through chemistry, physiology, and medicine to metaphysics (and beyond, to mysticism). Fechner was interested in the relation between mind and body, or matter and spirit, and he approached this problem by seeking quantitative laws that connect the mental and the physical. Weber had already suggested that the smallest change in the intensity of a physical magnitude required to produce a perceivable difference in sensation is not a fixed physical difference, but is proportional to the magnitude of the stimulus. Fechner generalized the law: the experienced intensity of a physical stimulus is equal to some constant times the log of the physical stimulus. Roughly: as a physical stimulus increases (say intensity of loudness or pitch in sound), equal increases in the magnitude of the physical stimulus will result in smaller and smaller increases in the felt sensation. The constant varies with the sense involved. This law can, of course, be tested, and it is approximately correct. The

[10] See, for example, 'Mental Events' and 'Three Varieties of Knowledge' in *A. J. Ayer: Memorial Essays*, Royal Institute of Philosophy Supplement 30, ed. A. Phillips Griffiths, Cambridge University Press, 1991, pp. 153–66.

decibel scale of loudness is an informal example: equal intervals on the decibel scale are (more or less) equal subjectively, but the ratio of two amounts of acoustical power is equal to 10 times the common logarithm of the power ratio.

Fechner had the right idea. If scientific methods can be applied to the mental, it is by proposing a solid theory and asking how it can be tested and interpreted empirically. Theories describe abstract structures; their empirical interpretations ask whether these structures can be discovered in the real world. Fechner's theory is relatively easy to interpret in some cases, which is perhaps not surprising, given the neurological basis of sensory discrimination. What we now know about neurons, neural nets, and the processing of information (so-called) that takes place in the sense organs and the brain, suggests that we should expect to find quantitative laws relating sensory discrimination and the physical magnitudes of stimuli. But there are closely related scalings of perceived sensations which are definitely surprising, at least to me. A good example is the perception of the relations among intervals in the pitch of sounds. The Greeks knew that if you divide a vibrating string in half, each half sounds an octave above the full string, and two thirds of the string produce the fifth above the full string. (Pythagoras is credited with discovering this.) But what is surprising is that if you sound two notes some arbitrary distance apart and ask a subject to tune a third note to the perceived mid-point, not only do different hearers arrive at approximately the same pitch, but pitches so determined are related in such a way as to produce an interval scale, that is, numbers can be assigned to various pitches in a way that keeps track of the relations between intervals, not on the basis of a physical magnitude, like string length or vibrations per second, but entirely on the basis of what is subjectively perceived. The theory that describes this fact has every right to be called a psychological theory, for it deals with nothing but the relations among psychological phenomena.

In a way, I have already given good examples of scientific theory in the field of psychology, one in the form of a general law relating the perceived intensity of sensory stimuli to physically measured aspects of the stimuli, the other in the form of the fundamental measurement of perceived intervals of pitch. But of course these examples do not speak to the concerns of those who ask whether, or in what way, psychology can be scientific. What they are interested in is the description, prediction, and explanation of intentional actions, and of associated attitudes such as intention, belief, desire, and linguistic meaning. Here I will consider a particular theory which I have proposed; I shall describe it in outline, and then ask in what respects it has the features of a scientific theory.

The theory I have in mind relates the concepts of belief, desire, and linguistic meaning. Since the theory treats belief in a quantified form, sometimes called subjective probability, and desire as measured on an interval scale (like Fahrenheit temperature or the subjective pitch scale I just mentioned), it includes a version of what is sometimes called decision theory; thus it is suited to the explanation of intentions and intentional actions. Unlike traditional decision theory in the form first given to it explicitly by Frank Ramsey, or the somewhat different version invented by Richard Jeffrey,[11] the theory I have in mind integrally includes a theory of meaning. It may therefore be called a unified theory of speech and action, or the Unified Theory for short.

The Unified Theory describes or defines an abstract structure. This structure has certain interesting and desirable properties which it is possible to prove. Thus one can prove, with respect to the part borrowed from decision theory, both a representation theorem and a uniqueness theorem. The first says in effect that numbers can be assigned to beliefs and desires which preserve the qualitative constraints imposed by the theory; the second says the numbers assigned to measure probabilities constitute a ratio scale and the numbers that track desires constitute an interval scale.[12] This is adequate to yield (at least 'in theory') predictions of intentional actions. The part of the theory that copes with linguistic meaning is in effect a modification of a Tarski-type theory of truth, and so is provably capable of supplying the truth conditions of all utterances of sentences in a language of which it treats. The final part of the theory joins decision theory and truth theory by a formal device which I shall not attempt to describe here.[13] The possibility of marrying the two theories depends on two things. The first is that decision theory shows how to extract both cardinal utilities and subjective probabilities from simple preferences. The second is that subjective probabilities, when taken as applied to

[11] I draw on Jeffrey's version in *The Logic of Decision*, 2nd edn., University of Chicago Press, 1983. F. M. Ramsey's original theory is reprinted in *Philosophical Papers*, ed. D. H. Mellor, Cambridge University Press, 1990.

[12] These remarks about the relevant scales apply strictly to Ramsey's theory; Jeffrey's theory is marginally different.

[13] For some details, see my 'The Structure and Content of Truth', *The Journal of Philosophy*, 10 (1990): 279–328.

sentences, are enough to yield a theory of meaning. There is thus a route, technically rather byzantine, but intuitively clear in each of its steps, from simple choices to a detailed interpretation of words, desires, and beliefs.

The possibility of such a theory rests on structures dictated by our concept of rationality. Both decision theory as I have used it, in the version developed by Richard Jeffrey, and theories of truth, for example, depend in part on logic. Jeffrey's decision theory, and Tarski's truth definitions, take an underlying logic for granted: these theories would be true only of perfect logicians. Beyond this, there is the assumption of a rational distribution of probabilities over propositions, and of a proportioning of degrees of belief in accord with the conditional probabilities: in other words, propositions are held true to the degree made rational by their evidential support. Thus the entire structure of the theory depends on the standards and norms of rationality.

These considerations cast considerable doubt on the scientific pretensions of the Unified Theory. But before I entertain doubts, let me dwell a bit more on the overall pattern. Like any scientific theory, the Unified Theory presents a clear and precise formal structure with demonstrable merits. There are only a few undefined concepts, and these are extensional. The basic primitive concept is the three-place relation between an agent and two sentences which holds when the agent would weakly prefer one sentence true rather than the other. This relation is extensional in the technical sense that a statement that this relation holds of three appropriate objects (an agent and two of that agent's sentences) retains its truth value (true or false) regardless of how those three objects are described. Yet if the observed pattern of such relations fits the terms of the theory, it is possible to infer the degrees of belief the agent accords his or her sentences, how much the agent would like those sentences to be true, and what the truth conditions (i.e., meanings) of those sentences are. In other words, the theory, if true of an agent, would serve to interpret the beliefs, values, and words of that agent.

This claim, even guarded as it is by the 'if true' clause, needs plenty of defense. It is a question, for example, whether belief, evaluation, and meaning are enough to support such broad-based interpretation without adding, say, intention or perception as further related but independent variables, not to mention the emotions. It is also uncertain whether a theory of truth is adequate to the interpretation of speech, even assuming that a theory of truth could be made to cover all the idioms of a natural language. But important as these matters are, I plan to leave them aside for now so that I can get on with the question whether a theory more or less like the Unified Theory can be thought of as scientific. My conclusion so far is: from a purely formal point of view, it is a powerful theory, and insofar as it corresponds to many of our intuitions concerning the nature of rationality, it is an attractive theory.

It is when we attend to the empirical interpretation of the theory that the basic questions and problems arise. Here I want to distinguish between the official story about how the theory can be interpreted, and an unofficial account. Officially, it is essential to be able to show how the theory can be interpreted without appeal to evidence that assumes the individuation of the contents of any propositional attitude. One such form of evidence is, as I mentioned, protocols that specify an agent's preference that one sentence rather than another be true. Given enough such evidence, a picture can be built of the agent's beliefs, desires, and meanings (that is, the truth conditions of his or her utterances). A finite amount of such evidence can only confirm the theory, of course; it cannot verify it. That is what we would expect. In brief outline, the official story takes this route:

Jeffrey's version of decision theory, applied to sentences, tells us that a rational agent cannot prefer both a sentence and its negation to a tautology, nor a tautology to both a sentence and its negation. This fact makes it possible for an interpreter to identify, with no knowledge of the meanings of the agent's sentences, all of the pure sentential connectives, such as negation, conjunction, and the biconditional. This minimal knowledge suffices to determine the subjective probabilities of all of the agent's sentences—how likely the agent thinks those sentences are to be true—and then, in turn, to fix the relative values of the truth of those sentences (from the agent's point of view, of course). The subjective probabilities can then be used to interpret the sentences. For what Quine calls observation sentences, the changes in probabilities provide the obvious clues to first order interpretation when geared to events and objects easily perceived simultaneously by interpreter and the person being interpreted. Conditional probabilities and entailments between sentences, by registering what the speaker takes to be evidence for his beliefs, provides the interpreter with what is needed to interpret more theoretical terms and sentences. This is the official story. Its merit lies not in its plausibility as an account of how we actually set about understanding others, but in the fact that it amounts to an informal proof of the adequacy of the theory to yield what is needed to support the interpretation of the basic propositional attitudes. (One should compare the official story of how Ramsey's decision theory yields sufficiently unique results to explain choice behavior on the basis of simple preferences.)

Unofficially, one can admit that as living, working interpreters, we never have enough of the sort of evidence needed to follow the official route, and we always have a great deal of other sorts of evidence. We make endless assumptions about the people we meet, about what they want, what they are apt to mean by what they say, what they believe about the environment we share with them, and why they act as they do. Our skills as interpreters come into play mainly when one or another of these assumptions turns out to be false, and by then we have much more than the poverty-stricken evidence the Unified Theory depends on. But this is as it should be. The point of the theory was not to describe how we actually interpret, but to speculate on what it is about thought and language that makes them interpretable. If we can tell a story like the official story about how it is possible, we can conclude that the constraints the theory places on the attitudes may articulate some of their philosophically significant features.

I have described in its most transparent form the art of applying the formal theory to an actual individual, with both interpreter and speaker outfitted with a mature set of concepts and the linguistic aptitudes for expressing them. All that is lacking at the start is a shared language, and prior knowledge of each other's attitudes. Since the theory and the official story of how it can be applied are already remote from actual practice, we must expect that the theory will throw only the most oblique light on the acquisition of a first language, and less still on the origins of speech. The most that can be said is that if we agree that the pattern of attitudes is as the theory depicts it, one can perhaps see that a creature properly endowed by nature could acquire it in the company of others already possessed of thought and speech. The theory may also prompt an interesting hypothesis about the origins of language; I shall mention this at the end.

I should emphasize how much belongs to the province of interpretation, of trying to give an empirical application to the formal theory. The intended application is to individuals, strictly speaking at a given time, since we can expect many of the values and beliefs of anyone to change swiftly as the world changes. The apparently quantitative ingredients, the measures of degree of desire and degree of belief, do not belong to the theory itself; like any theory of fundamental measurement, the numbers simply make use of the theory without being part of it. We could, if we pleased, use the theory simply as a device for recording the relations among the attitudes and the relations of the attitudes to the world, their semantics. But in the case of beliefs and the evaluative attitudes, it is convenient to represent these relations in the numbers, as the representation theorems for decision theories prove that we can.

Here a special feature of the Unified Theory emerges, one which may well excite suspicion. For what plays the role of the numbers when it comes to assigning *contents* to the words and attitudes of an agent? What is required is some potentially infinite supply of entities with a pattern or structure complex enough to provide a model for the attitudes. Given such a supply, we can then keep track of the roles of the attitudes and the truth conditions of sentences. Everyone who has a language has available such a set of entities, namely the (infinite) set of his or her own sentences; and these are all we have available for interpreting other people. It is obvious that we employ our own sentences whenever we attribute a particular belief or desire, intention or meaning, to someone else. This is not to say that my sentences are the *objects* of your attitudes; I merely use my sentences to keep track of what you think and mean, or to say, to myself or another, what you think and mean. The attitudes don't have objects in any psychological or epistemic sense. The attitudes are simply states, and no more require objects before the mind than sticks require numbers in order to have a certain length.

Now to return to the question with which I began: to what extent, or in what ways, is a theory like the Unified Theory scientific? Such a theory is not, I think it is clear, reducible to a science like physics or neurobiology: its basic concepts cannot be defined in the vocabulary of any physical science, and there are no precise bridging laws that firmly and reliably relate events or states described in the psychological vocabulary with events and states described in the vocabulary of a physical science. But it would be uninteresting to define science to be what can be reduced to physics. Are there other difficulties? Three features of the Unified Theory (and other theories like it) that have been thought to remove it from the domain of serious science are: its assumptions of holism and of externalism, and its normative properties.

The entire theory is built on the norms of rationality; it is these norms that suggested the theory and give it the structure it has. But this much is built into the formal, axiomatizable, parts of decision theory and truth theory, and they are as precise and clear as any formal theory of physics. However, norms or considerations of rationality also enter with the application of the theory to actual agents, at the stage where an interpreter assigns his own sentences to capture the contents of another's thoughts and utterances. The process necessarily involves deciding which pattern of assignments makes the other intelligible (not *intelligent*, of course!), and this is a matter of using one's own standards of rationality to calibrate the thoughts of the other. In some ways, this is like fitting a curve to a set of points, which is done in the best of sciences. But there is an additional element in the psychological case: in physics there is a mind at work making as much sense as possible of a subject matter that is being treated as brainless; in the psychological case, there is a brain at each end. Norms are being employed as the standard of norms.

The Unified Theory is holistic through and through. It is designed to assign contents to beliefs, utterances, and values simultaneously because these basic attitudes are so interdependent that it would not be possible to determine them one at a time, or even two at a time. Its treatment of each of these domains is also holistic: sentences are interpreted in terms of their relations to other sentences, beliefs in terms of their relations to other beliefs, and so on. Such holism is characteristic of any scheme of measurement: items owe their measure to their relations to other items. A meaning could no more be assigned to a single isolated sentence than a weight or location could be assigned to a single isolated object. The holism of the mental cannot, then, in itself be an obstacle to the scientific claims of a theory of the mental. Quite the reverse: the possibility of theory rests on holism.

The truth conditions of a speaker's utterances determine, and so depend in part, on the logical relations of the sentence uttered to other sentences. In the case of observation sentences, the truth conditions can also depend on the causal history of the situations in which the sentence was learned and used; this is one form externalism takes. Since perceptual externalism of this sort introduces an irreducibly causal element into the interpretation of the theory, the theory cannot hope to emulate physics, which has striven successfully to extrude all causal concepts from its laws. Externalism sets limits to how complete psychological explanation can be, since it introduces into the heart of the subject elements that no psychological theory can pretend to explain. On the other hand, this feature in itself makes psychological theory no less scientific than volcanology, biology, meteorology, or the theory of evolution.

Both Fodor and Chomsky have criticized the Unified Theory and the proposed method of its interpretation, which I have called *radical* interpretation (radical because it assumes no prior knowledge of the agent's propositional attitudes). Some of their criticisms seem to me to miss their mark.[14] Both Fodor and Chomsky observe that radical interpretation gives a completely wrong account both of how linguists study new languages and how children acquire a first language. Here they have understandably been misled by the age-old tendency of philosophers to discuss the theoretical question how a linguist or a child *could* learn an unknown or first language as if it were a practical question about how they actually do it. I have often explained that radical interpretation does not attempt to provide useful hints to real linguists, or to criticize their methods. Much less does it pretend to yield an insight into the mysterious (to me, at any rate) business of first-language acquisition.

Fodor and Chomsky criticize the fact that radical interpretation makes use of so much less information than is available to the informed and methodologically sophisticated linguist. This irritation is fed by their conviction that I hold that the evidence on which I say radical interpretation could be based is all the evidence that is legitimately available. Chomsky in particular thinks I ignore his discoveries about how much of the syntax of natural languages seems to be genetically programmed. I have argued, as I mentioned above, that it is one condition on the correctness of a theory of meaning that it be such that if an interpreter knew it to be true of a speaker, the interpreter could understand what the speaker said. Of course I denied that interpreters generally have, or at least know they have, such a theory; the theory is, rather, what the philosopher wants if he is to describe certain aspects

---

[14] The following discussion abbreviates a more detailed treatment of Fodor's criticism in my 'Interpreting Radical Interpretation', in *Philosophical Perspectives*, Vol. 8, *Logic and Language*, ed. J. E. Tomberlin, 1994, pp. 121–8. Also printed in *Reflecting Davidson: Donald Davidson Responding to an International Forum of Philosophers*, ed. R. Stoecker, de Gruyter, Berlin, 1993. Both these sources print the article by Jerry Fodor and Ernest Lepore, 'Is Radical Interpretation Possible?', to which I am replying.

The passages quoted from Chomsky come from *Inference, Explanation, and Other Frustrations: Essays in the Philosophy of Science*, ed. John Earman, University of California Press, pp. 108, 9.

of the interpreter's interpretive abilities. I then added, in an essay that particularly provoked Chomsky, 'It does not add anything to this thesis to say that if a theory does correctly describe the competence of an interpreter, some mechanism in the interpreter must correspond to the theory.'[15] Chomsky quotes this remark, and comments that 'from the standpoint of the natural sciences, [this] comment is utterly wrong-headed'. His subsequent discussion makes clear that what annoys him is that he thinks I am denying that there would be any interest in knowing what the mechanism is. But of course this is not my view, nor is this what I said. What I said was, and was intended as, a tautology: if a pill puts you to sleep, it adds nothing to say something about the pill had the power to put you to sleep. It would be vastly interesting to know more about the nature of our linguistic abilities, and the mechanisms underlying them. Who would deny it? If I have any doubts, they concern only the philosophical conclusions Chomsky and some of his followers have drawn from their results in this area.

Chomsky has accused me, and particularly Quine, of supposing that all we know about language must be based on behavioristic evidence. Quine has spoken for himself on this matter, but I would certainly deny the accusation; if we want to know everything about language, its acquisition and uses, there are no a priori limits on what evidence may be relevant. But I do share with Quine the conviction that our understanding of what speakers mean by what they say is partly based, directly or indirectly, on what we can learn or pick up from perceiving what they do. No matter how much grammar we come equipped with from the cradle, we must learn what the words of any particular language mean—we are not born speaking English or Hebrew or Mandarin; we must pick up our first language from those who already speak it. (The behaviorism I speak of is not, incidentally, reductive in nature: I do not expect any basic intentional predicates to be defined in non-intentional terms. The point simply concerns evidence.)

The criticisms Fodor and Chomsky have leveled at certain philosophers seem to me largely (though not entirely) based on their having read into those philosophers views they do not hold: I have tried to point out some instances. But there is also a failure to appreciate a difference in fundamental aims and interests. Chomsky apparently sees

[15] 'A Nice Derangement of Epitaphs', in *Philosophical Grounds of Rationality*, ed. R. Grandy & R. Warner, Oxford University Press, 1986, pp. 156–74. Reprinted in *Truth and Interpretation: Perspectives on the Philosophy of Donald Davidson*, ed. E. LePore, Blackwell, 1986.

me as trying to understand and explain the same phenomena he is, and therefore as proposing competing hypotheses. This seems altogether wrong. I want to know what it is about propositional thought—our beliefs, desires, intentions, and speech—that makes them intelligible to others. This is a question about the nature of thought and meaning which cannot be answered by discovering neural mechanisms, studying the evolution of the brain, or finding evidence that explains the incredible ease and rapidity with which we come to have a first language. Even if we were all born speaking English or Polish, it would be a question how we understand others, and what determines the cognitive contents of our sentences. It doesn't matter whether we call some of these projects scientific and withhold the term from others.

It does matter, however, in what ways the study of the attitudes I have been discussing is limited just as, in another context, it matters in what ways Chomsky's or Fodor's work is limited. (The limitations are, of course, different.) What are the most obvious shortcomings of the Unified Theory of thought and speech? Well, first and perhaps most striking is the fact that the formal theory (as opposed to features of its empirical application) says nothing at all about inconsistencies. It not only postulates perfect logic and a consistent and rational pattern of beliefs and desires, but it assumes rationality in the treatment of what we take to be evidence. Inconsistencies and failures of reasoning power must be accommodated by injecting large doses of what has been called charity in the fitting of the theory to actual agents.

Perhaps all straightforward irrationality shows up as inconsistency, but clearly not all inconsistency is what we normally call irrationality. The formal theory leaves no room for irrationality, and therefore is powerless to explain it. Any explanations of irrationality we care to proffer must work against the Unified Theory, not with it.

The Unified Theory, as I have described it, is static; it says nothing about the forms of rationality that deal with the incorporation of new information into a going system of thought. However, this is an area in which there is hope. Much work has been done, by Richard Jeffrey and Isaac Levi, for example, on making decision theory dynamic.

Finally, and perhaps most significantly, the interpretation of the formal theory does not rest entirely on ordinary intersubjective evidence. In measuring physical magnitudes, we can use the numbers to keep track of the properties of events and objects as publicly observed. The relevant properties of the numbers can also be agreed to by all concerned. But things are different when one mind tries to understand another. People are as publicly observable as anything else in nature, but the entities we use to construct a picture of someone else's thoughts must be our own sentences, as understood by us, or other entities with the same provenance and structure. The meanings of our sentences are indeed dependent on our relations to the world which those sentences are about, and our linguistic interactions with others. But there is no escape from the fact that we cannot check up on the objective credentials of the measure we are using as we can check up on our understanding of the numbers; we cannot check up on the objective correctness of our own norms by checking with others, since to do this would be to make basic use of our own norms once more.

Whether the features of a psychological theory I have been rehearsing, especially the last one, show that a psychological theory is so different from a theory in the natural sciences as not to deserve to be called a science I do not know, nor much care. What I am sure of is that such a theory, though it may be as genuine a theory as any, is not in competition with any natural science.

9 *What Thought Requires*

The true fly is dipterous, but it has halteres which have evolved from posterior wings. It had been thought that the astonishing rapidity with which a fly maneuvers must be due to a direct neural connection between the eyes and the wings, but recent studies suggest something more sophisticated.[1] It was known before that the halteres, which beat antiphase to the wings, act as gyroscopes which stabilize flight on all three axes by feeding information directly to the wing muscles. Remove a fly's halteres and it crashes. What is new is that apparently the visual system is directly connected to the halteres, which then control the wing muscles. This fancy setup distinguishes between the aerodynamic forces and the Coriolis forces acting on the wings, permitting the fly to evade the flyswatter with marvelous ease.

The fly serves to remind us that an organism can discriminate aspects of its environment with superb accuracy, and make use of the resulting information in complex ways that help keep it alive, without anything we would, or should, call thought.

Leibniz, who believed animals are machines, was asked why he was so reluctant to kill a bothersome fly. A fly is just a machine, Leibniz replied; but what a wonderful machine! It certainly would not be right, he thought, to destroy a manmade machine of comparable complexity.[2] Leibniz was right: designing such a machine is beyond the dreams of even today's technology. Leibniz also saw a profound difference between the fly (or any non-human creature) and man: man thinks, the fly does not. The fly's reaction to visual input is far too rapid

[1] Wai Pang Chan, Frederick Prete, and Michael H. Dickinson, 'Visual Input to the Efferent Control System of the Fly's "Gyroscope"' *Science*, 280 (1998), pp. 289–92.

[2] G. Guhrauer, *Gottfried Wilhelm Freiherr von Leibniz: Eine Biographie*, Breslau, 1846. I owe the reference to Benson Mates, *The Philosophy of Leibniz*, Oxford University Press, 1986, p. 15.

to involve thought. On the other hand, if a man managed to design such a machine, he might well be inclined to view his mechanical fly as calculating aerodynamic and Coriolis forces in order to maintain its stability during a double Immelman. But of course a machine that could do all that a fly can do, and no more, would not be calculating in the sense of giving thought to the matter. So we need to ask what would turn calculation, in the sense in which a fly or a computer can calculate, into thought?

We are just machines that are complex in ways flies are not, so the problem isn't one of transcending mere physical devices. I do not doubt that an artificer could, at least in principle, manufacture a thinking machine. The problem, for philosophy anyway, is what to aim for; what would show that the artificer had succeeded? I assume that you and I can tell, given enough time, and the right sort of environment, whether an object can think, and we can tell this without any clear idea of what is inside the skin. In this respect, Turing had the right idea, though his test was not conclusive for a variety of reasons. But what, more exactly, is it that we detect when we recognize a creature or object as a thinking being?

Animals show by their behavior that they are making fine distinctions, and many of the things they discriminate we do too. They recognize individual people and other animals, distinguish among various sorts of animal, find their way back to places they have been before, and can learn all sorts of tricks. So it is important to reflect on why none of this shows they have propositional attitudes: beliefs, desires, doubts, intentions, and the rest. Dumb beasts see and hear and smell all sorts of things, but they do not perceive *that* anything is the case. Some non-human animals can learn a great deal, but they do not learn *that* something is true.

Why doesn't the fact that a horse or a duck discriminates many of the things we do strongly suggest that they have the same concepts we do, or at least concepts much like ours? This is a suggestion many find persuasive, and it is apparently unavoidably seductive for most of us when we want to describe the activities of unthinking creatures. But there is little reason to take the suggestion literally. Someone could easily teach me to recognize a planet in our solar system (smaller than the sun and moon, untwinkling) without my having a clear idea what a planet is. A horse can distinguish men from other animals, but if it has a concept of what it is distinguishing, that concept is nothing like ours. Our concept is complicated and rich: we would deny that someone had the concept of a man who did not know something about what distinguishes a man from a woman, who did not know that fathers are men, that every man has a father and a mother, and that normal adults have thoughts. Creatures with propositional attitudes and creatures without such attitudes are alike in that both can be conditioned to respond differentially to many of the same properties, objects, or types of event. This misleads us into thinking similar processes are going on in the brains of both sorts of creature. And of course there is much that is similar. But a creature with propositional attitudes is equipped to fit a new concept into a complex scheme in which concepts have logical and other relations to one another. Speechless creatures lack the conceptual framework which supports propositional attitudes.

I think this is enough to ensure that some degree of holism goes with having concepts. Many concepts are fairly directly connected, through causality, with the world, but they would not be the concepts they are without their connections with other concepts, and without relations to other concepts, they would not be concepts. To say this is neither to suppose holism is so pervasive that no two people could, in any sense required for communication, have the same concept, nor is it to deny that the contents of some concepts are more directly attached to sensory moorings than others. We can appreciate why holism is not the disaster it has sometimes been portrayed as being if, instead of asking how the content of a concept or judgment is thought of by the creature that has the concept or judgment, we ask instead how an observer can size up the contents of the thoughts of another creature. This is, again, the Turing approach. So here I want to say something about how I think it is possible for one creature with a full basic set of concepts to come to understand another, for I think this will throw light on the central question I raised, which is how we can tell when a creature has a genuine concept.

There is no distinction to be made between having concepts and having propositional attitudes. To have a concept is to class things under it. This is not just a matter of being natively disposed, or having learned, to react in some specific way to items that fall under a concept; it is to *judge* or *believe* that certain items fall under the concept. If we do not make this a condition on having a concept, we will have to treat simple tendencies to eat berries, or to seek warmth and avoid cold, as having the concepts of a berry, or of warm, or of cold. I assume we don't want to view earthworms and sunflowers as having concepts. This would be a terminological mistake, for it would be to lose track of the fundamental distinction between a mindless disposition to respond differentially to the members of a class of stimuli, and a disposition to respond to those items *as* members of that class.

Given the task of deciphering a language we do not know, we will perforce start with perception sentences, sentences which a speaker will assent to or dissent from given a stimulus we too can perceive. As Quine put it,

Linguistically, and hence conceptually, the things in sharpest focus are the things that are public enough to be talked of publicly, common and conspicuous enough to be talked of often, and near enough to sense to be quickly identified and learned by name.[3]

Our first guess as to what is meant by a perception sentence will be a shot in the dark, but given how much alike people are, getting it right is often like hitting a barn door; the most casual guess is often correct. The simplicity of this mode of entry into an alien language should not leave us thinking that a concept so identified is defined by its external causes without the aid of theory or a supporting nexus of further concepts. A concept is defined by its typical cause only within the framework of a system of concepts that allows us to respond to certain stimuli as tables, friends, horses, and flies. A concept is defined for those who speak languages like ours by its typical causes, given that we are already in the world of language and conceptualization. But patterns of stimulation do not, in themselves, delineate the content of any sentence or concept. Only a very modest degree of holism is enough to lead to the conclusion that no simple story about the causal relations between mental states and the world can account for intentionality, much less specify the intentional contents of thoughts or utterances.

Concepts, and the sentences and thoughts that employ them, are in part individuated by their causal relations to the world and in part by their relations to each other. Thoughts, because they have propositional content, are unlike everything else in the world except for utterances in having logical relations to each other. There is only one way for an interpreter to spot these relations, and that is by noting patterns among the utterances to which a speaker awards credence. Thus the interpreter will note that a speaker who assents to 'It rained in Spain and we all got wet' will also assent to 'It rained in Spain' and 'We all got wet'; that a speaker who assents to 'John is taller than Sam'

[3] W. V. Quine, *Word and Object*, MIT Press, 1960, p. 1.

will also assent to 'Sam is shorter than John'; and so on. These examples illustrate the routes to different discoveries. The pattern of the first example holds no matter what sentences are substituted for 'It rained in Spain' and 'We all got wet', and so leads to the identification of the truth-functional connective for conjunction, one of the logical constants. The second pattern holds no matter what names are substituted for 'John' and 'Sam', and so leads to the recognition of a logical relation between the two two-place predicates, 'taller than' and 'shorter than'. The former discovery is far more important, since it uncovers one of the most basic sources of the creativity of language, a recursive rule. One can easily see how the other logical constants, at least those involved in the first-order predicate calculus, can be identified.

A more subtle problem for an interpreter is that of discerning relations of evidential support among a speaker's sentences. These relations can be uncovered, but only by invoking a version of decision theory which, by finding the subjective probabilities of sentences, allows the computation of conditional probabilities. Degrees of evidential support, while more variable from speaker to speaker than matters of logic and logical form, are essential to the identification of theoretical terms less directly keyed to perception than perceptual sentences, for they provide the ties that give substance, along with the structure provided by theory, to theoretical concepts.

I have been pursuing the twin questions of the relations between thought and language and the world on the one hand, and the sort of structure thought and language require on the other, in order to evaluate claims that one analysis or another of thought or language is satisfactory, or to decide what criteria to employ in judging whether a creature or device is thinking. How much structure should we demand? Here the fact that the structure of language mirrors the structure of propositional thought is a help. Possession of a concept already implies the ability to generalize since the point of a concept is that it is applicable to any item in an indefinitely large class. The fixed singular terms of a language are presumably finite in number, but demonstrative devices, whether combined with sortal predicates or not, provide the means for picking out an unlimited number of items. The truth-functional connectives, with their iterative powers, supply a further form of creativity. But is creativity enough? There is a good reason to think not. Consider a language consisting only of names, predicates, and the pure sentential connectives. Such a language has a finite vocabulary, but a potential infinity of sentences, so it is creative. But it is easy to give the semantics of such a language without introducing a concept of reference, and so without matching up either names or predicates with objects. The explanation is simple: given a finite vocabulary of names and predicates, the truth conditions of each of the finite number of sentences formed without the aid of connectives can be stated without considering the roles of the parts of sentences; the rest is truth tables. There is no compelling reason to credit a creature with so simple a language with an ontology.[4]

Should we nevertheless say a creature with these conceptual resources and no others has what we would call a language, or thoughts? A creature without the concept of an object, however good it is at discriminating what we call objects, is a creature without even the rudiments of the framework of thought. What calls for ontology is the apparatus of pronouns and cross reference in natural languages, what we represent by the symbolism of quantifiers and variables in elementary logic. These devices provide the resources for constructing complex predicates, and at this point semantics must map names and predicates on to objects.

If I am right that language and thought require the structure provided by a logic of quantification, what further conceptual resources is it reasonable to consider basic? I have no definite list in mind, but if the ontology includes macroscopic physical objects, including animals, as I think it must, then there will be sortal concepts for classifying the items in the ontology. There must be concepts for marking spatial and temporal position. There must be concepts for some of the evident properties of objects, and for expressing the various changes and activities of objects. If such changes and activities can be characterized in turn, then the ontology must also include events, and among the concepts must be that of the relation between cause and effect. I am inclined to make some major additions to this list, as I shall indicate in a moment, but this is enough to suggest that the domain in which thought can occur is fairly complex. It is the domain each of us inhabits, but one we have good reason to suppose is inhabited by no other animal on earth, and certainly by no machine.

Much of what I have said about the complexity and specificity of thought may be thought to be appropriate in connection with human

---

[4] Empirical evidence may, of course, suggest that someone can understand, and correctly utter, sentences he or she has never heard.

thought, but applicable only in that context. In other words, I am revealing a provincial attitude toward intensionality. Well, perhaps. There is a further consideration, however, that may reinforce the anthropomorphic perspective. The important question, after all, isn't whether some animals have a simpler or degraded set of concepts; it is the question whether they have concepts at all. There is a clear difference between being disposed to react in different ways to 'V's and 'W's, as octopodes can be trained to do, and having concepts, however vague and poor, of those letters. To have a concept is to classify items as instantiating the concept or not, to judge, however implicitly, that here is a 'V' and there is a 'W'. The difference lies in the idea of error. We can say, if we like, that an octopus has erred when it reacts to the 'V' as it was trained to react to the 'W'. That was not what *we* had in mind, and its action may deprive the octopus of a tasty reward. But on what grounds can we claim that the octopus did not grasp our concept? As Wittgenstein says, whatever the octopus does is in accord with some rule, that is, some concept or other, which is a way of saying there is no reason to suppose it has *any* concept. What the octopus did, when it chose a 'V' when we had trained it to choose a 'W', was not in accord with our idea of similar stimuli. But the judgment of resemblance is ours, not that of the octopus. So far as I can see, no account of error that depends on the classifications we find most natural, and counts what deviates from such as error, will get at the essence of error, which is that the creature itself must be able to recognize error. A creature that has a concept knows that the concept applies to things independently of what it believes. A creature that cannot entertain the thought that it may be wrong has no concepts, no thoughts. To this extent, the possibility of thought depends on the idea of objective truth, of there being a way things are which is not up to us. I do not see how any causal story about the sequence of stimuli reaching an isolated creature can account for this feature of conceptualization or intensionality, provided the story is told in the vocabulary of the natural sciences.

There is, I believe, a direction in which to look for a solution, and that direction has been pointed out by Wittgenstein. What is needed is something that can provide a standard against which an individual can check his or her reactions, and only other individuals can do this. To take the simplest case, consider two individuals jointly interacting with some aspect of the world. When the pair spot a lion, each hides behind a tree. If the individuals are in sight of one another, each also sees the other hide. Each is therefore in a position to correlate what he sees (the lion) with the other's reaction. If the situation is repeated, a consequence is that if one individual sees a lion when the other does not, the one who does not see the lion is apt to treat the first's reaction as a conditioned stimulus, and also hide. Now consider a situation in which each sees the same lion, but one of the individuals, because the light is poor, or a tree partially obscures the lion, reacts as he normally reacts to a gazelle. This turns out to be a mistake. This little skit cannot, in itself, explain conceptualization or grasp of the idea of error on the part of either observer. It does no more than indicate the sort of conditions in which the idea of error could arise. Thus it suggests necessary (though certainly not sufficient) conditions for conceptualization.

Tyler Burge has argued that the content of a perceptual belief is the usual or normal cause of that belief.[5] Thus the cause of the belief that a lion is now present is past correlations of lions with stimuli similar to the present stimulus. The difficulty with this proposal is that equally good answers would be that beliefs about lions are caused by the appropriate stimulation of the sense organs, or by the photons streaming from lion to eye, in which case the beliefs would be about stimulations or photons. There are endless such causal explanations, and each would dictate a different content for the same perceptual belief. It is natural to reply, and Burge does reply, that we have no idea how to characterize the various patterns of stimulated optic nerves that would be caused by a lion, aside from the way I just did it, by appealing to the role of lions. The force of this reply depends on the fact that we happen to have a single lion-concept, but no single concept for patterns of lion-caused firings of neurons. But nature with its causal doings is indifferent to our supply of concepts. When it is conceptualization that is to be explained, it begs the question to project our classifications on to nature.

Burge's suggestion fails two tests: it fails to pick out the relevant cause, and so gives no account of the content of perceptual sentences, and it fails to explain error. Adding a second person helps on both counts. It narrows down the relevant cause to the nearest cause common to two agents who are triangulating the cause by jointly observing an object and each other's reactions. The two observers don't share

---

[5] Tyler Burge, 'Cartesian Error and the Objectivity of Perception', in P. Pettit and J. McDowell (eds.), *Subject, Thought and Context*, Oxford University Press, 1986, pp. 117–36.

neural firings or incoming photons; the nearest thing they share is the object prompting both to react in ways the other can note. This is not enough to define the concept, as I said before, since to have the concept of a lion or of anything else is to have a network of interrelated concepts of the right sorts. But given such a network, triangulation will tend to pick out the right content for perceptual beliefs. Triangulation also creates the space needed for error, not by deciding what is true in any particular case, but by making objectivity dependent on intersubjectivity.

It is clear that for triangulation to work, the creatures involved must be very much alike. They must class together the same distal stimuli, among them each other's reactions to those stimuli. In the end, it is just this double sharing of propensities that gives meaning to the idea of classing things together. We say: that creature puts lions together into a class. How do we tell? The creature reacts in relevantly similar ways to lions. What makes the responses similar? Our concepts do; we have the concepts that define these classes. It takes another creature enough like the first to see and say this. The sharing of many discriminatory abilities explains why a considerable degree of holism is no obstacle to communication. This is also why Turing had the right idea about how to tell if a device (or animal) is thinking.

Here we have a reason why the third-person approach to language is not a mere philosophical exercise. The point of the study of radical interpretation is to grasp how it is possible for one person to come to understand the speech and thoughts of another, for this ability is basic to our sense of a world independent of ourselves, and hence to the possibility of thought itself. The third-person approach is yours and mine.

Triangulation depends not only on a plurality of creatures, but equally on shared external promptings. For this reason, among others, I think Kripke's account of what he takes to be Wittgenstein's 'skeptical solution' to the puzzle of rule-following is inadequate to serve as the whole story about conceptualization.[6] The problem is just the one we have been discussing: how to account for failure to apply a concept correctly, given that what one person might count as an error may just be another person applying a different concept. Kripke's suggestion is that if a learner fails to apply a concept (or word) as his teacher

---

[6] Saul Kripke, *Wittgenstein on Rules and Private Language*, Basil Blackwell, Oxford, 1982.

would, the learner has made a mistake. Unfortunately this does not distinguish between failure to apply a concept correctly and applying a different concept correctly—the very distinction in need of explication. Most of Kripke's examples also have another, related, flaw: they concern mathematical examples, and so lack the shared stimulus to provide the possibility of a shared content.

Ostensive learning, whether undertaken by a radical interpreter as a first step into a second language, or undergone by someone acquiring a first language, is an example of triangulation. The radical interpreter has, of course, the idea of possible error, and so do his informants, and the interpreter can assume he and they share most basic concepts. Thus a first guess is apt to be right, though there can be no assurance of this. Someone being initiated into the wonders of language and serious thought is also being initiated into the distinction between belief and knowledge, appearance and reality—in other words, the idea of error. Like triangulation, ostensive learning runs the risk of leaving unclear not only how the next step should go, but also what constitutes a wrong application of a concept at earlier steps. But neither the novice nor the sophisticated radical interpreter is in a position to question a teacher's or informant's early applications of a concept or word new to the learner. The teacher or informant may not be applying his own concepts correctly, but learner and interpreter must accept wrong steps as right until later in the game, since for them a concept is being given content. Erroneous ostensions on the teacher's part just lead the learner to learn a different concept from the one the teacher wished to introduce, and so will promulgate misunderstandings.

How will the learner or interpreter discover when he is applying a different concept than the one his teacher or informant had in mind, and when one of them is misapplying the same concept? Some answers to this question will appeal to the power of consensus, but this cannot be conclusive. Of course, consensus of *use*, where use is assumed to reflect what the teacher or society *means*, is just what the learner or radical interpreter needs to recognize, but consensus of *application* does not distinguish the two varieties of error. As far as I can see, nothing in the observable behavior of teacher or learner with respect to an isolated sentence can sort this out. Further distinctions depend on relations among uttered sentences. The relation of evidential support provides powerful clues. When the learner says 'That's a cow' when faced by a bull, is she erroneously applying the concept cow or correctly applying a concept that covers both cows and bulls? If she also learns what may be the truth conditions of 'That's an udder', one can test whether she assents to 'That's an udder' when presented with a cow but usually not when presented with a bull.

But the large and necessary step is learning to *explain* errors. It is when one has learned to say or to think, 'That looks green,' 'That man seems small,' 'I thought it was an oasis,' when one has said or thought that something blue was green, or that the large man in the distance was small, or that what looked like an oasis was a mirage, that one has truly mastered the distinction between appearance and reality, between believing truly and believing falsely. It is also at this point that the distinction becomes clear between falsely thinking a bull is a cow, and simply applying the word 'cow' to both.

Cognitive science aims, among other things, to deal with thought and thinking. Up to this point I have been chiefly concerned to speculate about the conditions thought must satisfy, about what constitutes the subject matter, or part of the subject matter, of cognitive science. But cognitive science also aims to be a science. Is thought, as I have described it, amenable to scientific study?

One reasonable demand on a scientific theory is that it should be possible to define a structure in such a way that instances of that structure can be identified empirically. This requires laws, or generalizations, which predict what will be observed given observed input. Some of the most impressive early work in psychology satisfied this condition. It was found, for example, that if a subject—just about any subject who was not deaf—was repeatedly asked to adjust a variable tone so that it sounded half way between two fixed tones, the subject made decisions that consistently defined an interval scale, in other words, a scale formally like the ordinary scales for temperature. This is not psychophysical measurement, since it does not relate a physical magnitude with subjective judgments; the tonal scale simply relates subjective judgments to other subjective judgments. Patterns of such judgments (approximately) instantiate the laws specified by the axioms which define an interval scale.

Bayesian decision theory, in the form which Frank Ramsey gave it,[7] is more subtle, but it is similar in that it relates judgments to judgments. Ramsey showed how, given only choices between wagers, it was possible to construct two scales, one for degrees of belief (sometimes

---

[7] Frank Ramsey, 'Truth and Probability', in *Foundations of Mathematics*, Routledge and Kegan Paul, 1931, pp. 156–98.

called subjective probabilities), and one for comparative degrees of perceived value. It is a question, of course, whether anyone's choices satisfy the conditions necessary for constructing such scales. As is well known, this is a very tricky question because of the mixture of normative and descriptive elements that enter into an attempt to give empirical application to the theory. Actual tests of Bayesian decision theory seldom show perfect consistency with the conditions; on the other hand, neither do they show many absurd deviations from them, and there are often persuasive arguments to explain the apparent deviations. What one can say is that 'given the right conditions', *ceteris paribus*, the laws of decision theory do describe how people make real choices. The fact is that we all depend on this. People will seldom risk their lives for a small reward and will pay quite a lot for a good chance at a large prize. These are laws of human behavior we depend upon, rough and fallible as they are.

In the same way the laws of logic are laws of thought—always, of course, given the right conditions, and so forth. Tarski-type truth definitions, modified to fit natural languages, describe the basic semantic structure that informs the human language ability. We do not know how to fit all the idioms of natural languages into the format Tarski provided, but a very impressive core can be handled. These three structures, of logic, decision theory, and formal semantics, have the characteristics of serious theories in science: they can be precisely, that is, axiomatically, stated, and, given empirical interpretation and input, they entail endless testable results. Furthermore, logic, semantics, and decision theory can be combined into a single unified theory of thought, decision, and language, as I have shown.[8] This is to be expected. Decision theory extracts from simple choices subjective scales for probabilities, i.e., degrees to which sentences are held to be true, and for values or the extent to which various states of affairs are held to be desirable. Radical interpretation, as I briefly described it above, extracts truth conditions, that is, meanings and beliefs, from simple expressions of assent and dissent. Formal semantics has logic built in, so to speak, and so does decision theory in the version of Richard Jeffrey.[9] Uniting the theories depends on finding an appropriate empirical concept, and one such concept is the relation between

[8] Donald Davidson, 'The Structure and Content of Truth', *Journal of Philosophy*, 87 (1990), pp. 279–328 (John Dewey Lectures).

[9] Richard Jeffrey, *The Logic of Decision*, University of Chicago Press, 1965 (2nd edn. 1983).

an agent, the circumstances of utterance, and two sentences, one of which the agent would rather have true than the other. The protocols for testing such a theory are like the protocols in the testing of decision theory except that the choices which express preferences are treated as awaiting interpretation rather than as already interpreted. Given the richness of the structure of the unified theory, it is possible to derive scales for subjective probability and desire, applied to sentences, and from these to determine the meanings of the sentences.

There is a widespread feeling among philosophers that we will not really understand the intensional attitudes, conceptualization, or language, until we can give a purely extensional, physicalistic account of them. Unless we can in this sense reduce the intensional to the extensional, the mental to the physical, so the theme runs, we will not see how psychology can be made a seriously scientific subject. Jerry Fodor argues that if intensional and semantic predicates 'form a closed circle', that is, can't be reduced to physical predicates, this

appears to preclude a physicalistic ontology for psychology since if psychological states were physical then there would surely be physicalistically specifiable sufficient conditions for their instantiation. But it's arguable that if the ontology of psychology is not physicalistic, then there is no such science.[10]

Fodor seems to indicate in a footnote that he is aware that psychological states and events may be physically describable one by one even though mentalistic predicates are neither definitionally nor nomologically reducible to the vocabularies of the physical sciences. But if this is the case, as I have argued, then the issue is not ontological; the question just concerns vocabularies.[11] Whether or not the ontology of psychology is physicalistic, my guess is that Fodor believes there can't be a science of psychology if its concepts can't be reduced, either definitionally or nomologically, to the concepts of the physical sciences.

It is easy to sympathize with this idea. Since psychology wants to explain perception, for example, it wants to explain how certain events physically described cause beliefs through the agency of the senses. Any laws concerning such interactions would, it seems, amount to partial nomological reductions of the mental vocabulary to the physical. (Psychophysical measurement has produced plenty of laws, but

[10] Jerry Fodor, *A Theory of Content*, MIT Press, 1992, p. 51.
[11] See *Essays on Actions and Events*, Oxford University Press, 1980.

these typically deal with the relations between physical quantities and sensations, not thoughts.) Any really complete scientific psychology would at many points have to relate the mental and the physical, by which I mean events and states described both in psychological and in physicalistic terms. A lot depends, of course, on how strict one wants the laws of such a science to be. With an ample sprinkling of 'other things being equal' and 'under normal conditions' clauses, we constantly utilize generalizations that relate the mental and the physical in everyday life. But here nothing like the laws of physics is in the cards.

I didn't finish discussing the unified theory of thought and language which I mentioned above. How much like a serious science could it be? Formally it's as clear and precise as any science. The difficulties lie in the application, the empirical interpretation. One trouble springs from its holism, though not quite in the way one would expect. All serious science is holistic. Whenever we assign a number to a physical magnitude we assume the correctness of the conditions which must hold to justify the form of measurement involved. In the ordinary measurement of length, for example, we assume that the relation of *longer than* is transitive. This assumption has no empirical content until we give an interpretation to this relation, and once we do this we are assuming that the operation we have specified for determining that one object is longer than another holds for all objects, observed or not, of the appropriate kind. If the law of transitivity fails in a single case, the entire theory of measurement of length is false, and we are not justified talking of physical lengths. Once one considers the further conditions imposed by the theory, one appreciates the thoroughly holistic character of almost any physical theory. What makes the empirical application of decision theory or formal semantics possible is that the norms of rationality apply to the subject matter. In deciding what a subject wants or thinks or means, we need to see their mental workings as more or less coherent if we are to assign contents to them. As in any science, we must be able to describe the evidence in terms the relevant theory accepts. The trouble with the study of thought is that the standards of rationality, outside of decision theory and logic at least, are not agreed upon. We cannot compare our standards with those of others without employing the very standards in question. This is a problem that does not arise when the subject matter is not psychological.

In one respect, the unified theory of thought and meaning which I described is a little better off than one might think. The important primitive term in that theory is the one expressing the attitude of preferring one sentence true rather than another. This is certainly a psychological concept, and a pretty complicated one. So there is no chance that the theory can be specified in physical terms. On the other hand, the theory is entirely stated in extensional terms. The relation of preferring true is a relation between an agent and two sentences, and it holds no matter how these entities are described. Of course, propositional attitudes are involved; they just aren't expressed, in the theory, in a way that individuates attitudes generally, and in a way that would make the theory circular. In testing the theory, one would have to devise a way of telling when an agent preferred one sentence true rather than another. This is not such a bad deal, for if the operation one hits on at first is wrong, the theory will yield nothing intelligible. The richness of the structure of thought and meaning will necessarily tease out a workable interpretation. This is the attitude we take to physical measurement and, in ordinary life, the attitude we actually take to the understanding of others.

10 A Unified Theory of Thought, Meaning, and Action

Any attempt to understand verbal communication must view it in its natural setting as part of a larger enterprise. It seems at first that this cannot be difficult, there being no more to language than public transactions among speakers and interpreters, and the aptitudes for such transactions. Yet the task eludes us. For the fact that linguistic phenomena are nothing but behavioral, biological, or physical phenomena described in an exotic vocabulary of meaning, reference, truth, assertion, and so on—mere supervenience of this sort of one kind of fact or description on another—does not guarantee, or even hold out promise of, the possibility of conceptual reduction.

There lies our problem. Some sort of reduction appears to be needed for understanding, yet significant reduction remains beyond reach in the case of language. The social scene, when depicted in terms that do not assume what is to be explained, is too large and casually related conceptually to what is characteristic of speech to reveal the secret of linguistic meaning. When we turn for enlightenment about the nature of language to the private and community interests that prompt language, we lose touch with the questions that interest us when we do not beg them. We need another strategy, another way of relating speech to its human setting. In this paper I sketch an alternative approach to a foundational account of language.

The immediate psychological environment of linguistic aptitudes and accomplishments is to be found in the propositional attitudes, states, or events that are described in intensional idiom: intentional action, desires, beliefs, and their close relatives like hopes, fears, wishes, and attempts. Not only do the various propositional attitudes and their conceptual attendants form the setting in which speech occurs, but there is no chance of arriving at a deep understanding of linguistic facts except as that understanding is accompanied by an interlocking account of the central cognitive and conative attitudes.

It is too much to ask that these basic intensional notions be reduced to something else—something more behavioristic, neurological, or physiological, for example. Nor can we analyze any of these basic three, belief, desire, and meaning, in terms of one or two of the others; or so I think, and have argued elsewhere.[1] But even if we could effect a reduction in this basic trio the results would fall short of what might be wanted simply because the end point—the interpretation, say, of speech—would be too close to where we began (with belief and desire, or with intention, which is born of belief and desire). A basic account of any of these concepts must start beyond or beneath them all, or at some point equidistant from them all.

If this is so, we cannot found the analysis of linguistic meaning on the non-linguistic purposes or intentions that prompt the use of language. Nor will it help to appeal to explicit or implicit rules or conventions, if only because these must be understood in terms of intentions and beliefs. There is no doubting, of course, the importance of showing how meanings and intentions are connected. Such connections give structure to the propositional attitudes and suit them to systematic treatment. But on my present plan, intention and intentional action won't directly explain meaning. Rather, meaning, belief, and desire will be treated as fully coordinate elements in an understanding of action. These broad, vague claims take shape in what follows.

The aim is a theory for the interpretation of a speaker's words, a theory that also provides a basis for attributing beliefs and desires to the speaker. The theory should not assume that any propositional attitudes of the speaker are available, at least in a fully individuated form. It will help to consider first Bayesian decision theory, as developed by Frank Ramsey,[2] which deals with two of our three fundamental elements, belief and desire. This theory will serve as a model for the kind of theory that we want, and also, of course, will contribute substantially to the design of the unified theory.

---

[1] For considerations in support of these claims, see my "Belief and the Basis of Meaning", *Synthese*, 27 (1974): 309–23; "Radical Interpretation", *Dialectica*, 27 (1973): 313–28; "Thought and Talk", in Samuel Guttenplan (ed.), *Mind and Language*, Oxford, 1975, pp. 7–23.

[2] F. P. Ramsey, "Truth and Probability", in *The Foundations of Mathematics*, New York, 1950.

The choice of one course of action over another, or the preference that one state of affairs obtain rather than another, is generally the product of two considerations: we value a course of action, or a state of affairs because of the value we set on its possible consequences, and how likely we believe those consequences are, given that we perform the action or the state of affairs comes to obtain. In choosing among courses of action or states of affairs, therefore, we choose one the relative value of whose consequences, when tempered by the likelihood of those consequences, is greatest. Courses of action are usually gambles, since we don't know for certain how things will turn out. So to the extent that we are rational we take what we believe to be the best bet available (we "maximize expected utility").

A feature of such a theory is that what it is designed to explain—ordinal preferences or choices among options—is relatively open to observation, while the explanatory mechanism, which involves degree of belief and cardinal values, is not taken to be observable. The issue therefore arises how to tell when a person has a certain degree of belief in some proposition, or what the relative strengths of his preferences are. The evident problem is that what is known (ordinal, or simple preference) is the resultant of two unknowns, degree of belief and relative strength of preference. If a person's cardinal preferences for outcomes were known, then his choices of courses of action would reveal his degree of belief; and if his degree of belief were known, his choices would disclose the comparative values he puts on the outcomes. But how can both unknowns be determined from simple choices or preference alone? Ramsey solved this problem by showing how to find a proposition deemed as probable as its negation on the basis of simple choices only. This single proposition can be used to construct an endless series of wager choices which yield a measure of value for all possible options and eventualities. It is then routine to fix the degrees of belief in all propositions.

Ramsey was able to turn the trick by specifying constraints on the permissible patterns of simple preferences or choices. These constraints are not arbitrary, but are part of a satisfactory account of the reasons for a person's preferences and choice behavior. They spell out the demand that an agent be rational, not in his particular and ultimate values, but in the pattern these form with one another and in combination with his beliefs. The theory thus has a strong normative element, but an element that is essential if the concepts of preference, belief, reason, and intentional action are to have application.

Pattern in what is observed is central to the ability of the theory to extract from facts that taken singly are relatively directly connected with what can be introspected in ourselves or observed to hold for others—to extract from such facts facts of a more sophisticated kind (degree of belief, comparisons of differences in value). From the point of view of the theory, the sophisticated facts explain the simple, more observable ones, while the observable ones constitute the evidential base for testing or applying the theory.

Because the constraints are sharply stated, various things can be proven about the theory. The intuition that the constraints define an aspect of rationality, for example, can be backed by a proof that only someone whose acts are in accord with the theory is doing the best he can by his own lights: a Dutch book cannot be made against him.

Bayesian decision theory does not provide a definition of the concepts of belief and preference on the basis of non-intensional notions. Rather, it makes use of one intensional notion, ordinal preference between gambles or outcomes, to give content to two further notions: degree of belief and comparisons of differences in value. So it would be a mistake to think the theory provides a reduction of intensional concepts to something else. Nevertheless it is an important step in the direction of reducing complex and relatively theoretical intensional concepts to intensional concepts that in application are closer to publicly observable behavior. Above all, the theory shows how it is possible to give a useful content to two basic and interlocking propositional attitudes without assuming that either one is understood in advance.

As a theory for explaining human actions, a Bayesian decision theory of the sort I have been discussing is open to the criticism that it presupposes that we can identify the propositions to which attitudes like belief and desire (or preference) are directed. But our ability to identify, and distinguish among, the propositions an agent entertains is not to be separated from our ability to understand what he says. We generally find out exactly what someone wants, prefers, or believes only by interpreting his speech. This is particularly obvious in the case of decision theory, where the objects of desire are often complex wagers, with outcomes described as contingent on specific events. Clearly, a theory that attempts to elicit the attitudes and beliefs which explain preferences or choices must include a theory of verbal interpretation if it is not to make crippling assumptions.

What we must add to decision theory, or incorporate in it, is a theory of interpretation for the agent, a way of telling what he means by his words. Yet this addition must be made in the absence of detailed information about beliefs, desires, or intentions.

A theory of verbal interpretation for a speaker (what I shall call a "theory of meaning") must give a meaning to each of the potential infinity of utterances in the repertoire of the speaker, and so a recursive theory is called for that derives the meaning of an utterance (or a sentence) from the meaning of its parts. In this respect, our theory of meaning must resemble decision theory, for decision theory also predicts choices among a potential infinity of alternatives.

Dispositions to speak one sentence or another are manifested in myriad ways. A conspicuous example is the manifestation of assent in the act of assertion. (Just as preference manifests itself in choice.) Suppose it were possible to tell, in one way or another, when a person assents to a sentence—when he holds it to be true. Honest assertion would serve, but so might many other acts and attitudes.

If such evidence could be seen to support a theory of meaning, notable progress would have been made. For though, as in the case of decision theory, the evidence would have an irreducibly intensional element (holding true), we would be starting with a single attitude that does not assume that we can detect the endless variety of propositional attitudes (beliefs, desires, intentions, and meanings) that a full-fledged theory hopes to end up with. From this point of view, the sort of theory of meaning I propose is better than theories that depend on detailed knowledge of the beliefs or intentions that accompany individual utterances. For such theories use for evidence facts as subtle and hard to identify as the facts they are intended to support. To restate my opening theme: we cannot assume we can make fine-grained distinctions among basic propositional attitudes of one sort (intentions, for example) in order to construct a theory of another range of propositional attitudes (meanings, for example) without assuming the harder questions have already been answered.

I would like a theory of meaning to be much like Ramsey's version of decision theory, but the best I know how to do falls seriously short of this goal. Nevertheless, I think one can see how something similar is possible, for we know in outline how to base a theory of meaning on assent to sentences as caused by events in the world. Such a theory will not only be a theory of meaning for the speaker but also a theory of belief, for sentence held true plus interpretation equals belief. Since to know that someone holds a sentence true is neither to know what the sentence means nor what belief it expresses, such a theory is not trivial. But putting the matter this way brings out a problem: just as choosing a course of action is the result of belief and desire, so holding a sentence true is the result of meaning and belief. How are we to distinguish the roles of each in the determination of sentences held true? We cannot hope to discover the interpretation first and then read off the beliefs, for it is the way beliefs are associated with sentences that constitutes the meanings of the sentences.

The problem is like the problem in decision theory, but the solution is not as neat. Ramsey devised an ingenious trick for fixing the subjective probability of one event exactly without knowing anything but simple preferences; with this start, utilities can be assigned generally as uniquely as the theory demands. In a combined theory of meaning and belief there is no such precise trick, and so the data can be accommodated by various theories of interpretation provided these theories are paired with appropriate theories of belief.[3] The consequent indeterminacy of interpretation is not on this account any more significant or troublesome than the fact that weight may be measured in grams or in ounces.

If we are to derive meaning and belief from evidence concerning what causes someone to hold sentences true, it can only be (as in decision theory) because we stipulate a structure. On the side of meaning, a plausible structure is given by a theory of truth of the sort suggested by Tarski, but modified in various ways to apply to a natural language. Such a theory may, I have argued, be considered adequate for interpreting the utterances of a speaker. (In fact it provides at best only the first step in interpreting what the speaker means, by specifying what his words mean in their most literal sense.)

On the side of belief it is less clear what structure to assume. But the guiding principles must derive here, as in the cases of decision theory or the theory of truth, from normative considerations. We individuate and identify beliefs, as we do desires, intentions, and meanings, in a great number of ways. But the relations between beliefs play a decisive constitutive role; we cannot accept great or obvious deviations from rationality without threatening the intelligibility of our attributions. If we are going to understand the speech or actions of another person,

---

[3] This is a way of stating one lesson we learn from Quine's indeterminacy of translation thesis.

we must suppose that their beliefs are incorporated in a pattern that is in essential respects like the pattern of our own beliefs. First, then, we have no choice but to project our own logic on to the beliefs of another. In the context of the present theory, this means we take it as a constraint on possible interpretations of sentences held true that they are logically consistent with one another. Put another way, the policy is to assume the speaker's beliefs are logically consistent (up to a point at least).

Logical consistency insures no more than the interpretation of the logical constants, however (whatever we take to be the limits of logic and the list of logical constants). Further interpretation requires the assumption of further agreement between speaker and interpreter. The assumption is certainly justified, the alternative being that the interpreter finds the speaker unintelligible. But it is hard to be precise about the rules for deciding where agreement most needs to be taken for granted. General principles are relatively simple to state: agreement on laws and regularities usually matters more than agreement on cases; agreement on what is openly and publicly observable is more to be favored than agreement on what is hidden, inferred, or ill observed; evidential relations should be preserved the more they verge on being constitutive of meaning.

It is uncertain to what extent these principles can be made definite— it is the problem of rationalizing and codifying our epistemology. But in one crucial area, that of evidential support, it is clear that progress is possible. It is obvious that a correct interpretation of a speaker's words will depend heavily on knowing to what extent the speaker counts the truth of one sentence in support of the truth of another. For the content of sentences or predicates more or less remote from what is immediately observed depends on what is taken to favor their truth or application, while the meaning of a sentence tied more directly to what is observed is partly determined by the theoretical truths its truth is taken to augment.

What is needed for an adequate theory of belief and meaning, then, is not merely knowledge of what causes a speaker to hold a sentence true, but knowledge of the degree of belief in its truth. It would then be possible to detect degrees of evidential support by noting how changes in the degree of credence placed on one sentence were accompanied by changes in the degree of credence placed on other sentences.

Degree of belief, however, is itself remote from what can generally be introspected by an agent or diagnosed by an interpreter; as we saw in discussing decision theory, degree of belief is a construction on more elementary attitudes. This is why Quine, in developing his theory of radical translation, depended on simple assent, and why, following Quine, I have depended on the closely related notion of holding true. These simple qualitative concepts, I have just been urging, are not adequate for constructing a theory of meaning (translation, interpretation).

Theory of meaning as I see it, and Bayesian decision theory, are evidently made for each other. Decision theory must be freed from the assumption of an independently determined knowledge of meaning; theory of meaning calls for a theory of degree of belief in order to make serious use of relations of evidential support. But stating these mutual dependencies is not enough, for neither theory can be developed first as a basis for the other. There is no way simply to add one to the other since in order to get started each requires an element drawn from the other. What is wanted is a unified theory that yields degree of belief, utilities on an interval scale, and an interpretation of speech without assuming any of them.

The problem is much like the problems posed in turn by decision theory and the theory of meaning, except that instead of two there are three items to be abstracted from evidence that does not depend, for its recognition, on what is to be explained. What is needed for the unified theory is therefore some simple propositional attitude which can plausibly be recognized to apply to an agent without detailed knowledge of the agent's beliefs, preferences, or verbal meanings, and from which we can extract a theory of degrees of belief, comparisons of differences in degree of desire, and a method for interpreting utterances.

I propose to take the following attitude as basic: the agent prefers one sentence true rather than another. The sentences must be endowed with meaning by the speaker, of course, but interpreting the sentences is part of the interpreter's task. What the interpreter has to go on, then, is information about what events in the world cause an agent to prefer that one rather than another sentence be true. Clearly the interpreter can know this without knowing what the sentences mean, what states of affairs the agent values, or what he believes. But the preferring true of sentences by an agent is equally clearly a function of what the agent takes the sentences to mean, the value he sets on various possible or actual states of the world, and the probability he attaches to those states contingent on the truth of the relevant sentences. So it is not absurd to think that all three attitudes of the agent can be constructed on the basis of the agent's preferences among sentences. At the same time, there are important respects in which the evidential base I am suggesting for a unified theory is superior to the evidential bases for decision theory or the theory of meaning. Decision theory is normally tested by asking a subject to choose between options described by an experimenter: in effect, the subject chooses between sentences, and the experimenter assumes he knows what those sentences mean to the subject. This assumption has been repeatedly challenged by experimental results. Our unified theory abandons the assumption by taking the data to be choices among the uninterpreted sentences.

In the case of theory of meaning, there is, of course, the fact discussed above, that it requires degrees of assent, and these are not directly given. But even if simple assent, or holding true, were sufficient basis for a theory of meaning, there is the difficulty that these attitudes have no obvious or direct connection with action or the springs of action in desire, preference, and intention. The problem is not so much that only action can be observed as that nothing can count as a reason for supposing someone assents to a sentence, or holds it true, that does not assume a lot about the agent's intentions or purposes or values. An empirical theory of meaning forces us to bring desire or preference, as well as belief, into the picture.

How is it possible to construct a unified theory from evidence about sentences preferred true? Here is a sketch of a possible procedure.

We have already seen (again in survey form) how to arrive at a theory of meaning and belief on the basis of knowledge about the degrees to which sentences are held true. So if we could derive degree of belief in sentences by appeal to information about preferences that sentences be true we would have a successful unified theory.

Ramsey's version of Bayesian decision theory makes essential use of gambles or wagers, and this creates a difficulty for my project. For how can we tell that an agent views a sentence as presenting a gamble until we are far along in the process of interpreting his language? A gamble, after all, specifies a connection, presumably causal, between the occurrence of a certain event (a coin comes up heads) and a specific outcome (you win a horse). Even assuming we could tell when an agent accepts such a connection, straightforward application of the theory depends also on the causing event (the coin coming up heads) having no value, negative or positive, in itself. It is also necessary to assume that the probability the agent assigns to the coin coming up heads is not contaminated by thoughts about the likelihood of winning a horse. In experimental tests of decision theory one tries to pick situations in which these assumptions have a chance of being true; but the general application we now have in mind cannot be so choosy.

We owe to Richard Jeffrey a version of Bayesian decision theory that makes no direct use of gambles, but treats the objects of preference, the objects to which subjective probabilities are assigned, and the objects to which relative values are assigned uniformly as propositions.[4] Jeffrey has shown in detail how to extract subjective probabilities and values from preferences that propositions be true.

Jeffrey's theory does not determine probabilities and utilities up to the same sets of transformations as standard theories. Instead of a utility function determined up to a linear transformation, in Jeffrey's theory the utility function is unique only up to a fractional linear transformation; and the probability assignments, instead of being unique once a number is chosen for measuring certainty (always One), are unique only to within a certain quantization. These diminutions in determinacy are conceptually and practically appropriate: they amount, among other things, to permitting somewhat the same sort of indeterminacy in decision theory that we have come to expect in a theory of linguistic interpretation. Just as you can account for the same data in decision theory using various utility functions by making corresponding changes in the probability function, so you can change the meanings you attribute to a person's words (within limits) provided you make compensating changes in the beliefs you attribute to him.

An obvious problem remains. Jeffrey shows how to get results enough like Ramsey's by substituting preferences among propositions for preferences among gambles. But propositions are meanings, or sentences with meanings; if we know what propositions an agent is choosing among, our original problem of interpreting language has once more been assumed to have been solved. What we need is to get Jeffrey's results given only preferences among uninterpreted sentences.

Fortunately this is not as wild a bootstrap proposal as it sounds. For Jeffrey's method for finding the subjective probabilities and relative desirabilities of propositions depends only on the truth-functional

---

[4] R. C. Jeffrey, *The Logic of Decision*, University of Chicago Press, 2nd edition, 1983.

structure of propositions—on how propositions are made up out of simple propositions by repeated application of conjunction, disjunction, negation, and the other operations definable in terms of these. If we start with sentences instead of propositions, then our problem will be solved provided the truth-functional connectives can be identified. For once the truth-functional connectives have been identified, Jeffrey has shown how to fix, to the desired degree, the subjective desirabilities and probabilities of all sentences; and this, I have argued, suffices to yield a theory for interpreting the sentences.

The basic empirical primitive in the method to be described is the agent's (weak) preference that one sentence rather than another be true; one may therefore think of the data as being of the same sort as the data usually gathered in an experimental test of any Bayesian theory of decision, with the proviso that the interpretation of the sentences among which the agent chooses is not assumed known in advance to the experimenter or interpreter.

The uniformity and simplicity of the empirical ontology of the system, comprising as it does just utterances and sentences, is essential to achieving the aim of combining decision theory with interpretation. I shall follow Jeffrey, whose theory deals with propositions only, as closely as possible, substituting uninterpreted sentences where he assumes propositions. Here, then, is the analogue of Jeffrey's *desirability axiom*, applied to sentences rather than propositions:

If $\text{prob}(s \text{ and } t) = 0$ and $\text{prob}(s \text{ or } t) \neq 0$, then   (D)

$$\text{des}(s \text{ or } t) = \frac{\text{prob}(s)\text{des}(s) + \text{prob}(t)\text{des}(t)}{\text{prob}(s) + \text{prob}(t)}.$$

(I write "prob(s)" for the subjective probability of s and "des(s)" for the desirability or utility of s.) By relating preference and belief, this axiom does the sort of work usually done by gambles; the relation is, however, different. Events are identified with sentences which on interpretation turn out to say the event occurs ("The next card is a club"). Actions and outcomes are also represented by sentences ("The agent bets one dollar", "The agent wins five dollars"). Gambles do not enter directly, but the element of risk is present, since to choose that a sentence be true is usually to take a risk on what will concomitantly be true. (It is assumed that one cannot choose a logically false sentence.) So we see that if the agent chooses to make true rather than false the sentence "The agent bets one dollar", he is taking a chance on the outcome, which may, for example, be thought to depend on whether or not the next card is a club. Then the desirability of the (truth of) the sentence "The agent bets one dollar" will be the desirability of the various circumstances in which this sentence is true weighted in the usual way by the probabilities of those circumstances. Suppose the agent believes he will win five dollars if the next card is a club and will win nothing if the next card is not a club; he will then have a special interest in whether the truth of "The agent bets one dollar" will be paired with the truth or falsity of "The next card is a club". Let these two sentences be abbreviated by "*s*" and "*t*". Then

$$\text{des}(s) = \frac{\text{prob}(s \text{ and } t)\text{des}(s \text{ and } t) + \text{prob}(s \text{ and } \sim t)\text{des}(s \text{ and } \sim t)}{\text{prob}(s)}.$$

This is, of course, something like Ramsey's gambles. It differs, however, in that there is no assumption that the "states of nature" that may be thought to determine outcomes are, in Ramsey's term, "morally neutral", that is, have no effect on the desirabilities of the outcomes. Nor is there the assumption that the probabilities of outcomes depend on nothing but the probabilities of the "states of nature" (the agent may believe he has a chance of winning five dollars even if the next card is not a club, and a chance he will not win five dollars even if the next card is a club).

The "desirability axiom" (D) can be used to show how probabilities depend on desirabilities in Jeffrey's system. Take the special case where $t = \sim s$. Then we have

$$\text{des}(s \text{ or } \sim s) = \text{des}(s)\text{prob}(s) + \text{des}(\sim s)\text{prob}(\sim s) \qquad (1)$$

Since $\text{prob}(s) + \text{prob}(\sim s) = 1$, we can solve for $\text{prob}(s)$:

$$\text{prob}(s) = \frac{\text{des}(s \text{ or } \sim s) - \text{des}(\sim s)}{\text{des}(s) - \text{des}(\sim s)}. \qquad (2)$$

In words, the probability of a proposition depends on the desirability of that proposition and of its negation. Further, it is easy to see that if a sentence *s* is more desirable than an arbitrary logical truth (such as "*t* or $\sim t$"), then its negation ("$\sim s$") cannot also be more desirable than a logical truth. Suppose that (with Jeffrey) we assign the number 0 to any logical truth. (This is intuitively reasonable since an agent is indifferent to the truth of a tautology.) Then (2) can be rewritten:

$$\text{prob}(s) = \frac{1}{1 - (\text{des}(s)/\text{des}(\sim s))}. \tag{3}$$

It is at once apparent that $\text{des}(s)$ and $\text{des}(\sim s)$ cannot both be more, or both be less, desirable than 0, the desirability of any logical truth, if $\text{prob}(s)$ is to fall in the interval from 1 to 0. If (once again following Jeffrey) we call an option good if it is preferred to a logical truth and bad if a logical truth is preferred to it, then (3) shows that it is impossible for an option (sentence) and its negation both to be good or both to be bad.

Taking "$\sim(s \text{ and } \sim s)$" as our sample logical truth, we can state this principle purely in terms of preferences:

$$\text{If des}(s) > \text{des}(\sim(s \text{ and } \sim s))\text{then} \tag{4}$$

$$\text{des}(\sim(s \text{ and } \sim s)) \geq \text{des}(\sim s), \text{ and}$$

$$\text{if des}(\sim(s \text{ and } \sim s)) > \text{des}(s) \text{ then}$$

$$\text{des}(\sim s) \geq \text{des}(\sim(s \text{ and } \sim s))$$

Since both negation and conjunction can be defined in terms of the Sheffer stroke "|" ("not both"), (4) can be rewritten:

$$\text{If des}(s) > \text{des}((t|u)|((t|u)|(t|u))) \text{ then} \tag{5}$$

$$\text{des}((t|u)|((t|u)|(t|u))) \geq \text{des}(s|s), \text{ and}$$

$$\text{if des}((t|u)|((t|u)|(t|u))) > \text{des}(s) \text{ then}$$

$$\text{des}(s|s) \geq \text{des}((t|u)|((t|u)|(t|u))).$$

The interest of (5) for present purposes is this. If we assume that "|" is some arbitrary truth-functional operator that forms sentences out of pairs of sentences, then the following holds: if (5) is true for all sentences s, t, and u, and for some s and t, $\text{des}(s|s) \neq \text{des}(t|t)$, then "|" must be the Sheffer stroke (it must have the logical properties of "not both"); no other interpretation is possible.[5]

Thus data involving only preferences among sentences the meanings of which are unknown to the interpreter has led (given the

---

[5] I am indebted to Stig Kanger for showing me why an earlier attempt at a solution to this problem would not work. He also added some needed refinements to the present proposal.

constraints of the theory) to the identification of one sentential connective. Since all logically equivalent sentences are equal in desirability, it is now possible to interpret all the other truth-functional sentential connectives, since all are definable in terms of the Sheffer stroke. For example, if it is found that, for all sentences s,

$$\text{des}(s|s) = \text{des}(\sim s),$$

we can conclude that the tilde is the sign for negation.

It is now possible to measure the desirability and subjective probability of all sentences, for the application of formulas like (2) and (3) requires the identification of only the truth-functional sentential connectives. Thus it is clear from (3) that if two sentences are equal in desirability (and are preferred to a logical truth) and their negations are also equal in desirability, the sentences must have the same probability. By the same token, if two sentences are equal in desirability (and are preferred to a logical truth), but the negation of one is preferred to the negation of the other, then the probability of the first is less than that of the second. This, along with appropriate existence axioms, is enough to establish a probability scale. Then it is easy to determine the relative desirabilities of all sentences.[6]

At this point the probabilities and desirabilities of all sentences have in theory been determined. But no complete sentence has yet been interpreted, though the truth-functional sentential connectives have been identified, and so sentences logically true or false by virtue of sentential logic can be recognized. It remains to sketch the methods that could lead to a complete interpretation of all sentences, that is, to the construction of a theory of truth for the agent's language. The approach is one I have discussed in a number of articles, and is inspired by the work of W. V. Quine on radical translation.[7]

For an agent to have a certain subjective probability for a sentence is for him to hold that sentence true, or false, or for him to have some determinate degree of belief in its truth. Since the agent attaches a meaning to the sentence, his degree of confidence in the truth of the sentence is also his degree of faith in the truth the sentence expresses. Beliefs, as manifested in attitudes to sentences, are the clue to meaning. We have already observed that logically equivalent sentences are

[6] For details see Jeffrey, *op. cit.*

[7] See chapter 2 of W. V. Quine, *Word and Object*, The Technology Press and John Wiley, 1960, and essays 9–12 in Davidson, *Inquiries into Truth and Interpretation*, Oxford University Press, 1984.

equal in desirability. This in itself is no direct help in getting at the meanings of logically equivalent sentences, though it does help, as we have seen, in interpreting the truth-functional sentential connectives. Patterns of sentences held true or false will also lead to the detection of the existential and universal quantifiers, and thus to the structures that account for entailments and logical truths in quantificational logic. To discover the structures that account for entailments and logical truths in quantificational logic is to uncover *logical form* in general, that is, to learn how sentences are made up of predicates, singular terms, quantifiers, variables, and the like. The symbol for identity should be easy to locate, given its role in promoting entailments based on substitution; someone who holds sentences of the forms "$a = b$" and "Fa" true will also hold a sentence of the form "Fb" true, whatever the predicate "F" means (unless it is intensional—one of the problems I am here overlooking).

Further steps in interpretation will require some elaboration of the empirical basis of the theory; it will be necessary to attend, not just to the agent's preferences among sentences, but also to the events and objects in the world that cause his preferences (and hence also his beliefs). Thus it will be the observable circumstances under which an agent is caused to assign high or low probabilities to sentences like "It is raining", "That's a horse", or "My foot is sore", that yield the most obvious evidence for the interpretation of these sentences and the predicates in them. The interpreter, on noticing that the agent regularly assigns a high or low degree of belief to the sentence "The coffee is ready" when the coffee is, or isn't, ready will (however tentatively pending related results) try for a theory of truth that says that an utterance by the agent of the sentence "The coffee is ready" is true if and only if the coffee is ready.

Pretty obviously, the interpretation of common predicates depends heavily on indexical elements in speech, such as demonstratives and tense, since it is these that allow predicates and singular terms to be connected to objects and events in the world. To accommodate indexical elements, theories of truth of the sort proposed by Tarski must be modified; the nature of these modifications has been discussed elsewhere.[8]

---

[8] See Alfred Tarski, "The Concept of Truth in Formalized Languages", in *Logic, Semantics, Metamathematics*, Oxford University Press, 1956. The application of Tarski's general approach to natural language is discussed in Davidson, *Inquiries into Truth and Interpretation*.

The interpretation of predicates less directly keyed to untutored observation will depend in large measure on conditional probabilities, which show what the agent counts as evidence for the application of his more theoretical predicates. Such evidence may also be expected to help account for errors in the application of observational predicates under less than ideal conditions.

The approach to the problems of meaning, belief, and desire that I have outlined is not, I am sure it is clear, meant to throw any direct light on how in real life we come to understand each other, much less how we master our first concepts and our first language. I have been engaged in a conceptual exercise aimed at revealing the dependencies among our basic propositional attitudes at a level fundamental enough to avoid the assumption that we can come to grasp them—or intelligibly attribute them to others—one at a time. My way of performing this exercise has been to show how it is in principle possible to arrive at all of them at once.

What makes the task practicable at all is the structure the normative character of thought, desire, speech, and action imposes on correct attributions of attitudes to others, and hence on interpretations of their speech and explanations of their actions. What I have said about the norms that govern our theories of intensional attribution is at crucial points crude, vague, or too rigid. The way to improve our understanding of such understanding is to improve our grasp of the standards of rationality implicit in all interpretation of thought and action.

IRRATIONALITY

11 *Paradoxes of Irrationality*

The idea of an irrational action, belief, intention, inference, or emotion is paradoxical. For the irrational is not merely the non-rational, which lies outside the ambit of the rational; irrationality is a failure within the house of reason. When Hobbes says only man has 'the privilege of absurdity' he suggests that only a rational creature can be irrational. Irrationality is a mental process or state—a rational process or state—gone wrong. How can this be?

The paradox of irrationality is not as simple as the seeming paradox in the concept of an unsuccessful joke, or of a bad piece of art. The paradox of irrationality springs from what is involved in our most basic ways of describing, understanding, and explaining psychological states and events. Sophia is pleased that she can tie a bowline. Then her pleasure must be due to her belief that she can tie a bowline and her positive assessment of that accomplishment. Further, and doubtless more searching, explanations may be available, but they cannot displace this one, since this one flows from what it is to be pleased that something is the case. Or take Roger, who intends to pass an examination by memorizing the Koran. This intention must be explained by his desire to pass the examination and his belief that by memorizing the Koran he will enhance his chances of passing the examination. The existence of reason explanations of this sort is a built-in aspect of intentions, intentional actions, and many other attitudes and emotions. Such explanations explain by rationalizing: they enable us to see the events or attitudes as reasonable from the point of view of the agent. An aura of rationality, of fitting into

A precursor of this paper was delivered as the Ernest Jones Lecture before the British Psycho-analytical Association on 26 April 1978. Dr Edna O'Shaughnessy commented, and I have profited from her informative remarks. I am also indebted for further useful suggestions to Dagfinn Føllesdal, Sue Larson, and Richard Wollheim.

a rational pattern, is thus inseparable from these phenomena, at least as long as they are described in psychological terms. How then can we explain, or even tolerate as possible, irrational thoughts, actions, or emotions?

Psychoanalytic theory as developed by Freud claims to provide a conceptual framework within which to describe and understand irrationality. But many philosophers think there are fundamental errors or confusions in Freud's thought. So I consider here some elements in that thought that have often come under attack, elements that consist of a few very general doctrines central to all stages of Freud's mature writings. After analysing the underlying problem of explaining irrationality, I conclude that any satisfactory view must embrace some of Freud's most important theses, and when these theses are stated in a sufficiently broad way, they are free from conceptual confusion. It perhaps needs to be emphasized that my 'defence' of Freud is directed to some only of Freud's ideas, and these are ideas at the conceptual, in contrast to the empirical, end of that vague spectrum.

Much that is called irrational does not make for paradox. Many might hold that it is irrational, given the dangers, discomforts, and meagre rewards to be expected on success, for any person to attempt to climb Mt Everest without oxygen (or even with it). But there is no puzzle in explaining the attempt if it is undertaken by someone who has assembled all the facts he can, given full consideration to all his desires, ambitions, and attitudes, and has acted in the light of his knowledge and values. Perhaps it is in some sense irrational to believe in astrology, flying saucers, or witches, but such beliefs may have standard explanations if they are based on what their holders take to be the evidence. It is sensible to try to square the circle if you don't know it can't be done. The sort of irrationality that makes conceptual trouble is not the failure of someone else to believe or feel or do what we deem reasonable, but rather the failure, within a single person, of coherence or consistency in the pattern of beliefs, attitudes, emotions, intentions, and actions. Examples are wishful thinking, acting contrary to one's own best judgement, self-deception, believing something that one holds to be discredited by the weight of the evidence.

In attempting to explain such phenomena (along with much more, of course) Freudians have made the following claims:

First, the mind contains a number of semi-independent structures, these structures being characterized by mental attributes like thoughts, desires, and memories.

Second, parts of the mind are in important respects like people, not only in having (or consisting of) beliefs, wants, and other psychological traits, but in that these factors can combine, as in intentional action, to cause further events in the mind or outside it.

Third, some of the dispositions, attitudes, and events that characterize the various substructures in the mind must be viewed on the model of physical dispositions and forces when they affect, or are affected by, other substructures in the mind.

A further doctrine about which I shall say only a little is that some mental phenomena that we normally assume to be conscious, or at least available to consciousness, are not conscious, and can become accessible only with difficulty, if at all. In most functional respects, these unconscious mental states and events are like conscious beliefs, memories, desires, wishes, and fears.

I hope it will be agreed that these doctrines are all to be found in Freud, and that they are central to his theories. They are, as I have said, far less strong and detailed than Freud's views. Yet even in reduced form, they require more defence than is possible, in the view of many philosophers. The criticisms I shall be attempting to meet are related in various ways, but they are essentially of two sorts.

First, the idea that the mind can be partitioned at all has often been held to be unintelligible, since it seems to require that thoughts and desires and even actions be attributed to something less than, and therefore distinct from, the whole person. But can we make sense of acts and attitudes that are not those of an agent? Also, as Sartre suggests, the notion of responsibility would lose its essential point if acts and intentions were pried loose from people and attached instead to semi-autonomous parts of the mind. The parts would then stand proxy for the person: each part would become a little woman, man, or child. What was once a single mind is turned into a battlefield where opposed forces contend, deceive one another, conceal information, devise strategies. As Irving Thalberg and others point out, sometimes it even happens that one segment protects itself from its own forces (thoughts).[1] The prime agent may appear as a sort of chairman of the board, arbiter, or dictator. It is not surprising that doubts have arisen as to whether these metaphors can be traded for a consistent theory.

---

[1] See Irving Thalberg, 'Freud's Anatomies of the Self', in *Philosophical Essays on Freud*, ed. R. Wollheim and J. Hopkins (Cambridge University Press, 1982).

A second, though related, set of worries concerns the underlying explanatory methodology. On the one hand, psychoanalytic theory extends the reach of teleological or reason explanation by discovering motives, wishes, and intentions that were not recognized before. In this respect, as has often been noted, Freud greatly increased the number and variety of phenomena that can be viewed as rational: it turns out that we have reasons for our forgettings, slips of the tongue, and exaggerated fears. But on the other side, Freud wants his explanations to yield what explanations in natural science often promise: causal accounts that permit control. In this vein, he applies to mental events and states terms drawn from hydraulics, electromagnetism, neurology, and mechanics. Toulmin, Flew, MacIntyre, and Peters among philosophers have at one time or another suggested that psychoanalytic theories attempt the impossible by trying to bring psychological phenomena (which require explanations in terms of reasons) under causal laws: they think this accounts for, but does not justify, Freud's constant use, when talking of the mind, of metaphors drawn from other sciences.[2]

It seems then, that there are two irreconcilable tendencies in Freud's methodology. On the one hand he wanted to extend the range of phenomena subject to reason explanations, and on the other to treat these same phenomena as forces and states are treated in the natural sciences. But in the natural sciences, reasons and propositional attitudes are out of place, and blind causality rules.

In order to evaluate these charges against psychoanalytic theory, I want first to rehearse part of what I think is a correct analysis of normal intentional action. Then we can consider irrationality.

A man walking in a park stumbles on a branch in the path.[3] Thinking the branch may endanger others, he picks it up and throws it in a hedge beside the path. On his way home it occurs to him that the branch may be projecting from the hedge and so still be a threat to unwary walkers. He gets off the tram he is on, returns to the park, and restores the branch to its original position. Here everything the agent does (except stumble on the branch) is done for a reason, a reason in the

---

[2] See, for examples, Antony Flew, 'Motives and the Unconscious', in *Minnesota Studies in the Philosophy of Science*, vol. 1, ed. H. Feigl and M. Scriven (University of Minnesota Press, Minneapolis, 1956); Alasdair MacIntyre, *The Unconscious* (Routledge, London, 1958); R. S. Peters, *The Concept of Motivation* (Routledge, London, 1958); Charles Taylor, *The Explanation of Behaviour* (Routledge, London, 1965).

[3] The example, though not the use I make of it, comes from Sigmund Freud, 'Notes upon a Case of Obsessional Neurosis', *Standard Edition*, x, 23.

light of which the corresponding action was reasonable. Given that the man believed the stick was a danger if left on the path, and a desire to eliminate the danger, it was reasonable to remove the stick. Given that, on second thought, he believed the stick was a danger in the hedge, it was reasonable to extract the stick from the hedge and replace it on the path. Given that the man wanted to take the stick from the hedge, it was reasonable to dismount from the tram and return to the park. In each case the reasons for the action tell us what the agent saw in his action, they give the intention with which he acted, and they thereby give an explanation of the action. Such an explanation, as I have said, must exist if something a person does is to count as an action at all.

The pattern of reason explanations has been noted by many philosophers. Hume puts it pithily: 'Ask a man why he uses exercise: he will answer, because he desires to keep his health. If you then enquire why he desires health, he will readily reply, because sickness is painful.'[4] The pattern is so familiar that we may miss its subtlety. What is to be explained is the action, say taking exercise. At the minimum, the explanation calls on two factors: a value, goal, want, or attitude of the agent, and a belief that by acting in the way to be explained he can promote the relevant value or goal, or will be acting in accord with his attitude. The action on the one hand, and the belief–desire pair which give the reason on the other, must be related in two very different ways to yield an explanation. First, there must be a logical relation. Beliefs and desires have a content, and these contents must be such as to imply that there is something valuable or desirable about the action. Thus a man who finds something desirable in health, and believes that exercise will make him healthy can conclude that there is something desirable in exercise, which may explain why he takes exercise. Second, the reasons an agent has for acting must, if they are to explain the action, be the reasons on which he acted; the reasons must have played a *causal* role in the occurrence of the action. These two conditions on reason explanations are both necessary, but they are not sufficient, since some causal relations between belief–desire pairs and actions do not give reason explanations. (This complication will not concern us here, though there are no doubt irrational actions that hinge on the complication.)

This much of the analysis of action makes clear why all intentional actions, whether or not they are in some further sense irrational, have

---

[4] David Hume, *An Inquiry Concerning the Principles of Morals*, ed. L. A. Selby Bigge (The Clarendon Press, Oxford, 1957), Appendix I, p. 293.

a rational element at the core; it is this that makes for one of the paradoxes of irrationality. But we also see that Freud can be defended on one important point: there is no inherent conflict between reason explanations and causal explanations. Since beliefs and desires are causes of the actions for which they are reasons, reason explanations include an essential causal element.

What can be said of intentional action can be extended to many other psychological phenomena. If a person intends to steal some Brussels sprouts, then whether or not he executes his intention, the intention itself must be caused by a desire to possess some Brussels sprouts and a belief that by stealing them he will come into possession of them. (Once again, the logical, or rational, aspect of the intention is obvious.) Similarly, most of our wishes, hopes, desires, emotions, beliefs, and fears depend upon a simple inference (usually, no doubt, unnoticed) from other beliefs and attitudes. We fear poverty because we believe it will bring what we hold to be evils; we hope it will rain because we believe rain will help the crops, and we want the crops to prosper; we believe rain will help the crops on the basis of induction or hearsay or reading; and so on. In each of these cases, there is the logical connection between the contents of various attitudes and beliefs, and what they cause.

The conclusion up to this point is that merely to label a psychological state or event as being or entailing what is loosely called a propositional attitude is to guarantee the relevance of a reason explanation, and hence an element of rationality. But of course if such states and events can be irrational, the element of rationality cannot prevent their being at the same time less than rational. Consider the case of an action where the agent acts counter to what he believes, everything considered, is better. (Aristotle called such behaviour a case of akrasia; other terms are 'incontinence' or 'weakness of the will'.) It is easy to imagine that the man who returned to the park to restore the branch to its original position in the path realizes that his action is not sensible. He has a motive for moving the stick, namely, that it may endanger a passer-by. But he also has a motive for not returning, which is the time and trouble it costs. In his own judgement, the latter consideration outweighs the former; yet he acts on the former. In short, he goes against his own best judgement.

The problem of explaining such behaviour has puzzled philosophers and moralists at least since Plato. According to Plato, Socrates argued that since no one willingly acts counter to what he knows to be best, only ignorance can explain foolish or evil acts. This is often called a paradox, but Socrates' view is paradoxical only because it denies what we all believe, that there are akratic acts. If Socrates is right—if such actions are ruled out by the logic of the concepts—then there is nothing puzzling about the facts to be explained. Nevertheless, Socrates (or Plato) has brought our problem to a head: there is a conflict between the standard way of explaining intentional action and the idea that such an action can be irrational. Since the view that no intentional action can be internally irrational stands at one extreme in the continuum of possible views, let me give it a name: the *Plato Principle*. It is the doctrine of pure rationality.

At an opposite extreme is the *Medea Principle*. According to this doctrine, a person can act against his better judgement, but only when an alien force overwhelms his or her will. This is what happens when Medea begs her own hand not to murder her children. Her hand, or the passion of revenge behind it, overcomes her will. Some such treatment of weakness of the will is popular.[5] And given the thesis, the term is suitable, for the will of the agent is weaker than the alien passion. Moralists particularly have been attracted to this view, since it suggests that no more is needed to overcome temptation than greater resolve to do the right. Just the same, it is a strange doctrine, since it implies that akratic acts are not intentional, and so not in themselves actions for which the agent can be held responsible. If the agent is to blame, it is not for what he did, but because he did not resist with enough vigour. What the agent found himself doing had a reason— the passion or impulse that overcame his better judgement—but the reason was not *his*. From the agent's point of view, what he did was the effect of a cause that came from outside, as if another person had moved him.

Aristotle suggested that weakness of the will is due to a kind of forgetting. The akrates has two desires; in our example, he wants to save his time and effort, and also wants to move the branch. He can't act on both desires, but Aristotle will not let him get so far as to appreciate his problem, for according to Aristotle the agent loses active touch with his knowledge that by not returning to the park he can save time and effort. It is not quite a case of a conscious and an unconscious desire in conflict; rather there is a conscious and an

---

[5] For further discussion of these issues, and references, see my 'How is Weakness of the Will Possible?', in Donald Davidson, *Essays on Actions and Events* (Oxford University Press, 1980).

unconscious piece of knowledge, where action depends on which piece of knowledge is conscious.

There are situations in which Aristotle's analysis is appropriate, and other situations ruled by the Medea Principle. But such situations are not the only ones, and they are not the defining cases of akrasia, where the agent acts intentionally while aware that everything considered a better course of action is open to him. For when the Medea Principle is at work, intention is not present; and in Aristotle's analysis, the agent is not aware of an alternative.

On reflection it is obvious that neither the Medea Principle nor Aristotle's analysis allows for straightforward cases of conflict, cases in which an agent has good reasons both for doing, and for refraining from, a course of action; or, what comes to the same thing, good reasons for doing each of two mutually exclusive things. Such situations are too familiar to require special explanation: we are not normally paralysed when competing claims are laid on us, nor do we usually suppress part of the relevant information, or drive one of our desires underground. Usually we can face situations where a decision must be made, and we decide best when we manage to keep all the considerations, the pros and the cons, before us.

What requires explaining is the action of an agent who, having weighed up the reasons on both sides, and having judged that the preponderance of reasons is on one side, then acts against this judgement. We should not say he has no reason for his action, since he has reasons both for and against. It is because he has a reason for what he does that we can give the intention with which he acted. And like all intentional actions, his action can be explained, by referring to the beliefs and desires that caused it and gave it point.

But although the agent has a reason for doing what he did, he had better reasons, by his own reckoning, for acting otherwise. What needs explaining is not why the agent acted as he did, but why he *didn't* act otherwise, given his judgement that all things considered it would be better.

A person who appreciates the fact that he has good reasons both for and against an action should not be thought to be entertaining a contradiction. It follows that moral principles, or the judgements that correspond to desires, cannot be expressed by sentences like 'It is wrong to lie' or 'It is good to give pleasure'. Not, that is, if these sentences are taken in the natural way to express universal statements like 'All lies are wrong' or 'All acts that give pleasure are good'. For one and the same act may be a lie and an act that gives pleasure, and so be both wrong and good. On many moral theories, this is a contradiction. Or to take an even simpler case, if it is right to keep promises and wrong to break them, then someone who through no fault of his own has made incompatible promises will do something wrong if he does something right.

The solution to this puzzle about the logic of practical reasoning is to recognize that evaluative principles are not correctly stated in the form 'It is wrong to lie'. For not all lies are wrong; there are cases when one ought to lie for the sake of some more important consideration. The fact that an action is a lie, or the breaking of a promise, or a consumer of time is a count against the action, to be weighed along with other reasons for the action. Every action we perform, or consider performing, has something to be said for it and something against; but we speak of conflict only when the pros and cons are weighty and close to being in balance. Simple deduction can tell me that if I wish to keep promise *A* I must be in Addis Ababa on a certain date, and if I wish to keep promise *B* I must be in Bora Bora at that same time; but logic cannot tell me which to do.

Since logic cannot tell me which to do, it is unclear in what respect either action would be irrational. Nor is the irrationality evident if we add that I judge that all things considered I ought to keep promise *A*, and yet I keep promise *B*. For the first judgement is merely conditional: in the light of all my evidence, I ought to do *A*; and this cannot contradict the unconditional judgement that I ought to do *B*. Pure internal inconsistency enters only if I also hold—as in fact I do— that I ought to act on my own best judgement, what I judge best or obligatory, everything considered.

A purely formal description of what is irrational in an akratic act is, then, that the agent goes against his own second-order principle that he ought to act on what he holds to be best, everything considered. It is only when we can describe his action in just this way that there is a puzzle about explaining it. If the agent does not have the principle that he ought to act on what he holds to be best, everything considered, then though his action may be irrational from *our* point of view, it need not be irrational from his point of view—at least not in a way that poses a problem for explanation. For to explain his behaviour we need only say that his desire to do what he held to be best, all things considered, was not as strong as his desire to do something else.

But someone who knowingly and intentionally acts contrary to his own principle; how can we explain that? The explanation must, it is evident, contain some feature that goes beyond the Plato Principle;

otherwise the action is perfectly rational. On the other hand, the explanation must retain the core of the Plato Principle; otherwise the action is not intentional. An account like this seems to satisfy both requirements: there is, we have agreed, a normal reason explanation for an akratic action. Thus the man who returns to the park to replace the branch has a reason: to remove a danger. But in doing this he ignores his principle of acting on what he thinks is best, all things considered. And there is no denying that he has a motive for ignoring his principle, namely that he wants, perhaps very strongly, to return the branch to its original position. Let us say this motive does explain the fact that he fails to act on his principle. This is the point at which irrationality enters. For the desire to replace the branch has entered into the decision to do it twice over. First it was a consideration in favour of replacing the branch, a consideration that, in the agent's opinion, was less important than the reasons against returning to the park. The agent then held that everything considered he ought not to return to the park. Given his principle that one ought to act on such a conclusion, the rational thing for him to do was, of course, not to return to the park. Irrationality entered when his desire to return made him ignore or override his principle. For though his motive for ignoring his principle was a reason for ignoring the principle, it was not a reason against the principle itself, and so when it entered in this second way, it was irrelevant as a reason, to the principle and to the action. The irrationality depends on the distinction between a reason for having, or acting on, a principle, and a reason for the principle.

Another, and simpler, example will make the point clear. Suppose a young man very much wishes he had a well-turned calf and this leads him to believe he has a well-turned calf. He has a normal reason for wanting to have this belief—it gives him pleasure. But if the entire explanation of his holding the belief is that he wanted to believe it, then his holding the belief is irrational. For the wish to have a belief is not evidence for the truth of the belief, nor does it give it rational support in any other way. What his wish to have this belief makes rational is that this proposition should be true: He believes that he has a well-turned calf. This does not rationalize his believing: I have a well-turned calf. This is a case of wishful thinking, which is a model for the simplest kind of irrationality. Simple as it is, however, the model has a complexity which is obscured by the ambiguity of the phrase 'reason for believing'.

In some cases of irrationality it is unlikely, and perhaps impossible, for the agent to be fully aware of all that is going on in his mind. If someone 'forgets' that today is Thursday because he does not want to keep a disagreeable social commitment, it is perhaps ruled out that he should be aware of this. But in many cases there is no logical difficulty in supposing the agent knows what is going on. The young man may know he believes he has a well-turned calf only because he wants to believe it, just as the man who returns to the park to replace the branch may realize both the absurdity and the explanation of his action.

In standard reason explanations, as we have seen, not only do the propositional contents of various beliefs and desires bear appropriate logical relations to one another and to the contents of the belief, attitude, or intention they help explain; the actual states of belief and desire cause the explained state or event. In the case of irrationality, the causal relation remains, while the logical relation is missing or distorted. In the cases of irrationality we have been discussing, there is a mental cause that is not a reason for what it causes. So in wishful thinking, a desire causes a belief. But the judgement that a state of affairs is, or would be, desirable, is not a reason to believe that it exists.

It is clear that the cause must be mental in this sense: it is a state or event with a propositional content. If a bird flying by causes a belief that a bird is flying by (or that an airplane is flying by) the issue of rationality does not arise; these are causes that are not reasons for what they cause, but the cause has no logical properties, and so cannot of itself explain or engender irrationality (of the kind I have described). Can there be other forms of irrationality? The issue is not clear, and I make no claims concerning it. So far my thesis is only that many common examples of irrationality may be characterized by the fact that there is a mental cause that is not a reason. This characterization points the way to one kind of explanation of irrationality.

Irrationality of this kind may turn up wherever rationality operates. Just as incontinent actions are irrational, there can be irrational intentions to act, whether or not they are acted out. Beliefs may be irrational, as may courses of reasoning. Many desires and emotions are shown to be irrational if they are explained by mental causes that are not reasons for them. The general concept applies also to unchanges. A person is irrational if he is not open to reason—if, on accepting a belief or attitude on the basis of which he ought to make accommodating changes in his other beliefs, desires, or intentions, he fails to make those changes. He has a reason which does not cause what it is a sufficient reason for.

We now see how it is possible to reconcile an explanation that shows an action, belief, or emotion to be irrational with the element of rationality inherent in the description and explanation of all such phenomena. Thus we have dealt, at least in a preliminary way, with one paradox of irrationality. But now a second source of paradox emerges which cannot be so easily dissipated.

If events are related as cause and effect, they remain so no matter in what vocabulary we choose to describe them. Mental or psychological events are such only under a manner of description, for these very events surely are at the same time neurophysiological, and ultimately physical, events, though recognizable and identifiable within these realms only when given neurophysiological or physical descriptions. As we have seen, there is no difficulty in general in explaining mental events by appeal to neurophysiological or physical causes: this is central to the analysis of perception or memory, for example. But when the cause is described in non-mental terms, we necessarily lose touch with what is needed to explain the element of irrationality. For irrationality appears only when rationality is evidently appropriate: where both cause and effect have contents that have the sort of logical relations that make for reason or its failure. Events conceived solely in terms of their physical or physiological properties cannot be judged as reasons, or as in conflict, or as concerned with a subject matter. So we face the following dilemma: if we think of the cause in a neutral mode, disregarding its mental status as a belief or other attitude—if we think of it merely as a force that works on the mind without being identified as part of it—then we fail to explain, or even describe, irrationality. Blind forces are in the category of the non-rational, not the irrational. So, we introduce a mental description of the cause, which thus makes it a candidate for being a reason. But we still remain outside the only clear pattern of explanation that applies to the mental, for that pattern demands that the cause be more than a candidate for being a reason; it must *be* a reason, which in the present case it cannot be. For an explanation of a mental effect we need a mental cause that is also a reason for this effect, but, if we have it, the effect cannot be a case of irrationality. Or so it seems.

There is, however, a way one mental event can cause another mental event without being a reason for it, and where there is no puzzle and not necessarily any irrationality. This can happen when cause and effect occur in different minds. For example, wishing to have you enter my garden, I grow a beautiful flower there. You crave a look at my flower and enter my garden. My desire caused your craving and action, but my desire was not a reason for your craving, nor a reason on which you acted. (Perhaps you did not even know about my wish.) Mental phenomena may cause other mental phenomena without being reasons for them, then, and still keep their character as mental, provided cause and effect are adequately segregated. The obvious and clear cases are those of social interaction. But I suggest that the idea can be applied to a single mind and person. Indeed, if we are going to explain irrationality at all, it seems we must assume that the mind can be partitioned into quasi-independent structures that interact in ways the Plato Principle cannot accept or explain.

To constitute a structure of the required sort, a part of the mind must show a larger degree of consistency or rationality than is attributed to the whole.[6] Unless this is the case, the point of the analogy with social interaction is destroyed. The idea is that if parts of the mind are to some degree independent, we can understand how they are able to harbour inconsistencies, and to interact on a causal level. Recall the analysis of akrasia. There I mentioned no partitioning of the mind because the analysis was at that point more descriptive than explanatory. But the way could be cleared for explanation if we were to suppose two semi-autonomous departments of the mind, one that finds a certain course of action to be, all things considered, best, and another that prompts another course of action. On each side, the side of sober judgement and the side of incontinent intent and action, there is a supporting structure of reasons, of interlocking beliefs, expectations, assumptions, attitudes, and desires. To set the scene in this way still leaves much unexplained, for we want to know why this double structure developed, how it accounts for the action taken, and also, no doubt, its psychic consequences and cure. What I stress here is that the partitioned mind leaves the field open to such further explanations, and helps resolve the conceptual tension between the Plato Principle and the problem of accounting for irrationality.

[6] Here as elsewhere my highly abstract account of the partitioning of the mind deviates from Freud's. In particular, I have nothing to say about the number or nature of divisions of the mind, their permanence or aetiology. I am solely concerned to defend the idea of mental compartmentalization, and to argue that it is necessary if we are to explain a common form of irrationality. I should perhaps emphasize that phrases like 'partition of the mind', 'part of the mind', 'segment', etc. are misleading if they suggest that what belongs to one division of the mind cannot belong to another. The picture I want is of overlapping territories.

The partitioning I propose does not correspond in nature or function to the ancient metaphor of a battle between Virtue and Temptation or Reason and Passion. For the competing desires or values which akrasia demands do not, on my account, in themselves suggest irrationality. Indeed, a judgement that, all things considered, one ought to act in a certain way presupposes that the competing factors have been brought within the same division of the mind. Nor is it a matter of the bald intervention of a fey and alien emotion, as in the Medea Principle. What is called for is organized elements, within each of which there is a fair degree of consistency, and where one element can operate on another in the modality of non-rational causality.

Allowing a degree of autonomy to provinces of the mind dissipates to a degree the problems we have discussed, but it generates others. For to the extent that the Plato Principle fails to explain the workings of the mind, mere causal relations replace it, and these explain best, or make most progress toward science, as they can be summarized in laws. But there is a question how far the workings of the mind can be reduced to strict, deterministic laws as long as the phenomena are identified in mental terms. For one thing, the realm of the mental cannot form a closed system; much that happens in it is perforce caused by events with no mental description. And for another, once we contemplate causal relations between mental events in partial disregard of the logical relations between the descriptions of those events, we enter a realm without a unified and coherent set of constitutive principles: the concepts employed must be treated as mixed, owing allegiance partly to their connections with the world of non-mental forces, and partly to their character as mental and directed to a propositional content. These matters bear directly on the important question what kind of laws or generalizations will be found to hold in this area, and therefore on the question how scientific a science of the mental can be: that is, however, a subject I have put to one side.

There is one other problem that springs from recognizing semi-independent departments within the same mind. We attribute beliefs, purposes, motives, and desires to people in an endeavour to organize, explain, and predict their behaviour, verbal and otherwise. We describe their intentions, their actions, and their feelings in the light of the most unified and intelligible scheme we can contrive. Speech yields no more direct access into this scheme than any other behaviour, since speech itself must be interpreted; indeed speech requires at least two levels of interpretation, there being both the question what the speaker's words mean, and the question what the speaker means in speaking them. Not that an agent knows directly what he believes, wants, and intends in some way that reduces observers to mere detectives. For though he can often say what is on his mind, an agent's words have meaning in the public domain; what his words mean is up to the interpreter as well as to him. How he is to be understood is a problem for him as it is for others.

What makes interpretation difficult is the multiplicity of mental factors that produce behaviour and speech. To take an instance, if we know that in speaking certain words a man meant to assert that the price of plutonium is rising, then generally we must know a great deal more about his intentions, his beliefs, and the meaning of his words. If we imagine ourselves starting out from scratch to construct a theory that would unify and explain what we observe—a theory of the man's thoughts and emotions and language—we should be overwhelmed by the difficulty. There are too many unknowns for the number of equations. We necessarily cope with this problem by a strategy that is simple to state, though vastly complex in application: the strategy is to assume that the person to be understood is much like ourselves. That is perforce the opening strategy, from which we deviate as the evidence piles up. We start out assuming that others have, in the basic and largest matters, beliefs and values similar to ours. We are bound to suppose someone we want to understand inhabits our world of macroscopic, more or less enduring, physical objects with familiar causal dispositions; that his world, like ours, contains people with minds and motives; and that he shares with us the desire to find warmth, love, security, and success, and the desire to avoid pain and distress. As we get to matters of detail, or to matters in one way or another less central to our thinking, we can more and more easily allow for differences between ourselves and others. But unless we can interpret others as sharing a vast amount of what makes up our common sense we will not be able to identify any of their beliefs and desires and intentions, any of their propositional attitudes.

The reason is the holistic character of the mental. The meaning of a sentence, the content of a belief or desire, is not an item that can be attached to it in isolation from its fellows. We cannot intelligibly attribute the thought that a piece of ice is melting to someone who does not have many true beliefs about the nature of ice, its physical properties connected with water, cold, solidity, and so forth. The one attribution rests on the supposition of many more—endlessly more.

And among the beliefs we suppose a man to have, many must be true (in our view) if any are to be understood by us. The clarity and cogency of our attributions of attitude, motive, and belief are proportionate, then, to the extent to which we find others consistent and correct. We often, and justifiably, find others irrational and wrong; but such judgements are most firmly based when there is the most agreement. We understand someone best when we hold him to be rational and sage, and this understanding is what gives our disputes with him a keen edge.

There is no question but that the precept of unavoidable charity in interpretation is opposed to the partitioning of the mind. For the point of partitioning was to allow inconsistent or conflicting beliefs and desires and feelings to exist in the same mind, while the basic methodology of all interpretation tells us that inconsistency breeds unintelligibility.

It is a matter of degree. We have no trouble understanding small perturbations against a background with which we are largely in sympathy, but large deviations from reality or consistency begin to undermine our ability to describe and explain what is going on in mental terms. What sets a limit to the amount of irrationality we can make psychological sense of is a purely conceptual or theoretical matter—the fact that mental states and events are the states and events they are by their location in a logical space. On the other hand, what constrains the amount and kind of consistency and correspondence with reality we find in our fellow men and women is the frailty of human nature: the failure of imagination or sympathy on the part of the interpreter, and the stubborn imperfection of the interpreted. The underlying paradox of irrationality, from which no theory can entirely escape, is this: if we explain it too well, we turn it into a concealed form of rationality; while if we assign incoherence too glibly, we merely compromise our ability to diagnose irrationality by withdrawing the background of rationality needed to justify any diagnosis at all.

What I have tried to show, then, is that the very general features of psychoanalytic theory that I listed as having puzzled philosophers and others are, if I am right, features that will be found in any theory that sets itself to explain irrationality.

The first feature was that the mind is to be regarded as having two or more semi-autonomous structures. This feature we found to be necessary to account for mental causes that are not reasons for the mental states they cause. Only by partitioning the mind does it seem possible to explain how a thought or impulse can cause another to which it bears no rational relation.

The second feature assigned a particular kind of structure to one or more subdivisions of the mind: a structure similar to that needed to explain ordinary actions. This calls for a constellation of beliefs, purposes, and affects of the sort that, through the application of the Plato Principle, allow us to characterize certain events as having a goal or intention. The analogy does not have to be carried so far as to demand that we speak of parts of the mind as independent agents. What is essential is that certain thoughts and feelings of the person be conceived as interacting to produce consequences on the principles of intentional actions, these consequences then serving as causes, but not reasons, for further mental events. The breakdown of reason relations defines the boundary of a subdivision. Though I talk here, with Freud, of parts and agencies, there does not seem to be anything that demands a metaphor. The parts are defined in terms of function; ultimately, in terms of the concepts of reason and of cause. The idea of a quasi-autonomous division is not one that demands a little agent in the division; again, the operative concepts are those of cause and reason.

The third feature on which we remarked was that certain mental events take on the character of mere causes relative to some other mental events in the same mind. This feature also we found to be required by any account of irrationality. It is a feature that can be accommodated, I argued, but in order to accommodate it we must allow a degree of autonomy to parts of the mind.

The three elements of psychoanalytic theory on which I have concentrated, the partitioning of the mind, the existence of a considerable structure in each quasi-autonomous part, and non-logical causal relations between the parts; these elements combine to provide the basis for a coherent way of describing and explaining important kinds of irrationality. They also account for, and justify, Freud's mixture of standard reason explanations with causal interactions more like those of the natural sciences, interactions in which reason does not play its usual normative and rationalizing role.

Finally, I must mention the claim that many mental phenomena which normally are accessible to consciousness are sometimes neither conscious nor easily accessible to consciousness. The reason I have said nothing about this claim is that I think the relevant objections to unconscious mental states and events are answered by showing that the theory is acceptable without them. It is striking, for example, that nothing in the description of akrasia requires that any thought or motive be unconscious—indeed, I criticized Aristotle for introducing something like an unconscious piece of knowledge when this was not necessary. The standard case of akrasia is one in which the agent knows what he is doing, and why, and knows that it is not for the best, and knows why. He acknowledges his own irrationality. If all this is possible, then the description cannot be made untenable by supposing that sometimes some of the thoughts or desires involved are unconscious.

If to an otherwise unobjectionable theory we add the assumption of unconscious elements, the theory can only be made more acceptable, that is, capable of explaining more. For suppose we are led to realize by a genius like Freud that if we posit certain mental states and events we can explain much behaviour that otherwise goes unexplained; but we also discover that the associated verbal behaviour does not fit the normal pattern. The agent denies he has the attitudes and feelings we would attribute to him. We can reconcile observation and theory by stipulating the existence of unconscious events and states that, aside from awareness, are like conscious beliefs, desires, and emotions. There are, to be sure, further puzzles lurking here. But these seem to be puzzles that result from other problems; unconscious mental events do not add to the other problems but are natural companions of them.

I have urged that a certain scheme of analysis applies to important cases of irrationality. Possibly some version of this scheme will be found in every case of 'internal' inconsistency or irrationality. But does the scheme give a sufficient condition for irrationality? It would seem not. For simple cases of association do not count as irrational. If I manage to remember a name by humming a certain tune, there is a mental cause of something for which it is not a reason; and similarly for a host of further cases. But far more interesting, and more important, is a form of self-criticism and reform that we tend to hold in high esteem, and that has even been thought to be the very essence of rationality and the source of freedom. Yet it is clearly a case of mental causality that transcends reason (in the somewhat technical sense in which I have been using the concept).

What I have in mind is a special kind of second-order desire or value, and the actions it can touch off. This happens when a person forms a positive or negative judgement of some of his own desires, and he acts to change these desires. From the point of view of the changed desire, there is no reason for the change—the reason comes from an independent source, and is based on further, and partly contrary, considerations. The agent has reasons for changing his own habits and character, but those reasons come from a domain of values necessarily extrinsic to the contents of the views or values to undergo change. The cause of the change, if it comes, can therefore not be a reason for what it causes. A theory that could not explain irrationality would be one that also could not explain our salutary efforts, and occasional successes, at self-criticism and self-improvement.

12 *Incoherence and Irrationality*

Irrationality, like rationality, is a normative concept. Someone who acts or reasons irrationally, or whose beliefs or emotions are irrational, has departed from a standard; but what standard, or whose, is to be the judge? If you deviate from my norms of rationality, and you do not share my sense of what is reasonable, then are you really irrational? After all, fully rational agents can differ over values. If rationality is just one more value or complex set of values, then calling someone irrational would seem to be no more than a matter of expressing disagreement with his values or norms.

No doubt we very often stigmatize an action, belief, attitude, or piece of reasoning as irrational simply because we disapprove, disagree, are offended, or find something not up to our own standards. I am not concerned with such cases in this paper. My interest here is entirely with cases, if such there be, in which the judgment that the works or thoughts of an agent are irrational is not based, or at least not necessarily based, on disagreement over fact or norm. One might be tempted to call it a judgment of objective irrationality. This suggests that we should limit ourselves to cases in which an agent acts, thinks, or feels counter to his own conception of what is reasonable; cases where there is some sort of inner inconsistency or incoherence.

Inner inconsistency is, however, hard to describe in any detail, and harder still to explain. The difficulty in describing inner inconsistency is created by the character of the so-called propositional attitudes: belief, desire, intention, and many of the emotions. Put briefly, the problem is this: one way in which propositions are identified and distinguished one from another is by their logical properties, their place in a logical network. But then it would not seem possible to have a propositional attitude that is not rationally related to other propositional attitudes. For the propositional attitude itself, like the proposition to which it is directed, is in part identified by its logical relations to other propositional attitudes. Suppose someone discovers that his rake is missing and comes to believe on slender evidence that his neighbor has stolen it. Is he (objectively) irrational? Certainly not if he deems his evidence sufficient, and has no evidence against his suspicion. But suppose he has far better evidence against his belief than for it. Still he is not irrational unless he appreciates that the evidence he has *is* evidence against his belief, and holds that the evidence against outweighs the evidence for his belief. But does even this suffice to show he is irrational if he does not accept what Carnap called "the principle of total evidence" which counsels an agent to accept the hypothesis supported by the totality of evidence he or she has?

Here we have reached an aspect of rationality so fundamental that we cannot make sense of an agent who does not generally reason in accord with it. And so we have reached a point where the distinction between the standards of rationality of the agent himself and of his critic merge. It is an "objective", though normative, judgment that someone whose reasoning is on some occasion not in accord with the principle of total evidence has reasoned irrationally. (This claim will in the end be modified.)

The difficulty in explaining irrationality is in finding a mechanism that can be accepted as appropriate to mental processes and yet does not rationalize what is to be explained. What makes trouble is that our normal way of explaining the formation of propositional attitudes, including intentions and intentional acts, is to state the reasons that caused the attitude or act. Thus many of Freud's explanations of apparently irrational thoughts and acts are intended to show that from the agent's point of view (enlarged to embrace unconscious elements) there were good reasons for his thinking or acting. The paradoxical consequence is that explaining irrationality necessarily employs a form of explanation which rationalizes what it explains; without the element of rationality, we refuse to accept the account as appropriate to mental phenomena. We look, or tend to look, not merely for causes and forces, but for causes that are reasons. To explain irrationality we must find a way to keep what is essential to the character of the mental—which requires preserving a background of rationality—while allowing forms of causality that depart from the norms of rationality. What is needed to explain irrationality is a mental cause of an attitude, but where the cause is not a reason for the attitude it explains.

Let me take another example: one drawn from real life, or at least from my life. One late Spring afternoon I was returning home from my work at Princeton University. It was a warm day, doors stood open. I lived in one of a row of attached houses in which faculty members were housed. I walked in the door. I was not surprised to find my neighbor's wife in the house: she and my wife often visited. But I was slightly startled when, as I settled into a chair, she offered me a drink. Nevertheless, I accepted with gratitude. While she was in the kitchen making the drink I noticed that the furniture had been rearranged, something my wife did from time to time. And then I realized the furniture had not only been rearranged, but much of it was new—or new to *me*. Real insight began when it slowly came to me that the room I was in, though identical in size and shape to the room I was familiar with, was a mirror-image of that room; stairs and fireplace had switched sides, as had the door to the kitchen. I had walked into the house next to mine.

Here is a case of gross factual error. Instead of using the evidence at hand in a natural way to support the obvious hypothesis, I somehow managed to accommodate the growing evidence against the assumption that I was in my own house by fabricating more and more absurd or far-fetched explanations. Was I being irrational in believing I was in my own house? Well, that belief by itself, however strange or odd, was surely not irrational or even foolish. But given the accumulating evidence against my belief? Of course it would have been irrational to believe I was in my own house on the basis of contrary evidence. But did I have contrary evidence? Not from *my* point of view, for I thought that my neighbor's wife was being exceptionally kind in offering me a drink in my own house; I thought my own wife had rearranged the furniture and even introduced some new furniture. I did not so much as entertain the hypothesis that I was not in my own house, and so did not make the possibly absurd mistake of supposing my evidence supported the hypothesis I was in my own house rather than in another.

Is there a point of view from which we can make out that my belief that I was in my own house was irrational? No doubt there is. I believe, like everyone else, that when I have to invent strange explanations of what I think I see or believe I should consider alternative hypotheses. If I had adhered to my own standards of hypothesis formation, of "inference to the best explanation" as Harman calls it, I would have wondered much sooner than I did whether my assumption that I was in my own house was correct. I clung to a premature assumption far too long, and in rearranging so many beliefs (subjective probabilities), I failed to apply Quine's principle of conservation: other things being equal, change as few expectations as possible when accommodating recalcitrant appearances. So there is a clear sense in which I held a pattern of beliefs not in accord with my own best standards of rationality. I was not aware of this. Nevertheless, I was in a state of *inner inconsistency*.

Suppose that, contrary to the facts, I had asked myself whether I was in my house or in my neighbor's house, and had acknowledged that the evidence, though not absolutely conclusive, favored the hypothesis that I was in my neighbor's house. Then I would again have been in a state of inner inconsistency *provided* I held to the general principle that one ought to adjust one's degree of belief in a hypothesis to what one deems to be the extent to which it is supported by all one's available evidence—what one takes to be the available evidence, of course, since one can do no better.

What this example, with its various applications, suggests is that no factual belief *by itself*, no matter how egregious it seems to others, can be held to be irrational. It is only when beliefs are inconsistent with other beliefs according to principles held by the agent himself—in other words, only when there is an inner inconsistency—that there is a clear case of irrationality. Strictly speaking, then, the irrationality consists not in any particular belief but in inconsistency within a set of beliefs (or within a set consisting of beliefs combined with principles, if principles are to be distinguished from beliefs). I think we must say much the same about intentions, intentional actions, and other propositional attitudes (usually, or perhaps always, in conjunction with beliefs or principles). They are never irrational in themselves, but only as part of a larger pattern.

We often do say of a single belief or action or emotion that it is irrational, but I think that on reflection it will be found that this is because we assume in these cases that there must be an inner inconsistency. The item we choose to call irrational is apt then to be the one by rejecting which things are most easily or economically brought back into line. If I buy a lottery ticket believing it will win, you may well be right in calling me irrational. But the belief that the ticket is a winning ticket cannot by itself make me irrational; after all, I might have, or legitimately think I have, inside information. In accusing me of irrationality you assume I have no such information;

you assume I know I have only one chance in many of winning, and in the light of *this* belief (and further beliefs and principles), my belief that I will win is absurd. My beliefs cannot be made to fit together according to my own views of how probabilities should be distributed over beliefs.

Or suppose that I am ashamed that I am not six feet tall. Such an emotion is, many would hold, an irrational emotion. If it is irrational, the reason must be something like this: one can be ashamed of having some trait only if one believes one has it and holds that having that trait is blameworthy. But something is blameworthy only if it is something for which one is responsible, and one cannot be responsible for not being six feet tall. If something like this account is correct, we again find that irrationality is a feature of a complex of attitudes, not of isolated parts of the complex. It may be that I think I *am* responsible for my not being six feet tall; then I am not, after all, irrational in being ashamed of not being six feet tall. Of course, my belief that I am responsible for my not being six feet tall may itself be inconsistent with other things I believe, in which case irrationality is present in another way. The point remains: we call a single attitude, belief, or action irrational only when we assume it conflicts with other beliefs or attitudes of the agent.

Here is an example of an irrational *action*. I stay up late arguing with a friend about politics even though I know I will not be able to change his mind (nor he mine) and I do not enjoy the clash of opinion. My action is an example of akrasia, since I am acting contrary to my own best judgment. No doubt there are reasons why I go on arguing: I am exasperated by my friend's false views and warped values (as I see them), and I cannot resist the desire to set him straight, even though I know I will not succeed. I have my reasons for acting as I do, then, but these reasons are outweighed, in my own sober judgment, by the reasons I have against continuing the argument. Once more, it is not the isolated item, in this case the action itself, that proves irrationality. The irrationality depends on the discrepancy between the action and the reasons I recognize as relevant to its performance.

As in the other examples, there is much more to say here, and the need for distinctions. Any action, for example, may be described in endless ways that are irrelevant to its irrationality even in context. But it is always relevant to questions of rationality and irrationality to consider the description of an action under which it is intentional.

An intention (or so I have argued[1]) consists in an evaluative judgment of a certain kind, and in the case of my ill-considered late night political argument, this judgment is literally inconsistent with the judgment enjoined by the "principle of continence" which says one should prefer (act on) the judgment based on all the considerations deemed relevant. Intentional actions entail the existence of intentions, and so acting with a certain intention can entail the existence of a judgment that is inconsistent with other attitudes and principles of the agent. Strictly speaking, then, we might want to say the irrationality lies in the inconsistency of the intention with other attitudes and principles rather than in the inconsistency of the action of which it is an intention with those attitudes and principles.

So far, my thesis (far from proven, of course) is that all (objective) irrationality is a matter of inner inconsistency. But there is a difficulty which brings us back to the question with which I began: what, or whose, standards are at stake? It may seem that this matter was settled when it was decided that irrationality is always inner; this might be taken to show that the standards that matter are those of the agent alone. However, here there lurks an unexplored and undefended assumption which might be put this way: why must *inconsistency* be considered irrational? (Alternatively, or perhaps equivalently, one could ask: who is to decide what consistency demands?) Isn't this just one more evaluative judgment, and one that an agent might reject? Emerson did not see consistency as an intellectual virtue. When sufficiently aroused, my father would sometimes reply to the accusation that he had contradicted himself by saying, "I'll contradict myself if I want to."

Let me take one more example. Imagine that you want to rent a house, and three houses are available, a large house that rents for $1,000 a month, a medium-sized house that rents for $800 a month, and a small house that rents for $600 a month. You prefer the large house to the medium-sized house, since the difference in cost is relatively small; you prefer the medium to the small on the same ground. But you also prefer the small to the large, since in this case the difference in cost is enough to outweigh considerations of size. Is the set of your preferences irrational? I may remind you that according to

---

[1] In essay 5 in *Essays on Actions and Events*, Oxford University Press, 1980. See also my replies to Michael Bratman, Paul Grice and Judith Baker, and Christopher Peacocke in *Essays on Davidson, Actions and Events*, ed. Bruce Vermazen and Merrill Hintikka, Oxford University Press, 1985.

rational decision theory your preferences form an inconsistent triad, and so you are irrational. Suppose you reply, "So what; those are *your* standards of rationality, not mine." "Well (I argue), decision theory (and common sense) says to choose an option available to you such that none is preferred to it. How can you do this, since whatever option you hit on, there is another you like better?" "Hold on (you retort), what *are* my options? If they are the large house and the medium, I take the large; if the medium and the small, I take the medium; if the large and the small, I take the small." "Aha! (I snort) And suppose I offer you all three; then what?" "Easy (you smile): I take the large." "But you prefer the small to the large." "Only (you reply) in case my choice is between the large and the small only; if the medium is also available, I prefer the large."

At this point there are several lines I might take. I might complain that it is irrational to change one's preference of the large over the small just because another option is available; but I may have trouble explaining why this is irrational. Or I may point out that a dutch book can be made against you: given your declared preferences, you can be offered a set of bets such that no matter what happens you lose by your own admission. Plenty of questionable assumptions are needed for this argument.

I am strongly inclined to think my mistake in this imagined exchange came right at the start: I should never have tried to pin you down to an admission that you ought to subscribe to the principles of decision theory. For I think everyone does subscribe to those principles, whether he knows it or not. This does not imply, of course, that no one ever reasons, believes, chooses, or acts contrary to those principles, but only that if someone does go against those principles, he goes against his own principles.

I would say the same about the basic principles of logic, the principle of total evidence for inductive reasoning, or the analogous principle of continence. These are principles shared by all creatures that have propositional attitudes or act intentionally; and since I am (I hope) one of those creatures, I can put it this way: all thinking creatures subscribe to *my* basic standards or norms of rationality. This sounds sweeping, even authoritarian, but it comes to no more than this, that it is a condition of having thoughts, judgments, and intentions that the basic standards of rationality have application. The reason is this. Beliefs, intentions, and desires are identified, first, by their causal relations to events and objects in the world, and, second, by their relations to one another. A belief that it is about to rain would lose much of its claim to be just *that* belief if it did not have some tendency to cause someone who had it and wanted to stay dry to take appropriate action, such as carrying an umbrella. Nor would a belief that it is about to rain plausibly be identified as such if someone who was thought to have that belief also believed that if it rains it pours and did not believe it was about to pour. And so on: these obvious logical relations amongst beliefs; amongst beliefs, desires, and intentions; between beliefs and the world, make beliefs the beliefs they are; therefore they cannot in general lose these relations and remain the same beliefs. Such relations are *constitutive* of the propositional attitudes.

I have greatly oversimplified by making it seem that there is a definite, and short, list of "basic principles of rationality". There is no such list. The kinds and degrees of deviation from the norms of rationality that we can understand or explain are not settled in advance. We make sense of aberrations when they are seen against a background of rationality; but the background can be constituted in various ways to make various forms of battiness comprehensible. So it would be a mistake to put too much weight on the examples of irrationality that I have chosen, and worse to worry whether I have in each case drawn the line between principles constitutive of rationality and potentially intelligible flaws in just the right place. The essential point is that the more flamboyant the irrationality we ascribe to an agent, the less clear it is how to describe any of his attitudes, whether deviant or not, and that the more basic we take a norm to be, the less it is an empirical question whether the agent's thought and behavior are in accord with it.

If this is so, then it does not make sense to ask, concerning a creature with propositional attitudes, whether that creature is *in general* rational, whether its attitudes and intentional actions are in accord with the basic standards of rationality. Rationality, in this primitive sense, is a condition of having thoughts at all. The question whether a creature "subscribes" to the principle of continence, or to the logic of the sentential calculus, or to the principle of total evidence for inductive reasoning, is not an empirical question. For it is only by interpreting a creature as largely in accord with these principles that we can intelligibly attribute propositional attitudes to it, or that we can raise the question whether it is in some respect irrational. We see then that my word "subscribe" is misleading. Agents can't *decide* whether or not to accept the fundamental attributes of rationality: if they are in a position to decide anything, they have those attributes. (It is no doubt for this reason that Aristotle held that an agent could not be *habitually* akratic; akrasia is deviation from a norm shared by all creatures capable of akratic acts.)

An agent cannot fail to comport most of the time with the basic norms of rationality, and it is this fact that makes irrationality possible. For if someone does on occasion think or act or feel in ways that offend against those norms, he must have departed from his own standards, that is, from his usual and best modes of thought and behavior. Inner inconsistency is possible just because there are norms no agent can lack. The inconsistency does not have to be recognized by the agent, though of course it may be, nor does the existence of inconsistency depend on the agent's being able to formulate the principles against which he offends. The possibility of (objective) inconsistency depends on nothing more than this, that an agent, a creature with propositional attitudes, must show much consistency in his thought and action, and in this sense *have* the fundamental values of rationality; yet he may depart from these, his own, norms.

To identify at least some irrationalities with inner inconsistencies, as I have in this paper, is not to explain, or even to go very far in describing, such psychological states; indeed, it makes the problems of description and explanation seem impossible. For if a person really is at a given moment harboring an inconsistent set of beliefs and attitudes, we must suppose that the views, values, and principles that create the conflict are at that moment all active tendencies or forces. It is not enough to think of one or more of the elements that create the conflict as potential and no more, or as creating a merely statistical preponderance of the rational over the irrational, where the irrational events are in the minority, but a minority expected in its numbers, and its members no more demanding explanation one by one than the events on the side of reason. Such a picture would not raise the problems here under discussion, since it would make inconsistency diachronic, not synchronic. Diachronic inconsistency is interesting in its own right, but not puzzling in the same way that synchronic inconsistency is.

Synchronic inconsistency requires that all the beliefs, desires, intentions, and principles of the agent that create the inconsistency are present at once and are in some sense in operation—are live psychic forces. It is by no means easy to conceive how a single mind can be described in this way.

We cannot, I think, ever make sense of someone's accepting a plain and obvious contradiction: no one can believe a proposition of the form (p and not-p) while appreciating that the proposition is of this form. If we attribute such a belief to someone, it is we as interpreters who have made the mistake. But if someone has inconsistent beliefs or attitudes, as I have claimed (objective) irrationality demands, then he must at times believe some proposition p and also believe its negation. It is between these cases that I would draw the line: someone can believe p and at the same time believe not-p; he cannot believe (p and not-p). In the possible case, of simultaneously, and in some sense actively, believing contradictory propositions, the thinker fails to put two and two (or one and one) together, even though this failure is a failure by his own (and our) standards. This is why I have urged, in several recent papers, that it is only by postulating a kind of compartmentalization of the mind that we can understand, and begin to explain, irrationality.[2]

In this paper, however, I have not attempted to describe or explain states of irrationality; I have been concerned only to show that judgments of irrationality do not have to be subjective; they may, on the contrary, be as objective as any of our attributions of thoughts, desires, and intentions.[3]

[2] For example in essay 2 in *Essays on Actions and Events*; "Paradoxes of Irrationality", in *Philosophical Essays on Freud*, ed. Richard Wollheim and James Hopkins, Cambridge University Press, 1982; and "Deception and Division", in *The Multiple Self*, ed. Jon Elster, Cambridge University Press, forthcoming.

[3] An earlier draft of the present paper was discussed by John McDowell at the 1984 meeting of the Institut International de Philosophie, and I have profited from his comments.

13 *Deception and Division*

Self-deception is usually no great problem for its practitioner; on the contrary, it typically relieves a person of some of the burden of painful thoughts, the causes of which are beyond his or her control. But self-deception is a problem for philosophical psychology. For in thinking about self-deception, as in thinking about other forms of irrationality, we find ourselves tempted by opposing thoughts. On the one hand, it is not clear that there is a genuine case of irrationality unless an inconsistency in the thought of the agent can be identified, something that is inconsistent by the standards of the agent himself. On the other hand, when we try to explain in any detail how the agent can have come to be in this state, we find ourselves inventing some form of rationalization that we can attribute to the self-deceiver, thus diluting the imputed inconsistency. Self-deception is notoriously troublesome, since in some of its manifestations it seems to require us not only to say that someone believes both a certain proposition and its negation, but also to hold that the one belief sustains the other.

Consider these four statements:

(1) D believes that he is bald.
(2) D believes that he is not bald.
(3) D believes that (he is bald and he is not bald).
(4) D does not believe that he is bald.

In the sort of self-deception that I shall discuss, a belief like that reported in (1) is a causal condition of a belief which contradicts it, such as (2). It is tempting, of course, to suppose that (2) entails (4), but if we allow this, we will contradict ourselves. In the attempt to give a consistent description of D's inconsistent frame of mind, we might then say that since D both believes that he is not bald and believes that he is bald (which is why (4) is false) he must then believe that he is bald and not bald, as (3) states. This step also must be resisted: nothing a person could say or do would count as good enough grounds for the attribution of a straightforwardly and obviously contradictory belief, just as nothing could sustain an interpretation of a sincerely and literally asserted sentence as a sentence that was true if and only if D was both bald and not bald, though the words uttered may have been 'D is and is not bald'. It is possible to believe each of two statements without believing the conjunction of the two.

We have the task, then, of explaining how someone can have beliefs like (1) and (2) without his putting (1) and (2) together, even though he believes (2) *because* he believes (1).

The problem may be generalized in the following way. Probably it seldom happens that a person is *certain* that some proposition is true and also certain that the negation is true. A more common situation would be that the sum of the evidence available to the agent points to the truth of some proposition, which inclines the agent to believe it (make him treat it as more likely to be true than not). This inclination (high subjective probability) causes him, in ways to be discussed, to seek, favour or emphasize the evidence for the falsity of the proposition, or to disregard the evidence for its truth. The agent then is more inclined than not to believe the negation of the original proposition, even though the totality of the evidence available to him does not support this attitude. (The phrase 'inclined to believe' is too anodyne for some of the states of mind I want it to describe; perhaps one can say the agent believes the proposition is false, but is not quite certain of this.)

This characterization of self-deception makes it similar in an important way to weakness of the will. Weakness of the will is a matter of acting intentionally (or forming an intention to act) on the basis of less than all the reasons one recognizes as relevant. A weak-willed action occurs in a context of conflict; the akratic agent has what he takes to be reasons both for and against a course of action. He judges, on the basis of all his reasons, that one course of action is best, yet opts for another; he has acted 'contrary to his own best judgement'.[1] In one sense, it is easy to say why he acted as he did, since he had reasons for his action. But this explanation leaves aside the element of irrationality; it does not explain why the agent went against his own best judgement.

[1] I discuss weakness of the will in essay 2 of *Essays on Actions and Events*, Oxford: Oxford University Press, 1980.

An act that reveals weakness of the will sins against the normative principle that one should not intentionally perform an action when one judges on the basis of what one deems to be all the available considerations that an alternative and accessible course of action would be better.[2] This principle, which I call the Principle of Continence, enjoins a fundamental kind of consistency in thought, intention, evaluation and action. An agent who acts in accordance with this principle has the virtue of continence. It is not clear whether a person could fail to recognize the norm of continence; this is an issue to which I shall turn presently. In any case, it is clear that there are many people who accept the norm but fail from time to time to act in accordance with it. In such cases, not only do agents fail to conform their actions to their own principles, but they also fail to reason as they think they should. For their intentional action shows they have set a higher value on the act they perform than their principles and their reasons say they should.

Self-deception and weakness of the will often reinforce one another, but they are not the same thing. This may be seen from the fact that the outcome of weakness of the will is an intention, or an intentional action, while the outcome of self-deception is a belief. The former consists of or essentially involves a faultily reached evaluative attitude, the latter of a faultily reached cognitive attitude.

Weakness of the will is analogous to a certain cognitive error, which I shall call *weakness of the warrant*. Weakness of the warrant can occur only when a person has evidence both for and against a hypothesis; the person judges that relative to all the evidence available to him, the hypothesis is more probable than not; yet he does not accept the hypothesis (or the strength of his belief in the hypothesis is less than the strength of his belief in the negation of the hypothesis). The normative principle against which such a person has sinned is what Hempel and Carnap have called *the requirement of total evidence for inductive reasoning*: when we are deciding among a set of mutually exclusive hypotheses, this requirement enjoins us to give credence to the hypothesis most highly supported by all available relevant evidence.[3] Weakness of the warrant obviously has the same logical structure

---

[2] What considerations are 'available' to the agent? Does this include only information he has, or does it also embrace information he could (if he knew this?) obtain? In this essay I must leave most of these questions open.

[3] See Carl Hempel, *Aspects of Scientific Explanation*, New York: Free Press, 1965, pp. 397–403.

(or, better, illogical structure) as weakness of the will; the former involves an irrational belief in the face of conflicting evidence, the latter an irrational intention (and perhaps also action) in the face of conflicting values. The existence of conflict is a necessary condition of both forms of irrationality, and may in some cases be a cause of the lapse; but there is nothing about conflict of these kinds that necessarily requires or reveals a failure of reason.

Weakness of the warrant is not a matter simply of overlooking evidence one has (though 'purposeful' overlooking may be another matter, and one that is relevant to self-deception), nor is it a matter of not appreciating the fact that things one knows or believes constitute evidence for or against a hypothesis. Taken at face value, the following story does not show me to have been self-deceived. A companion and I were spying on the animals in the Amboseli National Park in Kenya. Self-guided we did not find a cheetah, so we hired an official guide for a morning. After returning the guide to Park Headquarters, I spoke along these lines to my companion: 'Too bad we didn't find a cheetah; that's the only large animal we've missed. Say, didn't that guide have an oddly high-pitched voice? And do you think it is common for a man in these parts to be named "Helen"? I suppose that was the official uniform, but it seems strange he was wearing a skirt.' My companion: 'He was a she.' My original assumption was stereotyped and stupid, but unless I considered the hypothesis that the guide was a woman and rejected it in spite of the evidence, this was not a simple case of self-deception. Others may think of deeper explanations for my stubborn assumption that our guide was a man.

Suppose that (whatever the truth may be) I did consider the possibility that the guide was a woman, and rejected that hypothesis despite the overwhelming evidence I had to the contrary. Would this necessarily show I was irrational? It is hard to say unless we are able to make a strong distinction between lacking certain standards of reasoning and failing to apply them. Suppose, for example, that though I had the evidence, I failed to recognize what it was evidence for? Surely this *can* happen. How likely an explanation it is depends on the exact circumstances. So let us insist that there is no failure of inductive reasoning unless the evidence is taken to be evidence. And could it not happen that though the evidence was taken to be evidence, the fact that the totality of evidence made some hypothesis overwhelmingly probable was not appreciated? This too could happen, however unlikely it might be in a particular case. There are endless further questions that the tortoise can ask Achilles along these lines (there being as many gaps that unhappy reasoning may fail to close as happy reasoning must). So without trying to specify all the conditions that make for an absolutely clear case of weakness of the warrant, I want to raise one more question. Must someone accept the requirement of total evidence for inductive reasoning before his or her failure to act in accordance with the requirement demonstrates irrationality? Several issues are embedded in this question.

We should not demand of someone who accepts it that he or she always reasons or thinks in accordance with the requirement, otherwise a real inconsistency, an inner inconsistency, of this kind would be impossible. On the other hand, it would not make sense to suppose that someone could accept the principle and seldom or never think in accordance with it; at least part of what it is to accept such a principle is to manifest the principle in thinking and reasoning. If we grant, then, as I think we must, that for a person to 'accept' or have a principle like the requirement of total evidence mainly consists in that person's pattern of thoughts being in accordance with the principle, it makes sense to imagine that a person has the principle without being aware of it or able to articulate it. But we might want to add to the obvious subjunctive conditional ('a person accepts the requirement of total evidence for inductive reasoning only if that person is disposed in the appropriate circumstances to conform to it') some further condition or conditions, for example that conformity is more likely when there is more time for thought, less associated emotional investment in the conclusion, or when explicit Socratic tutoring is provided.

Weakness of the warrant in someone who accepts the requirement of total evidence is, we see, a matter of departing from a custom or habit. In such a case, weakness of the warrant shows inconsistency and is clearly irrational. But what if someone does not accept the requirement? Here a very general question about rationality would seem to arise: whose standards are to be taken as fixing the norm? Should we say that someone whose thinking does not satisfy the requirement of total evidence may be irrational by one person's standards but not (if he does not accept the requirement) by his own standards? Or should we make inner inconsistency a necessary condition of irrationality? It is not easy to see how the questions can be separated, since inner consistency is itself a fundamental norm.

In the case of fundamental norms the questions cannot be clearly separated. For in general the more striking a case of inner inconsistency seems to an outsider, the less use the outsider can make, in trying to explain the apparent aberration, of a supposed distinction between his own norms and those of the person observed. Relatively small differences take shape and are explained against a background of shared norms, but serious deviations from fundamental standards of rationality are more apt to be in the eye of the interpreter than in the mind of the interpreted. The reason for this is not far to seek. The propositional attitudes of one person are understood by another only to the extent that the first person can assign his own propositions (or sentences) to the various attitudes of the other. Because a proposition cannot maintain its identity while losing its relations to other propositions, the same proposition cannot serve to interpret particular attitudes of different people and yet stand in very different relations to the other attitudes of one person than to those of another. It follows that unless an interpreter can replicate the main outlines of his own pattern of attitudes in another person he cannot intelligibly identify any of the attitudes of that person. It is only because the relations of an attitude to other attitudes ramify in so many and complex ways—logical, epistemological and etiological—that it is possible to make sense of some deviations from one's own norms in others.

The issue raised a few paragraphs back, whether irrationality in an agent requires an *inner* inconsistency, a deviation from that person's own norms, is now seen to be misleading. For where the norms are basic they are constitutive elements in the identification of attitudes and so the question whether someone 'accepts' them cannot arise. All genuine inconsistencies are deviations from the person's own norms. This goes not only for patently logical inconsistencies but also for weakness of the will (as Aristotle pointed out), for weakness of the warrant and for self-deception.

We have yet to say what self-deception is, but we are now in a position to make a number of points about it. Self-deception includes, for example, weakness of the warrant. This is clear because the proposition with respect to which a person is self-deceived is one he would not accept if he were relieved of his error; he has better reasons for accepting the negation of the proposition. And as in weakness of the warrant, the self-deceiver knows he has better reasons for accepting the negation of the proposition he accepts, in this sense at least: he realizes that conditional on certain other things he knows or accepts as evidence, the negation is more likely to be true than the proposition he accepts; yet on the basis of a part only of what he takes to be the relevant evidence he accepts the proposition.

It is just at this point that self-deception goes beyond weakness of the warrant, for the person who is self-deceived must have a *reason* for his weakness of the warrant, and he must have played a part in bringing it about. Weakness of the warrant always has a *cause*, but in the case of self-deception weakness of the warrant is self-induced. It is no part of the analysis of weakness of the warrant or weakness of the will that the falling off from the agent's standards is motivated (though no doubt it often is), but this is integral to the analysis of self-deception. For this reason it is instructive to consider another phenomenon that is in some ways like self-deception: wishful thinking.

A minimal account of wishful thinking makes it a case of believing something because one wishes it were true. This is not irrational in itself, for we are not in general responsible for the causes of our thoughts. But wishful thinking is often irrational, for example if we know why we have the belief and that we would not have it if it were not for the wish.

Wishful thinking is often thought to involve more than the minimal account. If someone wishes that a certain proposition were true, it is natural to assume that he or she would enjoy believing it true more than not believing it true. Such a person therefore has a reason for believing the proposition. If he or she were intentionally to act in such a way as to promote the belief, would that be irrational? Here we must make an obvious distinction between having a reason to be a believer in a certain proposition, and having evidence in the light of which it is reasonable to think the proposition true. (Sentences of the form 'Charles has a reason to believe that *p*' are ambiguous with respect to this distinction.) A reason of the first sort is evaluative: it provides a motive for acting in such a way as to promote having a belief. A reason of the second kind is cognitive: it consists in evidence one has for the truth of a proposition. Wishful thinking does not demand a reason of either sort, but, as just remarked, the wish that *p* can easily engender a desire to be a believer in *p*, and this desire can prompt thoughts and actions that emphasize or result in obtaining reasons of the second kind. Is there anything necessarily irrational in this sequence? An intentional action that aims to make one happy, or to relieve distress, is not in itself irrational. Nor does it become so if the means employed involve trying to arrange matters so that one comes to have a certain belief. It may in some cases be immoral to do this

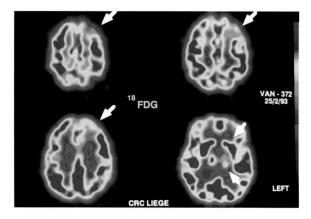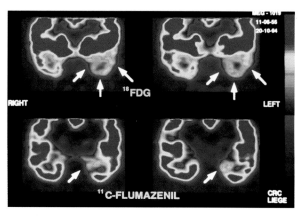

to someone else, especially if one has reason to think the belief to be instilled is false, but this is not necessarily wrong, and certainly not irrational. I think the same goes for self-induced beliefs; what it is not necessarily irrational to do to someone else it is not necessarily irrational to do to one's future self.

Is a belief deliberately begotten in the way described necessarily irrational? Clearly it is if one continues to think the evidence against the belief is better than the evidence in its favour, for then it is a case of weakness of the warrant. But if one has forgotten the evidence that at the start made one reject the presently entertained belief, or the new evidence now seems good enough to offset the old, the new state of mind is not irrational. When wishful thinking succeeds, one might say, there is no moment at which the thinker must be irrational.[4]

It is worth mentioning that both self-deception and wishful thinking are often benign. It is neither surprising nor on the whole bad that people think better of their friends and families than a clear-eyed survey of the evidence would justify. Learning is probably more often encouraged than not by parents and teachers who overrate the intelligence of their wards. Spouses often keep things on an even keel by ignoring or overlooking the lipstick on the collar. All these can be cases of charitable self-deception aided by wishful thinking.

Not all wishful thinking is self-deception, since the latter but not the former requires intervention by the agent. Nevertheless they are alike in that a motivational or evaluative element must be at work, and in this they differ from weakness of the warrant, where the defining fault is cognitive whatever its cause may be. This suggests that while wishful thinking may be simpler than self-deception, it is always an ingredient in it. No doubt it very often is, but there seem to be exceptions. In wishful thinking belief takes the direction of positive affect, never of negative; the caused belief is always welcome. This is not the case with self-deception. The thought bred by self-deception may be painful. A person driven by jealousy may find 'evidence' everywhere that confirms his worst suspicions; someone who seeks privacy may think he sees a spy behind every curtain. If a pessimist is someone

---

[4] In 'Paradoxes of Irrationality', in R. A. Wollheim and J. Hopkins (eds.), *Philosophical Essays on Freud*, Cambridge: Cambridge University Press, (1982), I assumed that in wishful thinking the wish produced the belief without providing any evidence in favour of the belief. In such a case the belief is, of course, irrational.

who takes a darker view of matters than his evidence justifies, every pessimist is to some extent self-deceived into believing what he wishes were not the case.

These observations merely hint at the nature of the distance that may separate self-deception and wishful thinking. Not only is there the fact that self-deception requires the agent to *do* something with the aim of changing his own views, while wishful thinking does not, but there is also a difference in how the content of the affective element is related to the belief it produces. In the case of the wishful thinker, what he comes to believe must be just what he wishes were the case. But while the self-deceiver may be motivated by a desire to believe what he wishes were the case, there are many other possibilities. Indeed, it is hard to say what the relation must be between the motive someone has who deceives himself and the specific alteration in belief he works in himself. Of course the relation is not accidental; it is not self-deception simply to do something intentionally with the consequence that one is deceived, for then a person would be self-deceived if he read and believed a false report in a newspaper. The self-deceiver must intend the 'deception'.

To this extent, at least, self-deception is like lying; there is intentional behaviour which aims to produce a belief the agent does not, when he institutes the behaviour, share. The suggestion is that the liar aims to deceive another person, while the self-deceiver aims to deceive himself. The suggestion is not far wrong. I deceive myself as to how bald I am by choosing views and lighting that favour a hirsute appearance; a lying flatterer might try for the same effect by telling me I am not all that bald. But there are important differences between the cases. While the liar may intend his hearer to believe what he says, this intention is not essential to the concept of lying; a liar who believes that his hearer is perverse may say the opposite of what he intends his hearer to believe. A liar may not even intend to make his victim believe that he, the liar, believes what he says. The only intentions a liar must have, I think, are these: (1) he must intend to represent himself as believing what he does not (for example, and typically, by asserting what he does not believe), and (2) he must intend to keep this intention (though not necessarily what he actually believes) hidden from his hearer. So deceit of a very special kind is involved in lying, deceit with respect to the sincerity of the representation of one's beliefs. It does not seem possible that this precise form of deceit could be practised on oneself, since it would require doing something with the intention that that very intention should not be recognized by the intender.[5]

In one respect, then, self-deception is not as hard to explain as lying to oneself would be, for lying to oneself would entail the existence of a self-defeating intention, while self-deception pits intention and desire against belief, and belief against belief. Still, this is hard enough to understand. Before trying to describe in slightly more and plausible detail the state of mind of the self-deceived agent, let me summarize the discussion up to here so far as it bears on the nature of self-deception.

An agent A is self-deceived with respect to a proposition p under the following conditions. A has evidence on the basis of which he believes that p is more apt to be true than its negation; the thought that p, or the thought that he ought rationally to believe p, motivates A to act in such a way as to cause himself to believe the negation of p. The action involved may be no more than an intentional directing of attention away from the evidence in favour of p; or it may involve the active search for evidence against p. All that self-deception demands of the action is that the motive originates in a belief that p is true (or recognition that the evidence makes it more likely to be true than not), and that the action be done with the intention of producing a belief in the negation of p. Finally, and it is especially this that makes self-deception a problem, the state that motivates self-deception and the state it produces coexist; in the strongest case, the belief that p not only causes a belief in the negation of p, but also sustains it. Self-deception is thus a form of self-induced weakness of the warrant, where the motive for inducing a belief is a contradictory belief (or what is deemed to be sufficient evidence in favour of the contradictory belief). In some, but not all, cases, the motive springs from the fact that the agent wishes that the proposition, a belief in which he induces, were true, or a fear that it might not be. So self-deception often involves wishful thinking as well.

What is hard to explain is how a belief, or the perception that one has sufficient reasons for a belief, can sustain a contrary belief. Of course it cannot sustain it in the sense of giving it rational support; 'sustain'

[5] One can intend to hide a present intention from one's future self. So I might try to avoid an unpleasant meeting scheduled a year ahead by deliberately writing a wrong date in my appointment book, counting on my bad memory to have forgotten my deed when the time comes. This is not a pure case of self-deception, since the intended belief is not *sustained* by the intention that produced it, and there is not necessarily anything irrational about it.

here must mean only 'cause'. What we must do is find a point in the sequence of mental states where there is a cause that is not a reason; something irrational according to the agent's own standards.[6]

Here, in outline, is how I think a typical case of self-deception may come about: in this example, weakness of the warrant is self-induced through wishful thinking. Carlos has good reason to believe he will not pass the test for a driving licence. He has failed the test twice before and his instructor has said discouraging things. On the other hand, he knows the examiner personally, and he has faith in his own charm. He is aware that the totality of the evidence points to failure. Like the rest of us he normally reasons in accordance with the requirement of total evidence. But the thought of failing the test once again is painful to Carlos (in fact the thought of failing at anything is particularly galling to Carlos). So he has a perfectly natural motive for believing he will not fail the test, that is, he has a motive for making it the case that he is a person who believes he will (probably) pass the test. His practical reasoning is straightforward. Other things being equal, it is better to avoid pain; believing he will fail the test is painful; therefore (other things being equal) it is better to avoid believing he will fail the test. Since it is a condition of his problem that he take the test, this means it would be better to believe he will pass. He does things to promote this belief, perhaps obtaining new evidence in favour of believing he will pass. It may simply be a matter of pushing the negative evidence into the background or accentuating the positive. But whatever the devices (and of course there are many), core cases of self-deception demand that Carlos remain aware that his evidence favours the belief that he will fail, for it is awareness of this fact that motivates his efforts to rid himself of the fear that he will fail.

Suppose Carlos succeeds in inducing in himself the belief that he will pass the test. He then is guilty of weakness of the warrant, for though he has supporting evidence for his belief, he knows, or anyway thinks, he has better reasons to think he will fail. This is an irrational state; but at what point did irrationality enter? Where was there a mental cause that was not a reason for what it caused?

There are a number of answers that I have either explicitly or implicitly rejected. One is David Pears' suggestion that the self-deceiver must 'forget' or otherwise conceal from himself how he came to

---

[6] The idea that irrationality always entails the existence of a mental cause of a mental state for which it is not a reason is discussed at length in 'Paradoxes of Irrationality'.

believe what he does.[7] I agree that the self-deceiver would *like* to do this, and if he does, he has in a clear sense succeeded in deceiving himself. But this degree and kind of success makes self-deception a process and not a state, and it is unclear that at any moment the self-deceiver is in an irrational state. I think self-deception must be arrived at by a process, but then can be a continuing and clearly irrational state. Pears' agent ends up in a pleasantly consistent frame of mind. Luckily this often happens. But the pleasure may be unstable, as it probably is in Carlos' case, for the pleasing thought is threatened by reality, or even just memory. When reality (or memory) continues to threaten the self-induced belief of the self-deceived, continuing motivation is necessary to hold the happy thought in place. If this is right, then the self-deceiver cannot afford to forget the factor that above all prompted his self-deceiving behaviour: the preponderance of evidence against the induced belief.

I have by implication also rejected Kent Bach's solution, for he thinks the self-deceiver cannot actually believe in the weight of the contrary evidence. Like Pears, he sees self-deception as a sequence, the end product of which is too strongly in conflict with the original motivation to coexist with an awareness of it.[8] Perhaps these differences between my views and those of Pears and Bach may be viewed as at least partly due to different choices as to how to describe self-deception rather than to substantive differences. To me it seems important to identify an incoherence or inconsistency in the thought of the self-deceiver; Pears and Bach are more concerned to examine the conditions of success in deceiving oneself.[9] The difficulty is to keep these considerations in balance: emphasizing the first element makes the irrationality clear but psychologically hard to explain; emphasizing the second element makes it easier to account for the phenomenon by playing down the irrationality.

I have yet to answer the question at what point in the sequence that leads to a state of self-deception there is a mental cause that is not

---

[7] See David Pears, 'Motivated Irrationality', in *Philosophical Essays on Freud* (see n. 4 above), and Pears, 'The Goals and Strategies of Self-Deception', in *The Multiple Self*, ed. J. Elster, Cambridge University Press, 1982. The differences between my view and Pears' are small compared to the similarities. This is no accident, since my discussion owes much to both of his papers.

[8] See Kent Bach, 'An Analysis of Self-deception', *Philosophy and Phenomenological Review*, 41, 1981, pp. 351–70.

[9] Thus I agree with Jon Elster when he says that self-deception requires 'the simultaneous entertainment of incompatible beliefs'. *Ulysses and the Sirens*, Cambridge: Cambridge University Press, 1979, p. 174.

a reason for the mental state it causes. The answer partly depends on the answer to another question. At the start I assumed that although it is possible simultaneously to believe each of a set of inconsistent propositions, it is not possible to believe the conjunction when the inconsistency is obvious. The self-deceived agent does believe inconsistent propositions if he believes that he is bald and believes he is not bald; Carlos believes inconsistent propositions if he believes he will pass the test and believes he will not pass the test. The difficulty is less striking if the conflict in belief is a standard case of weakness of the warrant, but it remains striking enough given the assumption (for which I argued) that having propositional attitudes entails embracing the requirement of total evidence. How can a person fail to put the inconsistent or incompatible beliefs together?

It would be a mistake to try to give a detailed answer to this question here. The point is that people can and do sometimes keep closely related but opposed beliefs apart. To this extent we must accept the idea that there can be boundaries between parts of the mind; I postulate such a boundary somewhere between any (obviously) conflicting beliefs. Such boundaries are not discovered by introspection; they are conceptual aids to the coherent description of genuine irrationalities.[10]

We should not necessarily think of the boundaries as defining permanent and separate territories. Contradictory beliefs about passing a test must each belong to a vast and identical network of beliefs about tests and related matters if they are to be contradictory. Although they must belong to strongly overlapping territories, the contradictory beliefs do not belong to the same territory; to erase the line between them would destroy one of the beliefs. I see no obvious reason to suppose one of the territories must be closed to consciousness, whatever exactly that means, but it is clear that the agent cannot survey the whole without erasing the boundaries.

It is now possible to suggest an answer to the question where in the sequence of steps that end in self-deception there is an irrational *step*. The irrationality of the resulting state consists in the fact that it contains inconsistent beliefs; the irrational step is therefore the step that makes this possible, the drawing of the boundary that keeps the inconsistent beliefs apart. In the case where self-deception consists in self-induced weakness of the warrant, what must be walled off from the rest of the mind is the requirement of total evidence. What causes

---

[10] I discuss the necessity of 'partitioning' the mind in 'Paradoxes of Irrationality'.

it to be thus temporarily exiled or isolated is, of course, the desire to avoid accepting what the requirement counsels. But this cannot be a *reason* for neglecting the requirement. Nothing can be viewed as a good reason for failing to reason according to one's best standards of rationality.

In the extreme case, when the motive for self-deception springs from a belief that directly contradicts the belief that is induced, the original and motivating belief must be placed out of bounds along with the requirement of total evidence. But being out of bounds does not make the exiled thought powerless; on the contrary, since reason has no jurisdiction across the boundary.

14 *Who is Fooled?*

According to the memoirs of former Secretary of State George Schultz, Ronald Reagan was aware that his agents were offering Iran a ransom of arms to obtain the release of hostages, and George Bush was a full participant in that decision, despite his repeated claims that he was "out of the loop". William Safire, who does not want us to forget these matters, claims that Schultz's evidence shows that "Reagan lied to himself, sticking to a script denying reality; Bush lied only to investigators and the public".[1] Safire does not say that Reagan lied not only to himself but also to investigators and the public; the "only" in "Bush lied only to investigators and the public" suggests this, but it also hints at the idea that since Reagan lied to himself, his behavior was less cynical, less knowingly self-serving, than Bush's. This would, of course, be the case only if Reagan, in lying to himself, succeeded in persuading himself that the deal in which he had connived was not an arms-for-hostages deal.

Suppose that Reagan did persuade himself that he had not agreed to and abetted an arms-for-hostages deal; to what extent would this diminish his responsibility? Well, to the extent that no memory at all of his original knowledge—the knowledge of which his lie relieved him—remained, he would not be guilty of lying to the investigators or the public, for he would not be deliberately saying what he had come to believe to be false. His fault would be rather in the original lie to himself. In this case we might think of him as the only victim of his deceit. But before we decide to hold him relatively blameless, we need to consider his motives in lying to himself, for a lie is an intentional act, and requires a motive. If the motive was to avoid either the political consequences of telling what he at first knew or

[1] William Safire, *The New York Times*, Thursday, Feb. 4, 1993, Section A, p. 23.

the pain of perjuring himself, then the motive included all that we despise in Bush's direct lie, for Reagan's intention, when he lied to himself, could be expressed as: intending to mislead the investigators and the public by persuading someone to whom the investigators and the public would appeal (himself) to say what he then knew to be false. Reagan would have lied to the messenger (Reagan) with the expectation (or intention) that the messenger (the future Reagan) would say in good faith what he (Reagan in the present) knew to be false. It is difficult to find any degree of exculpation in behavior that can be thus described.

But how accurate is this description? This partly depends, of course, on things we do not know, for example whether Reagan lied to himself primarily out of vanity—a wish to think well of himself, or in order to avoid the legitimate censure of others. But there are also conceptual problems. The first such problem concerns the clarity of the notion of lying to oneself. Is it possible to lie to oneself? In trying to answer this question, we must first ask what is involved in telling a lie to anyone. Telling a lie pretty clearly requires a speech act performed with the intention that someone be deceived, that is, misled with respect to the truth of some proposition.[2] In any case, the common assumption that lying involves a speech act already puts a strain on the idea of lying to oneself. Perhaps we can allow that silently addressing words to oneself is a form of speech, but the notion of action demands that this be done with an intention. We do sometimes repeat to ourselves exhortations like "No more cookies today!" or "I shall give up smoking for the next two months!", and these self-addressed remarks may be real acts, even if entirely silent. It is a question, though, whether this is what we typically have in mind when we speak of lying to oneself. We are inclined to think that if we lie to ourselves, we must be unaware that this is what we are doing. Is lying something one can do without knowing it? Maybe.

There is also a difficulty in identifying the proposition with respect to which the liar wishes to mislead. In many cases it is easy to recognize the ultimate intended deception. "It's solid gold" says the seller, intending to persuade the buyer that it is solid gold though the seller knows it is not. Suppose, however, that the seller believes the buyer knows him (the seller) to be a liar, and so says, "This is

---

[2] Here the phrase "misled with respect to the truth of some proposition" must, of course, fall under the scope of the intention: the proposition the liar intends his victim to believe may, contrary to the liar's belief, be true.

a worthless plated trinket; you shouldn't buy it", hoping the buyer will then insist on the purchase. Has the seller lied? He has uttered words literally true, though with the intention of misleading the customer both with respect to his own belief and with respect to the value of the object. While this may be as bad as a lie—or worse—it is not, I think, a genuine lie. The reason it is not helps to characterize the central concept of lying. In both stories the seller can accomplish his end only by asserting what he says, and assertion requires (among other things, no doubt) that the speaker represent himself as believing what he says: thus in saying "It's solid gold", he represents himself as believing what he does not; in saying it is a worthless trinket, he represents himself as believing what he actually believes. A liar must make an assertion, and so represent himself as believing what he does not.

The liar succeeds in deceiving his audience only if his intention to misrepresent what he believes is not discerned. On the other hand, there is an intention he must intend to be recognized, namely the intention to be taken as making an assertion, for if *this* intention is not recognized, his utterance will not be taken as an assertion, and so must fail in its immediate intention. (One cannot make an assertion without intending to be taken as making, and so intending to make, an assertion.) We can now see the difficulty in taking the notion of lying to oneself too literally: it would require that one perform an act with the intention both that that intention be recognized (by oneself) and not recognized (since to recognize it would defeat its purpose).

We had better, then, take the expression "lying to oneself" as a kind of metaphor—a dead metaphor, since we use it so often; at best, then, an idiom. William Safire may be politically astute and a whiz at language, but in this case he would have done better to say Reagan was self-deceived. The reason it is more plausible to hold that Reagan deceived himself than that he lied to himself is simply that, though the aim of lying to oneself, if this were possible, would be self-deception, there are less improbable techniques for achieving this end.

A lookout on the *Pinta* was, we are told, the first to sight land—an outlying island of America, but Columbus insisted that it was he. "This insistence has been variously interpreted by some as naked, mean greed, by others as honorable self-deception, born of the arrogance of lust for fame", writes Felipe Fernández in *The London Review of Books*.[3] Let us simplify the second suggestion to this: Columbus was

---

[3] Vol. 7, Jan. 1993, p. 3.

self-deceived, and his lust for fame helps explain his self-deception. What form can this explanation take, and what is it supposed to explain? If Columbus simply believed from the start that he was the first to sight land, he would have been wrong, but no one would have had to deceive him. We might explain his false belief as a case of wishful thinking, but wishful thinking may be as simple as a desire that something be the case begetting the belief that it is the case. Self-deception may involve wishful thinking, but it is more complicated. One complication is perhaps not important: in wishful thinking what we come to believe is also desired, while the self-deceived may come to believe what is distressing or feared. What is important is that to be self-deceived one must at some time have known the truth, or, to be more accurate, have believed something contrary to the belief engendered by the deception. To be self-deceived, Columbus must at one time have known, or at least believed, that he was not the first to sight land; Reagan at one time knew of the arms-for-hostages deal.

This original knowledge must, of course, have played a causal role in the self-deception. Columbus would not have needed to deceive himself if he had not known that it was not he who had made the fateful sighting. It was *because* he remembered the arms-for-hostages deal that Reagan "stuck to a script denying reality", to use Safire's words. We are apparently asking the belief that is to be rejected to serve as part of the motivation for the rejection. This may at first appear fairly straightforward. Someone has a belief he finds disagreeable or painful or ego-deflating. He thus has a reason to change things, to rid himself of the belief. He then acts, or thinks, in a way that causes him to reject the unwelcome thought. But to see this as straightforward is to neglect a distinction between two senses in which one can be said to have a reason for a belief. If one would be happier, prouder, more relaxed, less fraught if one had a certain belief, that is a reason, putting other considerations aside, to have the belief. But such a reason is not, in itself, a reason to suppose the desirable belief is true. It may or may not be rational for Columbus to believe he was first to sight the new land, but it would certainly not be rational for him to believe it solely on the grounds that he would like to believe it.

The explanation of self-deception remains not merely obscure, but apparently mired in contradiction. Self-deception requires that we do something with the intention of coming to believe what we do not believe; yet it provides us with no reason to hold the wished-for belief true: the agent is to perform an action with the intention of coming to believe what he does not believe. Since what drives the self-deceiver to perform this action is his unwanted doubt or belief, we seem to have to say the agent both believes and disbelieves the same proposition. If disbelieving a proposition entails not believing it, then the puzzle is ours: we would have to say that the agent did and did not believe the same thing. But however wild the pattern of beliefs we are willing to attribute to the self-deceiver, we must not fall into contradiction ourselves in describing his confusion.

We can, and should, escape from this particular difficulty by refusing to accept the entailment: we should not agree that believing the contradictory or contrary of a proposition entails not believing that proposition. It is possible for a person to believe contradictory propositions, not only when the contradiction is too subtle for normal detection, but also when the contradiction is obvious (for the contradiction must be obvious if it is to move someone to self-deceit). At the same time, we should balk at attributing to anyone belief in a plain contradiction. The distinction we need here is between believing contradictory propositions and believing a contradiction, between believing that p and believing that $not\text{-}p$ on the one hand, and believing that (p and $not\text{-}p$) on the other.

Still, it is hard enough to comprehend how it is possible to have beliefs that are contradictory. Why is this a problem? To see it as a problem—indeed, to see any form of irrationality as a problem—one must accept a degree of holism. If beliefs are atomic features of the brain, which can be individually added, changed, and deleted without regard to their propositional environment, as Jerry Fodor and Ernie Lepore seem to hold in their recent book on holism,[4] then any degree of inconsistency is possible. But if you think, as I do, that the mere possession of propositional attitudes implies a large degree of consistency, and that the identification of beliefs depends in part on their logical relations to other beliefs, then inconsistencies impose a strain on the attribution and explanation of beliefs (and, of course, other propositional attitudes). It is such considerations that make the attribution of a straightforward contradiction—a belief in an obvious contradiction—unintelligible. Of course we can say, "She thinks she is younger than she is"; but Russell showed us how to get out of this without saddling her with a contradiction. It is hard, but not impossible, to understand how someone can hold contradictory beliefs; hard, because there can

---

[4] Jerry Fodor and Ernie Lepore, *Holism: A Shopper's Guide*, Blackwell, Oxford, 1992.

scarcely be a better reason for supposing someone does not believe he is, say, stout, than that he believes he is not stout.

Even setting aside hard-line mental atomists, many philosophers have a hard time grasping why irrationality creates a conceptual difficulty; they regard someone who emphasizes the tie between rationality and explicability, and the centrality of consistency in rationality, as an obsessed rationalist who cannot understand any form of reason not based on simple logic. I want to plead guilty, and throw myself on the mercy of my (largely rational) readers—after, of course, explaining myself.

Here is why I am inclined to hold that all genuine cases of irrationality—akrasia, wishful thinking, self-deception, bad reasoning—involve inconsistency. Sticking to this condition may require a degree of verbal legislation, but legislation is sometimes the best way to promote order and clarity. Thus I do not want to call someone irrational because he has beliefs or desires that in themselves seem mad as long as the person has not arrived at these attitudes through faulty thinking, failure to take into account evidence he acknowledges, or willful disregard of contrary considerations. I have a cognitive view of evidence: it consists of beliefs, and does not include sensations. Sensations, no matter how complex or systematic, cannot be inconsistent with anything; unless they beget thoughts, they play no role in creating or constituting inconsistencies.

Let us consider possible exceptions. Is it irrational to hold oneself exempt from moral imperatives one applies to others? Not in itself, I would say, since one can easily construct a consistent rule that calls for special exemptions. But if one also believes that moral imperatives apply to everyone without exception, then one has inconsistent values. This is not a matter of conflicting values; conflict of values is not inconsistency. Is it irrational to agree that in every known case death by hemlock has been extremely messy and painful, but to fail to expect the next case to be the same? It all depends; but it is not necessarily irrational to have deviant standards of good inductive practice.

At this point someone is sure to ask who is to be the judge of rationality and consistency. The annoying answer is that this is a bad question, a question without an answer. There is no eternal, absolute standard. At the same time, we are not thrown back on your standards or mine; relativism is not the only alternative to standards independent of all thought and judgment. It is clear that in evading the question when a set of attitudes can be recognized as inconsistent, we are quickly driven back to basic logic; there comes a point at which intelligibility is so diminished by perceived inconsistency that an accusation of inconsistency loses application for lack of identifiable contents about which to be inconsistent. One must be able to think in order to be inconsistent. It is only by showing ourselves largely rational and consistent that we show ourselves capable of irrationality and inconsistency. An agent can fail in a particular case to generalize from evidence, but only because the agent, like every creature capable of thought, usually generalizes from evidence. Someone may have what I consider deviant inductive rules, but only because that person has standards of inductive reasoning that can be recognized as such. The first problem about self-deception, then, is that as a form of irrationality it undermines its own clarity of application. The contents of propositional attitudes are determined in part by their logical relations with other attitudes; to the extent that these relations of a particular attitude are broken or confused, the identity of that attitude, its content, is rendered less precise.

The second problem concerns explanation. Our normal mode of explanation of actions and beliefs is to review the reasons an agent had in acting, or the course of reasoning that led to the belief. Such explanations *rationalize* the action or belief by singling out other attitudes in the light of which the action or belief is reasonable—reasonable not only to the agent himself, but reasonable also to the explainer. This does not mean that every action or belief is reasonable everything considered; its reasonableness is only as seen in the light of the reasons that explain it. But now, given this mode of explanation, how are we to explain self-deception? The trouble is that what we want to say explains it can't rationalize it. Columbus' lust for fame may explain why he persuaded himself he was the first to sight land, but his lust for fame does not rationalize what he came to believe. There is no reason to suppose Columbus thought his lust for fame was a good reason to believe he was the first to sight land.

To take a step in the direction of resolving these problems I have made two proposals.[5] One is to allow that there is a mongrel form

---

[5] These proposals can be found in "Paradoxes of Irrationality", in *Philosophical Essays on Freud*, ed. R. Wollheim and J. Hopkins, Cambridge University Press, 1982; "Deception and Division", in *The Multiple Self*, ed. J. Elster, Cambridge University Press, 1986, pp. 79–92; and "Incoherence and Irrationality", *Dialectica*, 39, 1985, pp. 345–54 [Essays 11–13, this volume].

of explanation which, like explanations in both the social and the natural sciences, is causal, but unlike most explanations of actions and other intensionally described phenomena, does not rationalize what it explains. Such explanation accepts the idea that there may be mental causes of mental states or events for which they are not reasons. A simple example is wishful thinking: a desire or wish that a proposition be true causes a person to believe that it is true, but is not a reason for thinking it true. Self-deception is not this simple, since it requires the intention to alter one's beliefs, but self-deception, like wishful thinking, fits the mold: the desire to change a belief does cause the change, but is not a reason for counting the new belief true or the old one false.

The second proposal is meant to explain how it is possible at the same time both to accept and to reject a proposition—how it was possible for Reagan to know he had endorsed the arms-for-hostages deal and at the same time to believe he had not. Why didn't he juxtapose these two beliefs—though of course if he had, one or the other would have evaporated? I suggested the two obviously opposed beliefs could coexist only if they were somehow kept separate, not allowed to be contemplated in a single glance. I spoke of the mind as being *partitioned*, meaning no more than that a metaphorical wall separated the beliefs which, allowed into consciousness together, would destroy at least one.

This idea obviously echoes a long tradition: Plato, Aristotle, Augustine, Butler, Freud are just a few of those who have made semi-autonomous parts of the soul part of their philosophy of mind. But my echo is a feeble one. I do not assume that the divisions are fixed, or that they deserve such names as conscience, courage, intellect or id. More important, I do not think of the boundaries, however permanent or temporary, as separating autonomous territories. The territories overlap: there is a central core of mostly ordinary truths which the territories share (much as all rational creatures necessarily share a general, and mostly correct, picture of the world). Where territories differ is in the dissonant details. While Reagan's two "minds" shared most desires and beliefs and further attitudes, one contained the memory that he had agreed to the arms-for-hostages deal while the other denied he had any part in it. Of course this could not be the only difference: each of the contradictory beliefs needed a supporting phalanx of ideas. Producing support for the second belief was the task of self-deception.

The image I wished to invite was not, then, that of two minds each somehow able to act like an independent agent; the image is rather that of a single mind not wholly integrated; a brain suffering from a perhaps temporary self-inflicted lobotomy.

This highly abstract account of the logical structure of self-deception is not, and never was, intended as a psychologically revealing explanation of the nature or etiology of self-deception. Its modest purpose was to remove, or at least mitigate, the features that at first make self-deception seem inconceivable. The two main proposals were, to allow a hybrid form of explanation of mental phenomena, causal, but not rationalizing; and to distinguish firmly between accepting a contradictory proposition and accepting separately each of two contradictory propositions, the latter requiring, or perhaps just expressing, the idea of thoughts held apart.

It is natural to ask whether these suggestions, unprepossessing and schematic as they are, are so wooden and formalized as to correspond to nothing we can recognize in, or abstract from, actual or convincingly fictionalized accounts of self-deception. I am by no means certain what the outcome of an extended survey of cases would reveal with respect to my partial skeleton; I am pretty sure that no one scheme will fit all examples. But it may be illuminating to examine a few samples.

First a real case of what has been claimed to be mass self-deception. Paul Driver maintains that many of us—enough to establish and maintain a flourishing reputation—deceived ourselves about the originality and value of John Cage's work.[6] I shall express no opinion about the correctness of this claim; its validity obviously depends in part on the value of Cage's work. Suppose it is true that many of us are self-deceived about the value of Cage's work. How can our delusion be explained and described? Part of the explanation, according to Driver, is that Cage took himself so seriously that others tended to go along. He consistently represented himself as having been a student of Schönberg's, for example, though this was apparently a "public fantasy". Perhaps Cage told this story so often even he came to believe it; this would not be an unusual experience. If it worked in something like this fashion, the memory of the truth, being less pleasing than the fantasy, gradually caused, though it did not justify, the fantasy, and it seems clear that memory and fantasy-become-belief

---

[6] Review in *The London Review of Books*, vol. 7, Jan. 1993, pp. 3 ff.

had, during the period crucial to self-deception, to be kept on separate tracks.

How about the rest of us? Driver suggests, among other things, that we were embarrassed to admit we couldn't really make much of, or honestly admire, those pretentious minutes of silence, the sudden toneless bangs and twangs, the elaborately documented random noises. Maybe, we thought, this is what modern music is, or will become, and we do not want to be found out of touch with the newest thing, stuck with last week's fashions. Driver quotes Frank Kermode on how to recognize that one is in danger of deceiving oneself (he is thinking of poetry, but the same is to go for music): you sense, writes Kermode, a "certain ambiguity in your own response. *The Waste Land*, and also *Hugh Selwyn Mauberly*, can strike you in certain moments as emperors without clothes ... It is [with] your own proper fictive covering that you hide their nakedness and make them wise." Kermode has not exactly described self-deception, but a sign or frequent precursor: a wavering between two views, a recognition of the possibility of delusion. If you are struck by the suspicion that the emperor is without clothes, you are not yet deluded (assuming the emperor is in fact naked). The thought so far is of the threat, or lure, of being taken in. If this thought leads to your being taken in, you are self-deceived, for it is your own thought that has caused your final delusion. If you come to accept what you at first recognized as fantasy, and the recognition plays a causal role in the acceptance, you have satisfied one of my criteria for self-deception.

Dreaming, one is now told, can be bad for the heart. The most vivid dreams, the ones accompanied by REM, the dreams that come just before waking, or that wake us, produce many of the somatic changes the events we dream of would produce: rapid heart beat, secretion of adrenaline, various sexual responses. We cry out, convulse, kick, fit real sounds into our dream. (The toll such dreams take on us explains the fact, so speculation runs, that so many heart attacks occur early in the day.) If we think, with Freud and Delmore Schwartz, that we are in some sense responsible for our dreams, that they are motivated, then to the extent that we act them out we are self-deluded. But dreams aside, we can, often quite deliberately, summon up imagined scenes. At times this is a prelude to action: we imagine what the outcome of various possible courses of action will be, and act on the one that most attracts, amuses, or, in some cases, frightens us. This legitimate and useful exercise of the imagination is not altogether easy to distinguish from cases where we picture what we know to be false, or absurdly unlikely, or simply less desirable than some alternative, and act on its attraction. The compulsive gambler is an example. Akrasia is in this category.

In *Ulysses* Joyce, through his spokesman and representative, Stephen Dedalus, advances the theory that in *Hamlet* Shakespeare identifies himself with Hamlet's father, the deceived and dishonored ghost. There is evidence, we are told, that Shakespeare played the part of the ghost in early productions, and we know that he had a son named Hamnet. Here is Stephen's description of Shakespeare's fantasy:

—The play begins. A player comes on under the shadow, made up in the castoff mail of a court buck, a wellset man with a bass voice. It is the ghost, the king, a king and no king, and the player is Shakespeare who has studied *Hamlet* all the years of his life . . . in order to play the part of the spectre. He speaks the words to Burbage, the young player who stands before him . . . , calling him by a name:
  Hamlet, I am thy father's spirit
bidding him list. To a son he speaks, the son of his soul, the prince, young Hamlet and to the son of his body, Hamnet Shakespeare, who has died in Stratford that his namesake may live for ever.
  Is it possible that that player Shakespeare, a ghost by absence . . . speaking his own words to his own son's name . . . is it possible, I want to know, or probable that he did not draw or foresee the logical conclusion of those premises: you are the dispossessed son: I am the murdered father: your mother is the guilty queen. Ann Shakespeare, born Hathaway?[7]

If Shakespeare really foresaw this conclusion, and accepted it, he was deluded, for he was not about to be murdered, nor did he have reason to think he would be. His delusion, if that is what it was, coexisted, but could not have cohabited, with his grasp of truth. Someone doubts Stephen's account: Shakespeare merely made a mistake in marrying Ann Hathaway. "—Bosh! Stephen said rudely. A man of genius makes no mistakes. His errors are volitional and are the portals of discovery." A moment later we learn it was not his choice:

He chose badly? He was chosen, it seems to me. If others have their will Ann hath a way. By cock, she was to blame. She put the comether on him, sweet and twentysix. The greyeyed goddess who bends over the boy Adonis, stooping to conquer, as prologue to the swelling act, is a boldfaced Stratford wench who tumbles in a cornfield a lover younger than herself.[8]

[7] James Joyce, *Ulysses*, Random House, New York, 1937, pp. 186, 7.
[8] *Ulysses*, pp. 188, 9.

The confusion of Ann Hathaway with Athena (the "greyeyed goddess") may remind us of how Athena deceives Odysseus, quite obviously for the fun of it, when, deposited alone with an assortment of tripods and other gifts by his generous Phaeacian hosts, he ponders how to approach his wife and a palace full of hostile suitors. Athena disguises herself as a lad and enjoys the success of her deceit before she reveals herself and gives Odysseus some essential advice. The untrusting, flirtatious, affectionate relation between Athena and Odysseus is one of the more subtle subplots of the *Odyssey*. It strikes us as oddly modern, as if designed to leave us uncertain who it is that is fooled, and to what extent. Another quiet Homeric note sounds in the library scene in Joyce's *Ulysses*. Why, Stephen asks, did Shakespeare, a "lord of language", send another to woo for him? He answers:

Belief in himself has been untimely killed. He was overborne in a cornfield first . . . and he will never be a victor in his own eyes after nor play victoriously the game of laugh and lie down. Assumed dongiovannism will not save him. No later undoing will undo the first undoing. The tusk of the boar has wounded him there where love lies ableeding . . . . There is, I feel in the words, some goad of the flesh driving him into a new passion, a darker shadow of the first, darkening even his own understanding of himself.[9]

We recall an eerie scene in Homer's *Odyssey*. Odysseus has entered his palace in disguise. His old nurse, Euryclea, is washing his foot when suddenly she recognizes him by an old scar. Auerbach, in the first essay in *Mimesis*, calls our attention to the magical way in which Homer suspends the moment of recognition, without apology or comment, while we are told, in the present tense, the story of the ancient hunt and the wound inflicted by the boar.[10] The number of kinds and levels of disguise, of deception self- and other-imposed, of self-conscious and unsuspected cross identifications, gives some idea of the actual complexity and subtlety of self-deception in everyday life.

Who, then, is fooled? Well, first, Shakespeare, according to Stephen. Shakespeare was taken in by Ann Hathaway, as Hamlet's father was by his wife. In writing *Hamlet*, Shakespeare in part deceived himself (again if we accept Stephen's "theory"—a theory he will in a moment say he does not believe).

But who is Stephen? No one can doubt, one is not *allowed* to doubt, that Stephen is Joyce himself. *A Portrait of the Artist as a Young*

---

[9] *Ulysses*, p. 194.
[10] Erich Auerbach, "Odysseus' Scar", in *Mimesis*, Princeton University Press, Princeton, 1953.

Man is frankly autobiographical; and to a greater extent than in most autobiographical works, Joyce invents as much as records his past and himself. Stephen—or Joyce—also identifies with Shakespeare, not to mention God. Stephen speaks of Hamlet *pére* and Hamlet *fils*, "murdered and betrayed . . . Dane or Dubliner", and goes on,

> He found in the world without as actual what was in his world within as possible . . . . Every life is many days, day after day. We walk through ourselves, meeting robbers, ghosts, giants, old men, wives, widows, brothers-in-love. But always meeting ourselves. The playwright who wrote the folio of this world . . . the lord of things as they are . . . would be a bawd and cuckold too but that in the economy of heaven, foretold by Hamlet, there are no more marriages.[11]

Implicitly comparing Shakespeare's "exile" in London with his own (Joyce's, Stephen's) exile in Paris, Stephen says "Elizabethan London lay as far from Stratford as corrupt Paris lies from virgin Dublin" [p. 185]. Has no-one made out Hamlet to be an Irishman, someone asks. ("No-one" [ὅ υτισ] is, of course, Odysseus' alias when he wishes to deceive Polyphemus).

Does Joyce want us to see his Shakespeare, Stephen, himself, as self-deceived? Was Joyce to some extent self-deceived? Does it matter where we draw this line, or is there a line worth drawing? To the extent which at any moment we vividly imagine another life, that of a robber, ghost, giant, old man, etc., we have taken a first step toward accepting what we imagine. If we dwell on our fantasy, act out small parts of our imagined self, enjoy in our daydreams the excitements and triumphs we miss in reality, we are encouraging and motivating a degree of conviction in what, in the beginning, we know is false. The writer who, consciously or not, finds his characters writing their own plot, as in the case of Trollope, or finds his plot writing his own character, as in the case of Joyce, is doing what we all do when we fantasize or daydream, but doing it better. The author who thinks he is telling a secret truth about himself lends himself willingly to self-delusion: think of Proust, Genet, Dante, Lawrence, Byron, Philip Roth. The list is long.

—You are a delusion, said roundly John Eglinton to Stephen . . . . Do you believe your own theory?
—No, Stephen said promptly.

[11] *Ulysses*, p. 210.

But we are then allowed to overhear Stephen as he silently thinks: "I believe, O Lord, help my unbelief. That is, help me to believe or help me to unbelieve? Who helps to believe? *Egomen*. Who to unbelieve? Other chap."[12] Who is fooled?

Madam Bovary brilliantly dissects the stages of self-deception. Whether or not we are inclined to sympathize or identify with Emma Bovary, the account of how she persuades herself to accept absurdly unrealistic opinions of herself, her situation, and her behavior is unerringly convincing. It begins when she is barely older than a child. She reads *Paul et Virginie* and dreams of herself in the little bamboo hut, with faithful servant, loving small brother, exotic faraway scenes. At thirteen she enters a convent. At first she is swept away by the metaphors of betrothal, divine love, and marriage everlasting. She might at this point, we are told, have awakened to the lyric call of Nature, but since she comes from the country she prefers the picturesque:

She loved the sea only for its storms, green foliage only when it was scattered amid ruins. It was necessary for her to derive a sort of personal profit from things, she rejected as useless whatever did not minister to her heart's immediate fulfillment—being in search of emotions, not of scenery. (p. 49)

Soon she is secretly reading romantic novels; Flaubert is endlessly—enthusiastically—willing to give us the flavor of these novels:

They were all about love and lovers, damsels in distress swooning in lonely lodges, postilions slaughtered all along the road, horses ridden to death on every page, gloomy forests, troubles of the heart, vows, sobs, tears, kisses, rowboats in the moonlight, nightingales in the grove. (p. 50)

Flaubert and Joyce make a strange pair, two sentimentalists posing as realists. There are many pages of *Ulysses* that are in the style and tone Flaubert here and throughout ironically uses to convey the content of Emma's heated imagination. Joyce more sympathetically mimics the manner of penny novels to introduce us to the thoughts (and reading) of Gertie MacDowell, a young woman Leopold Bloom notices with interest on the beach. Gertie fantasizes harmlessly about Bloom; here is the texture of her thinking:

Here was that of which she had so often dreamed. It was he who mattered and there was joy on her face because she wanted him because she felt instinctively that he was like no-one else. The very heart of the girlwoman went out to him, her dreamhusband, because she knew on the instant it was him.[13]

<hr/>

[12] *Ulysses*, p. 211.   [13] *Ulysses*, p. 351.

Bloom and Gertie, the middle-aged man and the maiden, enjoy their unspoken mutual attraction and interaction, and part in good spirits, like Odysseus and Nausicaa. Such thoughts bring tragedy to the life of Madam Bovary. How does this happen? Gertie is in no danger—nor is Bloom—of losing touch with reality; reality only pushes Emma deeper into despair and a world of fantasy. This in itself would not be self-deception. What makes it self-deception is, first, her uninhibited longing for surroundings and experiences she imagines others to have, and that she believes are her due. Second, this longing engenders vivid imaginings of what she wishes and hopes for. Third, she more and more acts as if what she wants were the case. Finally, behaving in accord with a dream world, she gradually comes to believe it real. But since it is the actual world, which she detests, and which motivates and sustains the whole crazy construction, we must suppose—and this is how Flaubert describes it—that the two worlds, real and imagined, somehow occupy the same mind. Through the enormous energy of desire and weakness of will, the conflicting parts of the two worlds are kept from confronting, and so destroying, one another until the end.

When Emma returns to her father's farm after leaving the convent, "she regards herself as being utterly disillusioned, with nothing more to learn or feel" (p. 52). The appearance on the scene of Charles Bovary soon changes this: she comes to believe herself possessed at last of that wonderful passion about which she has dreamed. After playing briefly at being a happy homemaker, she awakens to the fact that her emotions do not match what she thought romantic love required. Sitting alone in a field she is suddenly overcome with regret: "O God, O God, why did I get married?" She tortures herself with what she imagines to be the exciting, fulfilled, lives of her old school friends.

In the development of her self-deception two things stand out: the steps she takes to nourish her illusions, both actions designed to this end, and the cultivation of conditions in which her fantasies blossom and reality is excluded; and the psychic energy that goes into keeping truth and illusion separate. After the ball at the chateau of the Marquis d'Andervilliers, the memory gives Emma something to "do": with time "some of the details vanished, but her yearning for it all remained" (p. 69). She thinks of the Viscount with whom she danced, and imagines him in Paris; she buys a guide to Paris and "traced her way about the capital with the tip of her finger, walking up the boulevards, stopping at every turning . . . she sought in Balzac and George Sand a vicarious gratification of her own desires" (p. 70). She is miserable. "Instead of turning her thoughts away she riveted them to it more firmly; she worked up her grief, and sought out its occasions" (p. 121). While Charles slept,

> she was awake in a very different dreamland . . . a coach-and-four had been whirling them [Emma and her lover—she deludes herself into thinking he will take her off forever] along for a week, towards a new world from which she would never return. On and on they drove, their arms entwined, in silence. Often from a mountain height they would suddenly catch sight of a splendid city below them . . . (p. 208)

When her lover rudely disillusions her, she is devastated, but takes solace in religion. Thinking she is going to die, she sees herself going off to heaven:

> This glorious vision remained in her memory as the most beautiful dream that could be dreamed . . . Amid the illusions that her wishes prompted, she glimpsed a realm of purity . . . she wanted to become a saint . . . she saw herself as possessed by the finest Catholic melancholy that ever ethereal soul could conceive. (p. 224)

Presently she takes another lover, Léon, a law-clerk with whom she had previously had an unconsummated flirtation. They urge each other on in inventing a romantic past, "For this is how they would have liked it all to be; they were both constructing an ideal of themselves and adapting their past lives to it" (p. 245, 6).

The effort to keep reality at bay shows constantly.

> So Paris swam before her eyes . . . . The teeming life that moved amid the tumult could, nevertheless, be divided and classified into separate scenes. Of these Emma saw only two or three, which shut out the rest, and represented, for her, the whole of humanity . . . there were private rooms in restaurants where you went for supper after midnight with a motley crowd of writers and actresses, all laughing in the candlelight . . . . Theirs was a higher life, . . . touched with the sublime. The rest of the world came nowhere, had no proper status, no real existence. In fact, the nearer home things came, the more she shrank from all thought of them. The whole of her immediate environment—dull countryside, imbecile petty bourgeois, life in its ordinariness—seemed a freak, a particular piece of bad luck that had seized on her; while beyond . . . ranged the vast lands of passion and felicity. (p. 71, 2)

Falling in love, she thinks, with Léon, she protects her secret life by taking better care of her dull husband. "Within she was all desire and rage and hatred . . . . She was in love with Léon; and she sought solitude that she might revel in his image undisturbed. It marred the pleasure of her daydreams to see him in the flesh" (p. 120). After her first seduction by Rodolphe, she ruminates ecstatically:

"I've a lover, a lover," she said to herself again and again, revelling in the thought as if she had attained a second puberty. At last she would know the delights of love, the feverish joys of which she had despaired. She was entering a marvelous world where all was passion, ecstasy, delirium .... She saw the sparkling peaks of sentiment beneath her, and ordinary life was only a distant phenomenon. (p. 175)

When Rodolphe's ardor starts to cool, it only increases her passion. Her reaction to rejection makes one think of Leon Festinger's theory of cognitive dissonance, which was inspired in part by the discovery, or insight, that people who have made an irreversible choice tend to continue to invest in that choice if the choice seems objectively to have been a mistake, with the apparent motive of demonstrating their wisdom to themselves.

Doing and thinking things with the conscious or unconscious aim of changing our own beliefs or other attitudes is not necessarily bad, or even what we would normally call irrational. John Dewey, who along with Aristotle had a dim view of the possibility of doing much to change one's own values, spoke many years ago about how, with luck and effort, it might be done (*Human Nature and Conduct*). His proposal had two parts: the first was that if you want to have a value or belief you do not have, you should act as if you already had it. The second part was to avert attention from the desired end and concentrate on the means. Don't keep repeating to yourself, "I will not smoke", but set out on an interesting expedition in a direction where no cigarettes are to be found. Dewey did not notice that his advice works better in the service of self-corruption. If your secret wish is to commit adultery, don't say to yourself, "I shall allow myself to be seduced"; just let him touch your hand.

Flaubert was a doctor's son. When he was thirteen he wrote a friend that he would be disgusted with life if he weren't writing a novel. Yet he was sometimes so annoyed with characters in *Madam Bovary* that he wrote whole scenes not intended for publication simply to relieve his feelings. But he was not annoyed with Emma. Though he claimed to make every possible effort to eliminate himself from this work, when he was asked who served as the model for Emma, he famously replied, "Madam Bovary, c'est moi!" Who was he fooling? Joyce injected himself into his work more obviously, but not enough to satisfy himself. At one point he asked Nora, his wife, to have an extra-marital affair so that he could write about the experience, his and hers.

The moral I draw from these examples is brief. Self-deception comes in many grades, from ordinary dreams through half-directed daydreams to outright hallucination, from normal imagining of consequences of pondered actions to psychotic delusions, from harmless wishful thinking to elaborately self-induced error. It would be a mistake to try to draw firm lines within these continua. But as we approach the classic cases like that of Emma Bovary, the formal structure I have postulated also seems to be revealed more and more clearly. Such analytic exercises do not, as some philosophers apparently think, necessarily distort or misrepresent the real thing. They do, of course, ignore the details and omit the color that give particular cases their interest and psychological persuasiveness. But the philosopher's exercises do not have to be false because they are pale and rational. Or am I fooling myself?

An Interview with Donald Davidson

by Ernie Lepore

Lepore: Tell me a bit about the early days.

Davidson: I was born in Springfield, Massachusetts, on 6 March 1917 to Clarence ('Davie') Herbert Davidson and Grace Cordelia Anthony. My mother's father's name was 'Anthony', but her mother had married twice and by coincidence both her husbands were named 'Anthony'. My mother had a half-brother who was directly descended from Susan B. Anthony, but I am not because I'm from the other 'Anthony'. I used to think I was related, because I knew my mother was named 'Anthony' and I knew Susan B. Anthony was in the picture, but it's false. My mother's family lived in Gloversville, New York, and at that time it was a great place for manufacturing gloves. My mother's father had a foundry in which he manufactured the stamps with which they stamped out the parts of gloves. They were moderately prosperous. They had five or six children, and they had a great big summer place on a lake. My father was born and grew up in Jersey City, New Jersey. He came from poor parents. His father was American-born, but his father, my great grandfather, came from Scotland with his family; and very shortly after he got to this country, he abandoned his family and disappeared into the West and was never heard from again. My grandfather worked much of his life as a Pullman car conductor. The Pullman car yards were then in the Bronx. So he lived quite near the yards. He'd be gone a lot of the time, because Pullman cars didn't

This 'interview' actually took place over two continents and several years. It's merely a part of what must be literally hundreds of hours of taped conversations between us from 1988 onwards. I put together what follows with Professor Davidson's approval, but he did not edit his own words for publication.—E. L.

belong to any railroad; they'd be leased, and they could be attached to any old train. I think he rather enjoyed that work. He was a very impressive-looking man, a great big man with a handlebar mustache.

My father went to Cornell University and he worked his way through college. We lived in the Philippines from shortly after I was born until I was about four years old. We lived about one year in Amherst (where my father taught elementary mathematics at the college), and then Swarthmore, and in Collingswood, which like Swarthmore was another suburb of Philadelphia. It wasn't until I was nine or ten that we moved to Staten Island and stayed put. I hadn't had any formal school training until then because my family moved all the time. My parents sent me to a public school, which I walked to for about three miles. But being a public school, they insisted that I start in the first grade. So, I was among kids that were three or four years younger than I was. I was much older than anyone else in the class. It was ridiculous. And furthermore, though I had no formal schooling, I was still way ahead of even my own age group. They had me doing penmanship. But I was at that school for only part of the year, and then a woman we always called 'Old Mrs Wilcox' whom my family knew and who had helped found the first and only progressive education school in Staten Island, the Staten Island Academy, just gave me a scholarship and supported me through the whole time I was there. There I started in the fourth grade, which was more or less my age group.

Lepore: When did you begin to think about philosophy?

Davidson: I was interested in philosophy from very young and thought about it when I was in high school. I was reading stuff of all different qualities. I read a lot of Nietzsche. I read Plato's *Parmenides*. I tried to read Kant's *Critique of Pure Reason*. All this was while I was in high school. Let me tell you why I tried to read the *Parmenides*. My high school [in Staten Island] had this set of the Jowett translations of Plato. I glanced at them and the *Parmenides* had all these one-line remarks; one guy would speak one line and another guy would speak another line, and I thought this would read like a play—that it would be very easy. In fact, it's all this mishmash about the one and the many. It's a hard book, whereas if someone had counseled me I would have started with Plato's *Apology* or something like that. I didn't know anything; instead I thought—I'll just put my mind to this and get through it.

Lepore: All your education was at Harvard? How is it that you went there?

Davidson: Hume Dow, my oldest friend, was the son of the Australian consul in New York City. We were great pals throughout high school. He introduced me to many things. He was a year older than I, and when he graduated he went off to Harvard University. That was part of the reason I went to Harvard. I had applied to colleges: Harvard University, Yale University, Dartmouth College, and Swarthmore College. Being the kind of person I was at that point, I took a week off from high school and went and visited all these schools. In each case I wrote to the Dean of Admissions and I said I'm looking your school over. Would you mind arranging for me to go to some classes and if possible I'd like to be put up in a dormitory to see what life is like on campus. No one had ever done this before, and they all responded positively. It was a scream. They didn't quite know how to react. They all arranged for me to go to classes; in the end, all the universities offered me scholarships, but Swarthmore offered me the best in the sense that it was a four-year scholarship. I was very tempted. But then the Harvard Club of New York City, a bunch of rich stockbrokers, interviewed me for a scholarship they offered each year. They interviewed fifty students. I was the very last person they interviewed. They talked to me; and at the end of the interview, they simply looked at each other, nodded, and said to me—you got it. It was the largest financial freshman scholarship available. It paid much more than tuition; it actually supported me while I was a student. Their parting words were—you better pass the college boards. In other words, Harvard hadn't admitted me yet. This club had just gone ahead and given me the scholarship. I got in. So, since I liked Harvard the best, and since this old pal of mine was there, I chose Harvard.

Lepore: You started Harvard in fall, 1935. Tell me about those early days at Harvard.

Davidson: From my point of view, Harvard was simply marvelous. When I was an undergraduate, I got really on very friendly terms with a lot of top-notch professors; the philosopher A. N. Whitehead took me under his wing; he would invite me to his apartment for afternoon tea all the time. I knew most of the people in the philosophy department: C. I. Lewis, Whitehead, later on Quine, Demos. I knew all the people in the classics department; I knew the chairman of the English department. I don't, for the most part, spend nearly as much time with my students as my teachers spent with me. It's just not in general done these days. I think it's partly because we all do so much traveling; and also so much time is taken up with correspondence. But back then these people actually invited me into their homes, regularly.

Lepore: But did you start off straight away in philosophy?

Davidson: Well, look, I was in fact an English major to begin with. I studied Shakespeare, seventeenth- and eighteenth-century poetry, the English novel. The Bible and Shakespeare was a very important course for me. I took courses with Harry Levin. That's how I got started on James Joyce. Levin wrote the first critical book on Joyce. Levin was beginning the comparative literature department at Harvard— the first one in the United States. He and Theodore Spencer, a great Shakespeare scholar, went into the history of ideas, tracing an idea from Homer through the Middle Ages and then on into the Renaissance. This program combined philosophy with literature and classics. These people in the history of ideas had a great influence on me. So did Whitehead, in fact, and it all fit together, because Whitehead by then was writing things like *Adventures of Ideas*. So, he too was very much into the history of ideas, which of course fit in very well with the kinds of things that Spencer was telling me about—for example, how the Homeric stories, especially the *Odyssey*, were being treated in the early Middle Ages, and later on in the Renaissance—how they became symbols for all sorts of things. He put me on to books like Arthur Lovejoy's *The Great Chain of Being*, which I just ate up. Boy, it turned me on. I had a very very strong historical approach to ideas.

Then when I returned after my second year in college to begin my third year, there were these very tough exams I had to take and pass in order to remain at Harvard. The examiners would give you one or two lines, for example, from Shakespeare and question you where did this line come from, who said it, what its role is in the play, etc. You had to know Shakespeare by heart. The same was true with the Bible. Everyone majoring in English had to do this. And then you had to choose an ancient and modern author. I chose Aeschylus and Goethe. And thus I did everything required to get a degree in English.

Lepore: Is this when you shifted into classics?

Davidson: Exactly. It's a characteristic of mine that anything I work on for very long I get interested in. It's a lucky characteristic to have.

I got into classics just by sheer accident. When I went to Harvard, you had to have Latin or Greek if you were going to get a B.A. (Bachelor of Arts degree); otherwise, you received a B.S. (Bachelor of Science degree). That was the only difference; no difference in the courses you took otherwise. If Harvard had offered Latin, I would have taken it. But Harvard assumed that you already knew Latin; I didn't. But they did offer beginning Greek. Now for no important reason whatsoever I wanted a B.A. and not a B.S. And so I took basic Greek. It was very well taught by teachers who were excellent, and so I continued with it. Already at Harvard in the first course you read Xenophon's *Anabasis*, which is very interesting. The second course you begin Homer. I loved it. You would do the *Iliad* in the first half of the year and the *Odyssey* in the second half of the year. Then I went on. I took a course on the dramatists. And then I did a wonderful course in Thucydides that was given by John Findlay. He was a brilliant teacher, absolutely marvelous. He just produced one beautiful sentence and paragraph after the other. He had a rhetorical flair. There weren't very many people majoring in classics. Harvard had this terrific classics department without any students to teach. So I got a lot of attention. After I shifted into classics and philosophy, I also had to take exams in philosophy and classics. Again, my idea was that if I had to take an exam on something, I wouldn't take the course. So, in fact, in undergraduate school, for example, I never took a course in logic; I just worked on it on my own.

Lepore: It seems you had a very broad education at Harvard.

Davidson: In fact I was spreading myself out through all this stuff. I also audited all the courses that there were on Greek art and architecture; and also on Romanesque architecture, and so in Greek I had a kind of advantage over others who were just classicists because I knew Greek philosophy, history, Greek art, and Greek architecture. I read all of Greek drama. I remember my senior year I persuaded Harvard to let me put on Aristophanes' *The Birds* in Greek. I played the lead, Peisthetairos, which meant memorizing 700 lines of Greek. Leonard Bernstein, who was also a senior in the class of 1938–39 and a friend (we used to play four-hand piano together), wrote an original score for the production and conducted it. Some of the music he wrote for that score, resurfaced in his ballet, *Fancy Free*. I also had a great interest in music. I audited advanced seminars on Beethoven. Yes, it was a wonderful education, absolutely marvelous.

Lepore: So were you a brilliant student?

Davidson: Not at all. I was good enough that I always had a scholarship, and one year I had three A's and a B+. If I had three and one-half A's and a B+ I would have been on a special list and gotten a free book or something like that. That didn't bother me, but I did miss out on several things. For example, the philosophy department had in mind to graduate me with a *summa cum laude*. And so they interviewed me, but something didn't go quite right and all I received was a *magna cum laude*. But my biggest failure came when I was a graduate student several years later. Harvard considered me for a Junior Fellowship. I was living with two guys who were Junior Fellows; Quine was also one of the Fellows. Whitehead was a Senior Fellow. I came as close as you can come without getting it. The way I know this is that these guys, who were my friends, they would go to the meetings and the folders of the candidates were there, and each week this pile would get smaller and smaller and they would tell me that I was still in the pile. In fact, I was the last one to be subtracted.

Lepore: But I'm not sure if I understand the importance of this to you.

Davidson: Well, you have to understand that practically every successful philosopher you have ever heard of who was at Harvard was a Junior Fellow. For example, Bert Dreben was a Fellow; Saul Kripke was a Fellow; Stanley Cavell was a Fellow. The Fellows were a richly endowed organization within the umbrella of Harvard. They had their own rooms in Elliot House, with its own dining rooms. To be a Junior Fellow meant to be fully supported for three years. The idea was that it would be given to people who did not yet have a degree, and one of the conditions was that they would not study for a degree; it was so prestigious to be a Junior Fellow that you didn't need a degree, and a lot of those guys don't have degrees. Kripke and Dreben don't have advanced degrees, and that's why. This rule was never absolutely rigid. For example, Quine got his degree so fast that he had his degree before he was a Junior Fellow. In fact, he was in the first batch of Junior Fellows along with B. F. Skinner. To be frank, I think in retrospect that they were right not to appoint me; at that point I didn't have the degree of achievement in any area that most of those guys had. They were brilliant people.

Lepore: What do you mean when you say 'brilliant'? Was it obvious that Quine was brilliant at that early age?

Davidson: You aren't kidding! Look, he had essentially no training in philosophy when he arrived at Harvard for graduate studies from Oberlin College. He had his Ph.D. within two years. There was nobody at Harvard who knew any serious logic; he went there because Whitehead was there; all Quine knew was *Principia Mathematica*. Whitehead had no interest in that sort of stuff by the time Quine arrived; nor did Russell by that time, for that matter. Look, Quine was obviously brilliant. In the third year of the Junior Fellowship, each Fellow was encouraged to go to Europe. Quine did, and that's when he met Carnap, which he says in his autobiography is the first philosopher to really impress him.

Lepore: Surely C. I. Lewis must have impressed Quine?

Davidson: I do think that C. I. Lewis had a tremendous influence on Quine, but Quine doesn't realize it. The explanation for that is that Quine had no training in philosophy and so when he took Lewis's course in epistemology, he took for granted this is what everybody knows about epistemology. Quine didn't realize that Lewis was any different from everyone else; pretty soon he worked out that there were some things he didn't agree with Lewis about, like the analytic–synthetic distinction. I don't think Quine would put it this way. As I said, I don't think he realized any of this, but you can find most of Quine's epistemology in C. I. Lewis minus the analytic–synthetic distinction. Epistemology naturalized is very close to the heart of C. I. Lewis. I don't think that Quine knows the extent to which there really is a sequence that starts with Kant and goes through C. I. Lewis and ends with Quine.

Lepore: Let's see what happened after you graduated from Harvard in spring, 1939? At some point you returned. How did that happen?

Davidson: After graduating, I had no plans for the future. I had a girlfriend with a car, so we set out for Hollywood where her father was the agent of a number of celebrities. I wrote some radio scripts for Big Town, a once-a-week private eye program starring Edward G. Robinson. We spent most of the summer of 1939 having fun, swimming, and riding horses. During the summer I got a call from Harvard asking me if I would accept a scholarship in philosophy with an emphasis in classics. A man named Teschemacher had just left a generous sum to establish such a fellowship available to philosophy graduate students at Harvard. No one else was interested in classical philosophy. I accepted. I don't know what I would have done otherwise.

Lepore: So now you are back at Harvard? What happens next?

Davidson: Now I had to get serious about philosophy. I had to take preliminary exams at the end of my second year. I took my first course in logic with Quine [fall, 1939], an advanced course which covered what was to become his *Mathematical Logic*. I don't think I was ever really any good at logic, at least not as good as many others were. Still, over the years I would rediscover how much I enjoyed solving simple mathematical and logical problems, though I always knew my gifts in this direction were slight.

Lepore: Who were your peers at Harvard while you were in graduate school?

Davidson: The two Rodericks, Chisholm and Firth, were there, and they were already as graduate students deeply into the problems of epistemology and could argue knowledgeably about sense-data. Henry Aiken was clearly being groomed to occupy a senior position in the faculty, something he had already done by the time I returned to Harvard after the war as a continuing graduate student. Arthur Smullyan was challenging Quine on quantified modal logic and chatting with Bertrand Russell about the nature of propositions when Russell visited Harvard. There was a great year in the early 1940s when Russell came and gave a seminar, to which Quine, Carnap, and Tarski all came.

Lepore: In addition to the course on mathematical logic, did you take any other courses with Quine as a young graduate student?

Davidson: Yes, indeed, and this second one changed my attitude to philosophy. Until then I had thought of philosophy as not as serious as science but more serious than art criticism. Quine's seminar on logical positivism, which I took as a first-year graduate student, turned me around. In later years, I often heard graduate students at Harvard complain about Quine's teaching; they found it clear and carefully worked out but uninspired. Quine himself has written that he did not much enjoy teaching, especially when it came to topics outside of logic. But he certainly turned me on, and in the process he turned me around. Under Quine's tutelage I discovered the magical satisfactions of contriving elementary formal proofs. More important to me in the long run was Quine's scrupulous attention to the distinctions between use and mention, the conditional and entailment, substitutional and ontic quantification. These implied a seriousness about the relations between semantics and logic which I absorbed without realizing at the time how few philosophers shared such concerns. When Quine came back from Europe in 1933, he was fired up by his encounters with the Vienna Circle, Tarski and especially Carnap. On his return to Harvard, Quine gave three lectures on Carnap which seemed openly to espouse all of Carnap's central doctrines; in any case there was no criticism. But by the time I was taking Quine's seminar on logical positivism years later as a graduate student, he had worked out his objections to the analytic–synthetic distinction, and to the reduction of ordinary statements about the physical world to statements about sense-data. This led to the rejection of Carnap's policy of tolerance with respect to general ontological issues. What mattered to me was not so much Quine's conclusions—I assumed he was right—as the realization that it was possible to be serious about getting things right in philosophy—or at least not getting things wrong. By comparison with most of the ideas I had studied as part of the history of ideas, the issues being debated by Quine and his opponents seemed to me clear enough to warrant interest in their truth values. The change in my attitude in philosophy began to seep into my thinking about ethics and the history of philosophy; I found in C. D. Broad's *Five Types of Ethical Theory* and Russell's book on Leibniz concerned with clarity and truth I was beginning to prize. I didn't know enough to be bothered by the historical inaccuracies; what I liked was the application of contemporary analytic methods and standards to material I had previously viewed as beyond or above being judged as true or false. C. I. Lewis's famous course on Kant had somewhat the same effect on me.

Lepore: You left Harvard at some point to go into the war. When and how did that happen?

Davidson: In fall of 1941, I was in my third year of graduate school, and it seemed pretty clear that we were going to get into the war. At first I was against the war. I had been brought up believing that the First World War was a capitalist plot to make money from munitions manufacturers, which may not be totally wrong.

Lepore: Really! Was your father a very political man?

Davidson: Yes, my father was political; in fact, both my parents were left wing, but not as left wing as I became. He thought, as many liberals did, that the First World War had been a very questionable enterprise all around. Maybe it doesn't look that way now, but it did to them. He was for a strong graduated income tax. He didn't think people ought to inherit money.

Lepore: Your politics doesn't come across in your writings. What sort of political leanings did you have in these early days?

Davidson: I was quite clearly what was called a 'fellow traveler'. My politics were like all my left-wing friends'. I never joined the Communist Party, but I followed the party line. Still, given a choice between becoming cannon fodder or making a pile of money, I chose the latter. And so I applied for admission to the Harvard Business School. They had an accelerated course for people to become junior executives who would run the factories. I thought that's for me. It was very hard, then as now, to get into Harvard Business School. I was both simultaneously being a graduate student in philosophy and attending the Harvard Business School. In fact, I was teaching sections in philosophy. I bought a bicycle so that I could get back between two sides of the river. I don't know if you know anything about what Harvard Business School was like? It's like going to law school. It's extremely intensive and very competitive. It's all based on the case system. At night you read a case, and you come in the next day and they call on people. You have to sit in a certain seat. The professor had a picture of you and he just looked down at his chart and picked you out. He would say—'Okay, you read the case. What was the decision and what would you do? Why would you do it?' It was an educational process. And these professors were very very skillful. It was terrific teaching. So I'm working my head off. I had a lot of energy. This was an accelerated program in two ways. It went straight through the summer, and they left out the course in advertising. The idea was that once you completed this program you would know how to set up a factory. They would give you the blueprints for a piece of machinery and say, okay, show us how you would set up a production line to manufacture this. We were supposed to learn how to do this. We were going to be the bosses.

Lepore: I'm sure most philosophers don't know this about you. How did you like business school?

An Interview with Donald Davidson   241

Davidson: I was a straight graduate student in philosophy for two years. The third year I was a graduate student in philosophy and at the same time was at the business school. I was actually third in my class at Harvard Business School; but in fact I never finished. I was a full year at the Business School and in my second year, something like forty-five days from when I would have graduated, I was called up by the Navy; I could have just said I didn't want to go, but I had volunteered. When Germany invaded Russia, we fellow travelers changed our minds about the nature of the war. Now there was a good and a bad side. This is before December 1942. I wasn't drafted; my lottery number was so low I would never have been drafted; indeed, no one who got into the Business School could be drafted. I actually volunteered. I could have said that I want to finish business school first and they would have let me. But I said, look, if I'm going to go to the war, I don't give a damn about this business stuff. I've always been glad I went to business school because it gave me an insight into how a lot of people think that I would have never known otherwise. And I liked the feeling that I could have done it. But I wouldn't have liked the people. After the war they said come back for a month and you could get your degree. I didn't go back.

Lepore: So you were in the war a long time?

Davidson: Absolutely. I was in three and a half years. I went in November of 1942 and got out about the summer of 1945.

Lepore: What rank did you enter the Navy as?

Davidson: I went in as an ensign. That's like a second lieutenant.

Lepore: That's because you were a college graduate?

Davidson: That's right. But I didn't have to go to boot camp because I was put into this accelerated program to become a teacher of recognition. In the summer of 1942, we had just invaded North Africa, and our ships had shot down forty planes or so, all of them our own. There were no enemy planes. So they needed people who could tell the difference. So they thought they'd better train people who could teach gunners how to recognize enemy plans. They very quickly picked a group of maybe thirty-five people. And not having any other idea of knowing how to do it, they picked people who looked as if they were going to be teachers—that included me. They sent us all to Ohio State, where there was a psychologist who thought he knew how to teach people well, if that's the right word, so that they can see a number on a screen that's exposed for only a hundredth of a second. And at first you don't see anything practically, and then after a while you can see something and you can write down some numbers. Now what you can teach people is that if you can see the thing for a hundredth of a second, you can write down thirteen numbers. He thought, well, in modern warfare, planes are coming at each other at about 1,000 miles an hour, you got to pick it up like that. So, the training consisted of showing us these black and white silhouettes for a hundredth of a second. I was the best person they ever had. I loved airplanes and ships, and I was extremely good at it. It had nothing to do with the hundredth of a second thing. When I came to train people, I discovered that wasn't the way to do it at all; I mean with silhouettes. You never see planes in perfect silhouettes. They come at funny angles. What's a much better way of identifying them is by how they move. So I got all these shots that they took from planes when they were shooting down other planes because, during the war, there was always a camera aimed in the same direction as the guns of the fighter—that is, straight ahead.

I was going to teach gunners how to distinguish allied planes from enemy planes. They gave us a little of the standard boot camp stuff on the side.

Lepore: Though it was a good cause, wasn't it a waste of time?

Davidson: Yeah. It was a terrible waste of time. But I did participate in the invasions of Sicily, Salerno, and Enzio. After we had driven the Germans out of North Africa, we had Malta, which was like an aircraft carrier for us. So I was in on the three big amphibious invasions before the big one in the north. Salerno was 6 September 1943; and Anzio was 22 January 1944. Still, it was a terrible waste of time. Most of it was incredibly boring.

Lepore: Did you stay in the Mediterranean the whole time?

Davidson: After one year in the Mediterranean, I knew more about plane recognition than anyone else. So they said you can go where you like, and I said, how about Florida? So I was sent to the naval air station in Jacksonville, Florida, around the end of 1943. I was there for almost a year. Then I was sent to Miami for a year, and that was pleasant. This was my third year in the Navy. I was now teaching pilots how to recognize enemy planes. I was able to rent a huge wonderful house on the beach just north of Miami. I commuted from there to the naval station. When I got back from the Mediterranean, I had quite a bit of money saved. Any car that was good at this time cost a fortune. So when I got back to the States, I bought this Plymouth convertible on Fifth Avenue in New York City right off the floor. This was the first extravagant thing of that kind I ever done in my life. I drove it to Florida.

Lepore: I'd like to know your impressions of the war.

Davidson: I didn't like risking my life, and what I was doing was very dangerous. More than half the ships in the flotilla were sunk with every one aboard. Destroyers are very very vulnerable. Their skins are so thin that a machine gun bullet will go through it. Inside they are full of mines and other sorts of explosive materials. Practically anything in them will blow up. All you had to do is tap them and that's the end of it. I kept changing from one ship to another. They were always putting me on the lead ship. I was lucky. I hated the idea of being killed. I wasn't fighting so much; I so much disliked the concept. On these ships, almost everyone was confused, and everything confusing. One thing that stands out in my mind very clearly—I think the first time it ever happened we were sitting in this harbor in North Africa getting organized to invade northern Sicily. There were hundreds of ships in this harbor—and the Germans came over at night to bomb us—all these search lines—but the main thing you would see is all this incredible anti-aircraft stuff going on—of all sizes: 20 mm, 40 mm, five-inch guns. The sky was full of tremendous fireworks. I love fireworks.

Lepore: But it's difficult for me, given what I know about your personality, to imagine you being bossed around, but being in the military means being bossed around.

Davidson: There isn't all that much bossing. There is plenty that you have to do. Fortunately I was spared a lot of that by my peculiar situation. A ship had so many officers who were to do one thing. But I didn't occupy any known role, so to speak. I was just an attached officer who theoretically could tell the difference between a friendly plane and an enemy plane. The captains didn't know what to do with me. Since they had no theory about what I should do, I spent some of the time in the messroom, trying to teach pilots to distinguish friendly from enemy planes. So I didn't suffer in the same way that others might have. I tried to explain to the captains of the ships I was on what I thought I could do. After they tried me out, they were pretty impressed that I could do this.

Lepore: Okay, so the war is over. You are out of the Navy. It's 1946. What do you do now?

Davidson: By then I was married. I had met my wife, Virginia Bolton, at my sister's wedding in 1941. She was the sister of the man my sister married. At that time, Virginia was married to someone else, to a German, who had come to this country to escape the war. I got married just as I graduated from the training school at Ohio State, at the beginning of my Navy career, on New Year's Eve, 1942. My wife Virginia moved back to New York City while I was at sea. She was with me in Jacksonville and Miami. After I left the military, in December 1945, I was released from the Navy, though theoretically still in the Navy, Virginia and I just fooled around in Mexico for months while I just thought about what I wanted to do. I did a lot of drawing and painting, and a lot of writing. One of the few dreams I never had was that I could become a painter, but I had certainly thought that I might be a writer. I had this experience writing radio scripts right after undergraduate school at Harvard and I knew a lot about literature. But after writing a few chapters of a prospective novel, I concluded that I was never going to be a great writer. I now think in a way I was very naive. I think I thought you try as hard as you can, and either it's okay or it's not. I didn't appreciate then the importance of persistence, something I have come to appreciate in philosophy.

Lepore: Was it at this point that you decided to go back to philosophy?

Davidson: Yes. I hadn't done anything for three and a half years with philosophy. Being in the service was just like being marooned. When I went back to Harvard after the war, in March 1946, all I had to do was write my dissertation; I finished all the course work and prelims before I went into the service. But I wondered what is it that I could possibly write on. C. I. Lewis said to me, 'Look, you lost three years. You got to get going.' He was more worried about it than I was. So, I thought, OK, I don't see how I'm going to do it. So, I just rushed through. I wrote on Plato's *Philebus*. It's an interesting dialogue. I've written about it recently in my paper 'Plato's Philosopher'.

Lepore: What's special about this dialogue?

Davidson: Socrates drops out of the Platonic dialogues pretty early. The *Philebus* is the only one in which he becomes the major figure again. This is twenty years after having dropped out. Secondly, it's the only late dialogue in which Plato uses the elenctic method of question/teaching that he uses in the early dialogues, and it's about ethics, which is the subject of all the early dialogues.

Lepore: You recently published your dissertation, didn't you?

Davidson: Yes, Garland Press has recently published many Harvard dissertations in philosophy. However, they charge outrageous prices for it. Plus what I wrote in my dissertation is quite dull. I rushed it. However, I made $600 on royalties from it after the first year. So, someone is buying it.

Lepore: Back to Harvard.

Davidson: The first draft of my dissertation wasn't accepted. At that point, summer, 1946, I was assisting Quine in his logic course. I had first met and started studying with Quine before the war during my first year of graduate school. I took his math logic course. That was my first logic course. As soon as I started studying with him, we became friends. In fact, at the end of my first year as a graduate student, summer of 1940, Quine and I spent the summer in Mexico.

Lepore: I can't imagine Quine being enthusiastic about your writing a dissertation on the Philebus?

Davidson: Well, the way to put it is that we remained friends through all of it. He was a little mystified by my writing on this. He never talked to me about it.

Lepore: So there you are back at Harvard.

Davidson: My second time around as a graduate student I simply wasn't earning any money. My wife Virginia was supporting us. She was making magazine layouts for some magazine in Boston. She worked the whole time I was in the Navy. Anyway, I thought I had to start earning some money and get a job. When I was an undergraduate, I studied with Raffaello Demos—the person who taught Greek philosophy at Harvard. The teaching assistant for my section was John Goheen. This was my freshman year. Goheen is my oldest friend in philosophy. By the time I completed by first draft of my dissertation, Goheen was teaching at Queens College in New York City. Goheen offered me a job at Queen's College. Although my dissertation had not been accepted yet, I was offered several jobs. But I liked Goheen and I liked the idea of being in New York City. So, I took the job at Queens in September 1946. I was only an instructor, not even an assistant professor.

Lepore: What was it like teaching at Queens?

Davidson: Queens was a superior campus. It was in what was then the Catholic area of Queens. At the time Goheen came there from Harvard, his first job too, he was asked to form the philosophy department. So there I was teaching at Queens fifteen hours a week, plus extra time with students who wanted to be tutored. The first year I was living in Flushing (Queens). But we wanted to be in Manhattan. Since I was a veteran, I was at the top of the list to get into Peter Stuyvesant Town, just north of Greenwich Village, as they were building it. They were Federal apartments, and we were able to pick out the apartment we wanted. We chose the top floor, and we stayed there a couple of years. Then I had a year off 1948–49 because the Ford Foundation used to give a boost to people in the services that they thought were worthy in one way or another. Quine got one of these special year-off fellowships as well. I spent that year in California, partly because Goheen was already out there staying with relatives in southern California in Riverside, and we had this great plan of writing a history of philosophy. It never got anywhere. Actually what I did with that year was write my dissertation. I was just over thirty. That was a nice year. That's the year I learned how to fly. There was an airport near where we were living in Pomona. I first taught myself how to fly when I was quite young, in my cellar. I built a little machine. It was a box that you put your knees in with foot peddles and a throttle. The throttle controlled the speed of a fan which was sitting in front of me flowing in my face. There was also a joy stick which controlled the position of a model airplane facing away from me. The wind is going by it, and it had these control surfaces that I could work with the throttle.

Lepore: How did you know about flying?

Davidson: I had been fascinated by this since I was a little kid. I would put myself to sleep at night by putting myself through maneuvers. The first time I got in a plane I could fly. While I was in the Navy teaching all these guys at Jacksonville and Miami, I would talk these guys into taking me up. So we got in these little planes, and they would leave me up in the cockpit flying. In Jacksonville I was flying these PBY2s, which is called the Catalina, a two-engine plane. But earlier than that I flew a PBY4, which is the Mariner, which is a much bigger plane. But when I got to Miami, they were flying fighters—much more high-powered planes. I used to get them to take me up in these, and I would try all these various maneuvers. So there I was in California. I was being paid by the GI Bill to attend graduate school, and I had only used up a little of it during the three months I was at Harvard. So I had money left and I used it to train to fly. I wasn't teaching in California. After I got my solo license, I could go anywhere I wanted, and I flew all over the south-west. I flew to San Francisco; I flew to Death Valley; I had some wonderful adventures. I loved it. Flying then was much more fun than it is now.

Lepore: Did you return to Queens at the end of that year?

Davidson: I finished my dissertation fairly early in 1949. I went back to Queens in fall, 1949, and everything had changed. The old president had retired and been replaced by this awful man Theobald, who was their in-house Catholic and he wanted to get rid of the whole philosophy department and hire a bunch of Catholics, which he eventually did. So, I had some interesting scraps where the president called me on the carpet and I fought with him and told him off. In the summer of 1950, Virginia and I went to Europe. We rented a house in the south of France. And the Quines visited us there. And he had the manuscript of 'Two Dogmas of Empiricism' with him, which I read and commented on. I returned to Queens that fall, and then in the middle of the year, January 1951, Goheen, who had left Queens to go to Stanford to become chairman, offered me a job at Stanford.

Lepore: Who was at Stanford at that time?

Davidson: Pat Suppes had arrived at Stanford in September 1950. I went in January 1951. The philosophy department consisted of Goheen, Suppes, myself, and several other people. There was a man named Mothershed, who was married to a very wealthy woman. There was a quite interesting man named John Reed. Reed taught ethics. He was married to a woman who was a psychologist and ran a clinic at Berkeley. After the first year I was there, he decided, while he was teaching full-time, he would go to medical school; he completed the first year of medical school and then was hired by Johns Hopkins University to teach in their psychiatry department. He was a very very smart guy. It was not an absurd thing for Hopkins to do. So he left. Reed was in his fifties when he left.

Lepore: Your move to Stanford, career-wise, was a lateral move. Stanford did not have any philosophical reputation at this point?

Davidson: It was coming up very fast but I didn't think about things that way. I didn't worry about tenure; I didn't worry about up and down, but I did think very much of geography. I loved moving out there.

Lepore: Did you have a nice place to live in?

Davidson: Oh boy. We felt as if we were rich. Virginia was by then a professional potter, and she made some money, not much. She never in fact made a lot of money. However, we rented a huge house in Mountain View. It was enormous, and we had the idea that we were going to buy some property and build a house. So, we lived in the rented house for a year. I was an assistant professor, and I didn't have tenure or anything else. We bought seven acres of land for $7,000 in the hills, in what became part of Woodside. During Christmas vacation I designed a house. Virginia was a draughtsman; she made the blueprints, and we hired guys to pour the concrete. We were able to move into the house. We completed the garage first. It had a lot of windows in it and we lived in that while we completed the rest of the house. But it didn't take us long. The land and the house cost us something like $18,000. I was making very little money, less than $6,000 a year. But the money went a long way. We were very lucky to fall into that piece of land. A superb piece of land way out in the middle of nowhere but very close to a country road which was kept up, and there were power lines off to one side. So no problem about getting electricity; the people that sold us the land installed a water system. We had a little water company among seven of us. We bought our water wholesale from the California Water Company and pumped it up the hill in a pipe we had installed. It was cheaper than being in the city. So it was a very good deal. That house is now [1988] worth more than $2,000,000.

Lepore: OK. It's 1952. You are in your mid-thirties, and you still don't have a philosophical project. I recall from earlier conversations that Suppes and McKinsey had you doing various decision theory problems. But that's hardly a project.

Davidson: That's right. It was very sweet of them to teach me decision theory and measurement theory. After I learned a bit, they said, let's write this article together, 'Formal Theory of Value', which appeared in *Philosophy of Science*. Then I made this little discovery—the Ramsey result I describe in 'Belief and the Basis of Meaning' and elsewhere. I should say I rediscovered this result of Ramsey's. Suppes realized immediately better than I did what its potential was. So we published that, and then we did this experimental work together. That all told took a couple of years.

Lepore: Suppes is about the same age as you?

Davidson: He's actually younger. But he thought of me as someone he was teaching. But in fact McKinsey was the guy who was teaching both of us. He was one of the inventors of quantified modal logic, though he didn't publish much of his stuff. We hired him because he was with the RAND corporation in Santa Monica, and there was all this stuff about his being a bad security risk because he was a homosexual. So they took away his security clearance, and Stanford hired him. Then McKinsey committed suicide. By then he had already been invited to write this article for the Schilpp Library of Living Philosophers volume on Carnap. He was a natural to choose to write something on *Meaning and Necessity*, since he knew all about quantified modal logic, and he was to write about the method of intension and extension. He said to me, 'Look, I know the logic, but you know the philosophy. Why don't we write it together?' I said OK, and then he died.

Lepore: 'Carnap on Extension and Intension' was your first serious philosophical publication. I always assumed that Quine arranged that?

Davidson: No, he had nothing to do with that. At that point in my career, Quine knew who I was, but we were not seeing anything of each other, or corresponding or anything like that.

Lepore: I've both taught that article and written on it. It's not dull, but it's long and plodding. Still, one can see some of your lifelong interests beginning to appear in it, even though that article was written some thirteen years before 'Truth and Meaning'.

Davidson: Well, I was simply teaching myself that subject when I wrote that piece. It was many years from when I finished writing that essay and it was published. I didn't know anything about Carnap when

I started writing it. I was spending all my time at Stanford teaching all these basic courses. I taught everything at Stanford. In that sense it was like Queens. I taught ancient philosophy, the later dialogues of Plato; I taught modern philosophy, Descartes, Hume, and so forth; I taught epistemology; I taught philosophy of language. At the same time I was in charge of the graduate program. When I showed up at Stanford, they were just giving MAs. After I arrived, each year I would travel around the country picking up students. Very quickly, by the mid-1950s, we picked up a lot of very good students. It didn't take long.

Lepore: But still you had no serious philosophical project. I suppose you had the decision theory.

Davidson: Yes, but I never thought of it as my life work. It engaged me. You don't understand me. I get interested in things. I found the work in decision theory pleasant. Also, I was working up a lot of stuff. For example, on 11 November 1954 I gave a talk on Carnap's method of intension and extension to which Tarski came. Those early years at Stanford, I was doing also all that psychological stuff. I was giving talks to psychologists and economists, and a lot of other sorts of talks as well. I gave a talk on use and meaning at an APA [American Philosophical Association] meeting in 1953, a talk on metaphor in 1954, a talk on meaning and music in 1954. At a Western Psychological Association meeting in 1954 I gave a talk on the experimental study of some factors influencing decision making in conflict situations. The American Mathematical Society, that year, I gave a talk on quantitistic axiomatization of subjective probability. I gave a talk in December 1954 on meaning and music to an aesthetics group. But getting back to the piece for the Carnap volume. It took me a lot of time; you have to realize I didn't really understand it very well, and I just had to think and think about that stuff. Even to get the most basic stuff straight in my head. After I sent the article in, but before the Schilpp volume came out, Carnap invited me down to Los Angeles to talk about it. He was extremely sweet. He was a lovely man and very impressive. It was wonderful training writing that article, and at the same time each year I was teaching the philosophy of language course, and that was a big help too. Also, I was teaching the introductory ethics course. I did that for seventeen years at Stanford.

Lepore: There were many interesting, stimulating people at Stanford, at least visiting at this time: for example, David Wiggins, Dagfinn

Føllesdal, Michael Dummett, David Pears. Who brought all these foreign philosophers to Stanford?

Davidson: I did that. It was all my doing. There was no one else to do these things. There was no one else to teach the basic courses, and there was no one else who even knew whom to invite. In the early days, I was in charge of speakers. I invited Ryle, with whom I got to be friends, Austin, Strawson, Anscombe, Dummett, Pears, Wiggins, Hampshire, Grice. Dummett came a number of times, at least two times, maybe three.

Lepore: How did you know whom to invite?

Davidson: Because I read. I read the truth paper by Dummett. I read everything. I was teaching philosophy of language every year and I read a lot of it; I was consuming a huge amount of stuff. How I had the energy and time to do all that, I have no idea.

Lepore: I'm sorry to keep returning to this same theme, but I, and I'm sure most other philosophers, think of you as a programmatic philosopher. No one else comes to mind right away who is as deeply entrenched in a philosophical program as you are. Now such programs don't spring *ex nihilo*, and here we are already up to 1955 and I still don't see a program forming. I can see traces of your philosophical work in the decision-theoretic projects that you contributed to with Suppes and McKinsey, but it's merely traces. Also, Quine hasn't shown up at Stanford yet. So, you didn't even know about *Word and Object*. I just don't have any historical sense from where your philosophical ideas sprang.

Davidson: I can easily help with this. I was building up more and more a picture in two areas. One was philosophy of action, and the other was philosophy of language. I was very inhibited so far as publication was concerned.

Lepore: One thing that must strike all students of your work is how relatively late in your career you began to publish on the topics for which you are so well known. This is especially interesting when one knows, as I do now, how many public presentations you were giving before you began to publish—for example, at APA's, very public events. So, I'm wondering what you mean by saying you were 'very inhibited so far as publication was concerned'? What was that all about?

Davidson: What's there to say? Lots of people have that. There is a sense in which I retained some of the attitude which I had as an undergraduate, which is that philosophy is something to view from afar. Although I was teaching philosophy and enjoyed doing it and did it with confidence, I didn't really see myself as a player. And I probably found something frightening about the idea that the minute I actually published something, everyone was going to jump on me. And part of the reason why Suppes and McKinsey took me under their wing is because they thought this guy really ought to get some stuff out. They certainly eased the thing for me by writing things with me. So Suppes and McKinsey helped me over that to some extent, and the Carnap paper, as you see, accidentally fell to me. Now it just takes two more elements. Dan Bennett, my graduate student, was writing his dissertation with me, and he went off to England for the year and found out about what Elizabeth Anscombe and Stuart Hampshire were working on. He came back to Stanford and wrote a dissertation on the philosophy of action. I was reading it, thinking about it, and so forth. I thought I saw that these guys had made a mistake in thinking that, given the properties that reason-explanations have, that somehow reasons couldn't be causes. At that point Mary Mothersill, who happened to be on the program committee of the American Philosophical Association, invited me to be on the program of the Eastern Division meetings, and so I wrote 'Actions, Reasons and Causes'. I remember thinking that a pile of bricks was going to fall on me after that presentation. I didn't realize that if you publish, as far as I can tell, no one was going to pay any attention.

Lepore: Well, they did to that paper!

Davidson: Ultimately, but it takes a little while before they respond. Here's an interesting fact: once the replies came in, they were all positive, and it was many years before I started getting negative responses to it.

Lepore: There are so many things going on in 'Actions, Reasons and Causes', it's hard to believe there wasn't a decade's work and thought already behind it before it was written.

Davidson: Well, there wasn't a decade behind it, but there were several years of sort of stitching it together and working with Dan Bennett. I was reading all the things that he was reading: Anscombe, Hampshire, and all these other Red Book philosophers.

Lepore: What was the second element?

Davidson: The other thing that happened—here I've been stewing about belief sentences. I really had a hang-up about belief sentences, and I thought about that for one solid year. Writing the Carnap piece got me thinking about these kinds of sentences. Just at the right moment, I discovered the logician Alfred Tarski's paper on the concept of truth. I read the *Wahreitsbegriff*. It took me six months to work myself through it. But when I understood it, it really turned me on. Still, I might not really have appreciated it if I hadn't done the stuff in decision theory. I had an appreciation for what it's like to have a serious theory, and I think the other people who were working in philosophy of language didn't have an appreciation for what it was like to have a serious theory. So, look, there were these two kinds of people in very different ways—there were people like Tarski, who knew what a serious theory was like alright, but didn't have much philosophical interest—Tarski didn't come at it from a philosophical point of view—and he wasn't especially interested in the semantics for natural languages or anything like that. On the other hand, there were all these people working on the semantics of natural language, but they didn't have any idea of what a theory was. I saw how to put these two things together. It came to me as if the heavens had opened and then I started writing a whole bunch of things.

Lepore: There are a few things here I don't get. Surely Carnap was interested in natural languages, and he knew Tarski's work and he knew about natural languages. What was missing in Tarski's work that you saw, at least according to your hypothesis?

Davidson: There are a lot of mysteries of that sort, where you say, how could so-and-so not have recognized such-and-such? How could so many people have failed to see what a problem the semantics of adverbs were, for example? There are just endless things like this where you can ask yourself. These people had what it took to recognize the problem and so forth—your example of Carnap is an excellent example—he wrote this series of three books while at the University of Chicago. The first one was on formal syntax, the second one on formal semantics—in which he develops a Tarski-type theory of truth—and the third is his *Meaning and Necessity*. It seems to me that he forgot the second book before when he wrote the last book. Alonzo Church had brought Frege to his attention and he was fascinated with all this apparatus of intension and extension, but why did he not remind himself of Tarski, which he clearly did not?

Then there is Quine. He was never into Tarski and he still isn't; I think he still doesn't appreciate Tarski. How can someone as smart as Quine, who has known Tarski all his life, knows everything that's there, who wrote this wonderful little article on an application of Tarski's theory of truth; he understood everything about it; how come he still doesn't really use it?

Lepore: Well, with Carnap there is this gray area between doing semantics and doing logic. For example, *Meaning and Necessity*, despite its title, is really about inference. It's about why one sentence implies another; and all that that talk about state descriptions is doing is sustaining inference. In your paper 'In Defense of Convention T' you make very clear that these two projects get accidentally conflated. Tarski is a focal point here because he was interested in both projects, but he is not philosophical in a way to appreciate that his work on the truth theory hooks up with philosophical problems surrounding natural languages.

Davidson: That doesn't answer my questions.

Lepore: The reason I got excited about your paper 'Truth and Meaning' is because, as I've said in print, even if one doesn't accept truth-conditional semantics, one must be impressed by this paper because it lays down conditions of adequacy, and as far as I can tell, they simply didn't exist anywhere else prior. The whole idea that one has to construct a theory is novel in that paper. The notion of theory, of course, has been around in philosophy for a long time. But this notion was ambiguous in philosophy at this stage. It might mean 'analysis', as in standard accounts in the theory of knowledge. Here's an interesting fact: no theory of knowledge I know of issues in theorems of the form, for example: Donald Davidson knows that Italy is in Europe. So clearly theories in epistemologists' mouths don't mean the same thing as it did when you used the term in 'Truth and Meaning'. The use of 'theory' as in 'theory of knowledge' is a very idiosyncratic use of theory. Think about a theory of physics or chemistry. You don't get an enumeration of truths or an analysis of the concept of matter in the theory of physics. So where the notion of theory in the theory of knowledge comes from is an interesting peculiarity of contemporary epistemology. But still, a philosopher like Carnap had the notion of theory in the right sense. What I think he lacked were clear conditions of adequacy. Here's a good question: if you go back and read *Meaning and Necessity* and ask yourself what were the conditions of adequacy here—that would be a good project—if we had the answer to that question, we would have an answer to the question how Carnap missed the boat.

Davidson: The same point can be made with Hans Reichenbach, with respect to his logic book, *Symbolic Logic*. When I first started getting into this, I couldn't believe that I had hit on something that hadn't been pretty obvious to these guys. So I started working my way through the literature. I went back to the logicism, the *Logische Syntax der Sprache* and so forth. I thought somebody here must have had the idea.

Lepore: It was around. If you read C. I. Lewis, in particular, his argument about how translation couldn't be sufficient for determining meaning since one could know a grammar book for Arabic and have an Arabic dictionary but still one wouldn't thereby understand Arabic. But that's not enough. Lewis has this brilliant observation but he doesn't take it anywhere.

Davidson: I had the same experience when I got interested in events. I simply couldn't believe that nobody had ever really faced the problem, especially someone like Whitehead, whose whole philosophy, the philosophy of process, was about events and he was a logician. I thought there must be something there. But I found nothing.

Lepore: I guess, like others, I always thought that the 'Action, Reasons, and Causes' literature was much more closely related to the 'Truth and Meaning' literature than it in fact is. But I also associate your interest in action theory to your former student Dan Bennett's return from Oxford. Now that was eight years before another student, John Wallace, showed up at Stanford, and I tend to associate your interest in philosophy of language with Wallace's arrival at Stanford.

Davidson: It's true that there was about eight year's difference between Bennett's departure and Wallace's arrival at Stanford. But I wrote up a lot of 'Truth and Meaning' long before it was published.

Lepore: Well, if one studies the Carnap piece you wrote, you can see some of what's going on in 'Truth and Meaning' already forming in that earlier piece. Also, I recall your saying, and it certainly makes good sense, that some of the ideas that occupy you in 'Truth and Meaning', and certainly in 'Radical Interpretation' and 'Belief and the Basis of Meaning', are provoked by your work in the laboratory with Suppes and McKinsey—for example, your interest in the presentation problem in experimental decision theory. I expect that McKinsey and Suppes didn't know what was bothering you. But this is clearly a place where your interest in the philosophy of language is brought to bear on your interest in action theory (decision theory).

Davidson: Well, in fact, these interests all grew up together. It wasn't so much the presentation problem at first that connected the two. It was rather events—thinking about events. In the very beginning these two things were somewhat separate. 'Actions, Reasons, and Causes' was simply a result of my realizing that no one had a good argument against causal theories of action. Then I became interested in practical reasoning, and that led to 'How is Weakness of the Will Possible?' All these were written while I was teaching the course in the philosophy of language. I think I was slower to write that stuff up in the philosophy of language partly because I lacked confidence. I thought that's a much harder field. The guys that were in action theory were in a somewhat muddled state. None of them knew any logic. There I felt greater confidence. I really thought I saw clearly what they were in a muddle about. Whereas in philosophy of language I thought that with these really smart people it's not going to be so easy to set things straight. In the beginning those two things were somewhat separate. However, it's obvious how these two interests just overlapped. Because in philosophy of action the analysis of propositional attitudes had always been very central, and I was very much into the problem of the individuation of actions. So that led to my doing semantics. Though I started out on each of the projects separately.

Lepore: It was around this time that John Wallace showed up at Stanford as your graduate student fresh out of Yale. What was his influence on you?

Davidson: My basic ideas in philosophy of language were worked out before Wallace came along. But he was a great help to me because he knew more logic than I did, for one thing, and he was very enthusiastic, in fact, very positive about it. He got very excited about my project. His dissertation contributed to it. But he didn't get me started in the way that Dan Bennett actually got me started on action theory. Still, it was great having John Wallace around. I didn't yet have a whole lot of confidence. I thought that if I got an idea that works here in philosophy of language, then undoubtedly a whole lot of other people had it. This is a natural reaction. And I had to publish a few things before I discovered that at least I didn't have something absurdly wrong. So Wallace was great, because he was enthusiastic and very smart, and by talking with him, a lot of things got straightened out. He had insights that were extremely useful.

Lepore: I'd like to stay with the 'Truth and Meaning' paper for a while. Many philosophers are unclear about your position in that paper. Are you a revisionist, saying that all there is to a theory of meaning is what a theory of truth provides? Or are you a reductionist, in the sense that meaning is truth? The idea there is that in your theory it appears that the predicate 'is true' occupies the place the predicate 'means that' once did. So, they wonder whether your idea is to try to reconstruct all meaning facts by appeal only to truth facts. That is, are you claiming that there are no meaning facts above and beyond truth facts? My inclination, on the basis of having read you all these years and having talked to you so much over the years, is to say that you never thought about your program in this way. Rather, you thought about there being a certain project, interpreting and understanding speakers, and that it's an open question what we must use to do that. But it is true that in 'Truth and Meaning' there are passages that if you come to that article with a certain vocabulary you can find evidence for each of these different ideas.

Davidson: Well, what's not in 'Truth and Meaning' but what lies behind it is the years of teaching philosophy of language without anyone to give me any guidance, really without any background in the subject. So I started out as many people did in those days, reading Ogden and Richards's *The Meaning of Meaning* and Charles Morris. Now what looked like the central problem to them was to define the concept of meaning: x means y, where x is a word or a phrase or sentence and God knows what y was supposed to be—and you wanted: iff what? That is how a lot of people were thinking about philosophy of language. Really smart people sought analyses of particular locutions, but never said anything about how you could tell whether you had come up with a correct solution or on what grounds you criticize these things aside from just *ad hoc* arguments. So I think perhaps I felt more frustrated by this situation that I found the subject to be in than I think other people did. On the one hand, so many issues seemed rather sharp: What is meaning? How do you even think about it? Where do you start? And somewhere along the line I discovered Tarski and I thought: you don't even want to ask the question what is meaning. It's the wrong question. It was a huge shift of perspective to get away from worrying about what it is to talk about the meaning of a predicate. Reading Tarski made me realize that there's a way to get around all that—and somewhere along there Quine showed up at the Center for Behavioral Studies at Stanford. At that point they invited people who were at the center to bring up an associate, and I had a term off and I agreed to just come and read a manuscript version of what was to become his *Word and Object*. I really didn't do anything else that term except read it over and over again, trying to understand what was going on. And when I did, I thought it was terrific. And I saw again that it was a whole way of approaching problems in the philosophy of language that other people hadn't caught on to, hadn't even thought about, and it seemed much more promising, and so I sort of slowly put what I thought was good in Quine with what I had found in Tarski. And that's where my general approach to the subject came from. But you wouldn't see it the way I saw it unless you came into the whole subject at the time I did in the late 1950s. No one really knew what to do about the subject, even though everyone was really fascinated by it.

Lepore: So Quine had very little influence on your philosophy of language until relatively late, until you were in your forties. This I think would be a great surprise to many readers of your work.

Davidson: That's right. My philosophy of language didn't grow out of my relationship with Quine at all. Once I got interested in the subject in a deep way, I went back and read Quine fresh with open eyes, and I started teaching this stuff. I had become well versed in Quine, but *Word and Object* was something new, and it really was very hard for me to grasp exactly what was going on in it. I read the first couple of chapters over and over and over again, just trying to take it in.

Lepore: Well, even here I think readers might leave with the not so uncommon impression that Davidson's philosophy of language is really just modified Quine. That would be a mistake. Quine, according to me, has a very different perspective from yours. He starts off clearly from a revisionist point of view. As early as his paper 'The Problem of Meaning in Linguistics', he's telling us that only very few features of our ordinary concept of meaning are salvageable. You don't think that at all. I don't see a revisionist perspective in your writings. Lastly, there is the Richard Montague tradition, which brings us back to Carnap's *Meaning and Necessity*. Carnap was really trying to devise theories of meaning, and he wasn't trying to analyze meaning by saying that meaning is an associated idea, or is associated behavior, or any of the other familiar analyses we present in introductory philosophy of language courses. So what, then, is the difference between your program and the Carnapian program, which is, after all, much older? Carnap wasn't doing model theory. He says he is trying to devise a semantics for natural languages. Here's another way of putting this point. According to Michael Dummett, Frege was trying to provide a theory of meaning in your sense long ago. However, this is difficult to believe. If you read the Klemke anthology on Frege—which I believe was an important and influential collection of essays on Frege as recently as twenty years ago [i.e. 1970]—you clearly don't get anything like Dummett's perspective on Frege. So clearly, just from a historical (or if you like a sociological) point of view, all along others were not thinking about Frege as Dummett counsels us to. And in fact I can't help, to the contrary, but wonder how much you actually influenced Michael's interpretation of Frege, at least with respect to reading Frege as attempting to devise theories of meaning in your sense.

Davidson: I think the idea that there was a way of thinking philosophically about meaning tied to the idea of getting a serious semantic theory for as much of natural language as you could—well, I was the first person to say that, and I say it in 'Truth and Meaning'. There I suggested that my dream was to try to do for the semantics for natural language what Noam Chomsky was doing for the syntax of natural language. But he didn't have quite the same concept of a theory as I did. He knew what it was like to give a recursive definition of a sentence, for example. But when I was writing that paper, I couldn't believe no one thought about it that way. So I looked about in Carnap, in Reichenbach, and in Quine, and none of them was even describing this as a project. Tarski discouraged everybody by saying, of course, you can't do this for natural language. Quine never thought of it in terms of a theory at all. Of course, his discussion of translation could, if you think of it now with a little twist, could be redescribed or re-expressed in a Tarski-like way But he certainly wasn't thinking about it this way at the time he was first writing about it in *Word and Object*.

Lepore: By now you are getting ready to leave Stanford.

Davidson: I was at Stanford eighteen years. I started there in 1951, and I left in 1968. In that period Stanford went from being a more or less invisible university to being a top university. That was a period when there was a tremendous amount of money available in certain areas. And the upper administration at Stanford was full of people who were scientists, and they just decided to take a chance in hiring senior people who had big grants. They were taking a chance because the money these new people brought might dry up. But this way they were able to get a terrific faculty very rapidly.

Lepore: But by the time you left Stanford, the philosophy department had grown in stature, and it was attracting very good graduate students. Still, you had not really published a lot by this time, and yet you clearly had a big influence on that department and on its graduate students.

Davidson: The reason I had an influence on the graduate students was that there wasn't anyone else teaching these central subjects: epistemology, philosophy of language, even ethics. All these are central topics. So naturally the graduate students revolved around me. I was the only person teaching those subjects, and also I was full of ideas; I was reading everything coming out and trying to digest it. I would write these ideas up, and I would pass my material out. I was full of topics to write dissertations on, and also I brought the graduate students there; I was director of graduate students for years and years and years, and I would go around the country recruiting them. I would talk to the administration in order to get more fellowships.

Lepore: But when did you begin to attract attention outside of Stanford?

Davidson: As soon as 'Actions, Reasons and Causes' came out, I started getting offers from all over the country. Once that paper came out, I was invited to all sorts of things, and I was giving papers all over the country all of the time. I had stuff ready to read, but I was slow in sending it out for publication. Also, a lot of people in England knew about me. I had invited them all to Stanford. David Wiggins and I agreed about a lot of stuff at this point. He was the first philosopher in England to catch on to what I was doing. He was actually in a younger generation of philosophers that I had influenced, but I knew the older generation as well. I knew Gilbert Ryle and J. L. Austin. All these people I knew quite well. They would be invited to Stanford for a quarter or to give a talk, and no one else on the faculty paid any attention to them. I had a lot of students who were interested in what these English people were doing. Wiggins and Dummett were invited over and over again, and later on David Pears. Even John Wisdom visited. They enjoyed visiting Stanford, and there wasn't anyone else they got to know except me.

Lepore: So leaving Stanford must have been extremely difficult?

Davidson: It was a huge thing. For one thing I loved my house and I loved the area. But I thought the politics of the university were dominated by the scientists, and I kept trying to get them to hire other people in philosophy. Pat Suppes, who by then was in the administration, had the idea, which I don't think was absurd, that the philosophy department should be full of formal people who addressed standard philosophical subjects from a formal perspective. But I, instead, wanted to be surrounded by people who were really steeped in the subject, whether they had a formal background or not. Suppes, instead, wanted logicians who knew something about other subjects. We hired Jaakko Hintikka, who knew something about epistemology and the history of philosophy from a logical point of view. We hired Dagfinn Føllesdal, who knew something about Continental philosophy, but don't forget that he was a logician, a student in fact of Quine's. And so on. I wanted something different. I was interested in philosophy of mind, in epistemology. I was operating on my own except for my own graduate students. I wanted the kind of challenge that this didn't provide.

Lepore: And so you left Stanford for Princeton? Do you think your work changed significantly after you arrived at Princeton? That's not obvious to a reader.

Davidson: I think so. Almost at once I was invited to give the John Locke Lectures at Oxford, which at that point were pretty prestigious. That came at the end of the academic year 1969–70. I spent that year at the SCSBS [Stanford Center for Social and Behavioral Sciences] and during that year I wrote about six of my best-known papers. I had just spent two years at Princeton. Those papers were definitely better as a result of my mixing it up with David Lewis, Gil Harman, Tom Nagel. I was suddenly in the midst of a bunch of very active people. All those people influenced me, including older ones like Stuart Hampshire and Gregory Vlastos. I think it was a good idea to get into an atmosphere where I wasn't the only person dealing with these topics. It's easy to convince yourself that you have everything right if you have no one around who is in a position to challenge you, and I knew Stanford was not the best intellectual environment. At Princeton, a lot of people would come to my seminars. I talked a lot of philosophy with Gil Harman and Carl Hempel, and just psychologically it made a difference to me. It was sort of like going from high school to Harvard.

Lepore: You have a tendency to work and rework papers before releasing them for publication.

Davidson: Yes, that's true. In 1969, I went to Australia, and I gave the David Gavin Lectures. These are Australia's John Locke Lectures, the big lecture series at the University of Adelaide. [Others to lecture in this series have been Ryle, Quine, Feigl, Lewis Hempel, Dennett, and Putnam.] The Australian philosopher J. J. C. Smart was reading my stuff, and he arranged for my invitation. These lectures constitute at least half of the lectures in my collection *Actions and Events*. The same is true of my John Locke Lectures. All but one of these ended up in my collection *Truth and Interpretation*. That's a considerable body of stuff. Enough to fill two volumes. The one of my Locke Lectures that isn't there is the one that ultimately became my first American Philosophical Association Presidential Address, 'On the Very Idea of a Conceptual Scheme'. I worked on that paper for seven years. I read all these papers all over the world for several years before they were published.

Lepore: In retrospect, do you think the move to Princeton was a good one for you?

Davidson: I think being at Stanford for me was psychologically very good. I was fifty when I arrived at Princeton. If I had gone straight to Princeton, there is no chance I would have built up all this stuff in all these areas because there were people there who knew stuff about it. It was only because I was at Stanford and nobody was doing those things that it gave me a chance to move in any direction I felt without anyone to oppose me.

Lepore: After Princeton there was the move to the research institution—the Rockefeller University in New York City.

Davidson: I only taught full-time at Princeton for two years. They had brought me in as chairman of the philosophy department. They thought people like Tom Nagel and Gil Harman and even Paul Benacerraf were too young to be chairman. I think that was a mistake on their part. After that, although I was at the Rockefeller, I was offici-ally on the staff at Princeton, not just a visitor. I had this special title, 'Lecturer with the rank of Professor'. About Rockefeller, first I have to tell you that all of my moves in one way or another were partly related to women, except going to Stanford. While Virginia, my first wife, and I were at Stanford, our marriage got worse. Virginia was very eager to go back to the East Coast, much more eager than I was. I had good reasons to leave Stanford, and she really wanted to go. These two things co-operated. She felt that the West Coast was nowhere artistic-ally. She was quite wrong about that. In fact, the West Coast was quite active at that point in a way in which the East Coast wasn't, and in fact she didn't get the kind of boost that she thought she was going to get by going to the East Coast. In fact, she did better on the West Coast. But her desire to go back to the East Coast was partly an expression of her dissatisfaction with our relationship. But Princeton was backwater, and that was one reason for moving from Princeton to the Rockefeller. The second reason was my reason. There was all this stuff I wanted to write about, and who wouldn't want a job where you didn't have to do anything you didn't want? [Rockefeller University, being a research institution, had no official students or classes. Each faculty member was required to do no more than his individual research.] So, I made an arrangement with Princeton that I would teach there one semester each year. That gave me the opportunity to teach the way I like. So I never stopped teaching. The main thing I worried about was that I would lack the stimulation I got from teaching. Teaching keeps you moving. So I asked myself a lot, would I really flourish under those condi-tions? And I interviewed a lot of people who were at the Rockefeller or, more importantly, had left it—for example, Robert Nozick and Sydney Shoemaker. Those were the main ones. I saw the danger very clearly, but I thought it would be cowardly not to accept an offer with such opportunity. It was grand, truly grand. Anything you wanted to do, they didn't just let you do it, they would help you do it—pay your transportation, etc. And so I went to the Rockefeller in 1969–70, right after I spent a year at the Stanford Center for the Behavioral Sciences.

Lepore: Well, let's see, you spent eighteen years at Stanford. You began there fairly young, and you left there to become chairman of arguably the best philosophy department in the world. Now a lot of people come right out of graduate school, moving ahead full steam, publishing in quality journals regularly, being offered jobs at the top universities, etc. That wasn't true of you.

Davidson: No, it wasn't. Part of it had to do with the years in the Navy. I was losing touch all those years I was in the Navy. I didn't feel behind, because I didn't even have the concept of an active career. It was only after being at Stanford for a while that I began to have ideas that were interesting and that I started feeling uptight about not publishing. But two things happened. Pat Suppes, who was younger than I, was publishing up a storm and getting promotion after promotion, and it was impossible for me not to notice this. The other that goaded me into publishing was that my students started publishing my ideas. They weren't stealing from me. No, quite the contrary. I began to say, I better get something out myself. But if there's one thing that distinguishes my generation from yours in philosophy anyway, it is that people now in graduate school form the concept of what it's like to be a professional operator, to have a career, and publish and so forth, and I just never went through that. I don't know whether this distinguishes me from my friends or not, or whether we were all that way. I can say that whatever successes came my way, I haven't aimed for them, and they always surprised me; and still when somebody introduces me as having done this and this, and having accomplished such-and-such, I'm actually embarrassed. I think, 'Who, me?'

Lepore: I'd like to ask you about your writing style, if I might. How would you describe your writing style?

Davidson: I begin most of my papers with either a problem or a question. I think the only thing I can say about my style is that I sometimes find it incredibly hard to start writing. I often imagine the first sentence and then ask myself, 'Wait! What comes next?' Pretty soon, I'm writing the whole paper in my head, and any problem in the composition or organization of the text stops me from even writing the first sentence for fear that I would be somehow trapped. When I do finally write something, I often find that the first couple of pages, which usually sort of ease me into the subject, are better left out. So, I'll throw away these painfully constructed early pages completely.

Lepore: But it's my impression that your papers undergo many revisions. Is this not true?

Davidson: I don't do a great deal of revising. I always believe that I have a pretty clear idea about how a paper is going to go before I start writing. However, in the throes of composing a paper, I find that I regularly think about the paper. When I'm trying to go to sleep or when I'm half asleep, ways of putting things often occur to me, or when I'm not in the midst of writing, a new idea or a solution for some problem of organization will come to me. I find that these relaxed moments are essential in my composing process.

Contents List of Volumes of Essays

by Donald Davidson

Volume 2

Inquiries into Truth and Interpretation

Volume 3

Subjective, Intersubjective, Objective

Volume 4
Problems of Rationality

Volume 5

Truth, Language, and History

Index

274 *Index*